The Fundamentals of Small Group Communication

To our families, for their continued
support throughout our academic careers.

—Scott and Carolyn

The Fundamentals of Small Group Communication

Scott A. Myers
West Virginia University

Carolyn M. Anderson
The University of Akron

SAGE Publications
Los Angeles • London • New Delhi • Singapore

For information:

Sage Publications Inc.
2455 Teller Road
Thousand Oaks, California 91320
E-mail: order@sagepub.com

Sage Publications India Pvt. Ltd.
B 1/I 1 Mohan Cooperative
   Industrial Area
Mathura Road, New Delhi 110 044
India

Sage Publications Ltd.
1 Oliver's Yard
55 City Road
London EC1Y 1SP
United Kingdom

Sage Publications Asia-Pacific Pte. Ltd.
33 Pekin Street #02–01
Far East Square
Singapore 048763

Printed in the United States of America

Library of Congress Cataloging-in-Publication Data

Myers, Scott A.
The fundamentals of small group communication / Scott A. Myers, Carolyn M. Anderson.
     p. cm.
Includes bibliographical references and index.
ISBN 978-1-4129-5939-1 (pbk.)
   1. Communication in small groups. I. Anderson, Carolyn M. II. Title.

HM736.M94 2008
302.3′4—dc22   2007035193

Printed on acid-free paper

08   09   10   11   12   10   9   8   7   6   5   4   3   2   1

Acquiring Editor:	Todd R. Armstrong
Editorial Assistant:	Katie Grim
Production Editor:	Sarah K. Quesenberry
Copy Editor:	Melinda Orman
Typesetter:	C&M Digitals (P) Ltd.
Proofreader:	Gail Fay
Indexer:	Marilyn Augst
Cover Designer:	Edgar Abarca
Marketing Manager:	Carmel Schrire

Brief Contents

Detailed Contents

List of Tables, Figures, and Assessment Tools

Tables

Figures

Assessment Tools

About the Authors

Scott A. Myers (PhD, Kent State University, 1995) is an associate professor and PhD graduate studies coordinator in the department of communication studies at West Virginia University (WVU). Prior to WVU, he taught at Buena Vista University, Kent State University, McNeese State University, and Creighton University. At WVU, he teaches undergraduate and graduate courses in small group communication, instructional communication, and communication theory. His research interests center on the student-instructor relationship in the college classroom and the relational maintenance behaviors used by adult siblings. His work has been published in several disciplinary and interdisciplinary journals, including, among others, *Communication Education, Communication Quarterly, Communication Research Reports,* and *Psychological Reports.* He is a former editor of *Communication Teacher* and served as the executive director of the Central States Communication Association from 2004 to 2006.

Carolyn M. Anderson (PhD, Kent State University, 1992) is a professor and interim director in the School of Communication at the University of Akron. She primarily teaches and researches small groups and leadership, health, and organizational communication. One specialty area is group research. She has studied or taught in China, Cuba, and Poland. Her articles have appeared in regional, national, and international journals. Many of her convention papers have earned top awards. Prior to receiving her doctorate, she worked in business for many years as a member of work teams, a project leader, and an entrepreneur. She provides service to the community as a public speaker, consultant, and organizational trainer.

Preface

I f you are like many people, the phrase *working in a small group* evokes a contradictory reaction. On one hand, you recognize that working in a small group provides you with many opportunities, such as the opportunity to develop further your social, communication, and critical thinking skills; the opportunity to work with and learn from others; and the opportunity to become adequately prepared for your future educational, community, and vocational endeavors. On the other hand, you know that working in a small group presents its challenges, including issues with task coordination, the emergence of conflict, and working with others who are uncooperative, fail to participate or contribute to the group task, or do not attend group meetings.

To capitalize on these aforementioned opportunities and confront these challenges, learn how to become an effective small group member—the aim of this textbook. We advise that to become an effective small group member, you not only must understand the small group communication process; you also must recognize the role you play in shaping how the groups to which you belong complete their tasks and how you develop relationships with group members.

To reach this end, this textbook contains 12 chapters that address three general themes associated with effective group membership. The first theme centers on the need to develop a basic knowledge of the small group communication process by becoming aware of the features that constitute the small group communication process (Chapter 1), how group members proceed through the small group socialization process (Chapter 2), the impact of group members' communication and personality traits on small group communication (Chapter 3), the various ways through which group member diversity emerges (Chapter 4), and the models that explain how small groups develop (Chapter 5). The second theme revolves around the need to recognize the features that impact how group members accomplish a task. These features include examining the characteristics of a task (Chapter 6), choosing the appropriate procedure group members can use to make decisions and solve problems (Chapter 7), identifying the roles needed to successfully complete a task (Chapter 8), and uncovering the ways in which all group members can engage in leadership (Chapter 9). The third theme focuses on the need to realize not only how relational issues affect how group members achieve task accomplishment but also how group members relate to one another as both individuals and group members. These relational issues include the verbal, nonverbal, and listening behaviors group members use to create relational communication (Chapter 10); the styles group members use to handle group conflict (Chapter 11); and the means through which group members establish a supportive communication climate (Chapter 12). Two included appendixes focus on tying the chapters' concepts together (Appendix A) and the tools needed to design and deliver a small group presentation (Appendix B).

To facilitate your reading of the textbook, each chapter follows a similar pattern. Each chapter begins with a list of five objectives that you should be able to accomplish once you have read the chapter. A case study then provides you with an introduction to the chapter topic and content. The chapter begins with an introduction that identifies the primary points and ends with a section titled "A Final Note About . . ." that precedes a conclusion. We also included a list of the references cited in the chapter should you decide you would like to explore a particular topic further. Throughout the chapter, a series of application questions appear: three questions focus on how the chapter content applies to your work group, one question inquires about the ethical component of small group membership, and five discussion questions at the end of the chapter that ask you to reflect on the chapter content in regard to any group to which you belong. In some chapters, we included assessment tools so you can assess how your communication behaviors impact your small group experiences. We formatted essential terms in bold and also included them in the glossary.

We hope that after you read this textbook, you not only will have gained a greater understanding of how to move toward becoming an effective group member but also will work actively toward maximizing your effectiveness the next time you work in a small group.

Enjoy!

—*Scott and Carolyn*

Acknowledgments

Working on this textbook required the assistance of several primary, learning, and work groups.

Without the members of these groups and their energy, dedication, and enthusiasm, we might not have finished this project on time or kept our sanity. As such, we extend our gratitude to our colleagues, our friends, and our students who helped us, in some way, complete this textbook. Several individuals deserve extra-special recognition for their contributions to this project.

First, we offer a resounding thank-you to our friends Katie Neary Dunleavy of LaSalle University for coauthoring Chapter 4 and Sally Vogl-Bauer of the University of Wisconsin–Whitewater for coauthoring Appendix A. Both Katie and Sally provided us with a much-needed and extremely appreciated perspective, evident in the content, style, and tone of their chapter and appendix, respectively.

Second, we appreciate the input from the COMM 112 students enrolled at West Virginia University during the spring 2007 semester. Their feedback provided us with several suggestions on how to improve the textbook. These students include Brandon Barber, Chantal Biancheri, Kevin Birkner, Christopher Byrd, Adam Cagle, Adam Castleman, Katie Cooper, Sean Coveleski, Alex Demeo, Jennifer Ferraro, Matt Ford, Heather Fowler, John Hatfield, Monica Hogge, Amanda Jo Huffman, Abby Humberson, Sarah Johnson, Daniel Joyce, Andrew Keeney, Justin Knight, David Lawson, Will Lively, Christopher Mahdavi, James Mahood, Vince McDermott, Katie Minan, Nick Myers, Colin O'neill, Jessica Poe, Eric Saffell, Lauren Sarna, Lisa Scarbrough, William Sebok, Jake Segall, and Shane Smith.

Third, we value the contributions made by several groups composed of COMM 112 students enrolled at West Virginia University during the spring 2007 semester. Each group designed an application activity for one of the 12 chapters; look for these application activities in the Instructor's Manual. These groups, and the members who contributed to the activity, follow:

Group 1—IMPULSE: Billy Davis, Amanda Jo Huffman, Megan Morris, Justin Suder

Group 5—The Small Groupies: Amy Arnett, Adrienne DeMinico, Adam Johnson, Ashley Murray

Group 6—The Communi-vaders: Katherine Austin, Mike Dent, Sarah

Johnson, Nick Myers

Group 7—The Communicateers: Olorunlogbon Ayo, Damia Dobbs, Patrick Jones, Darla Nething, Frank Vicendese

Group 9—The Five Little Piggies: Robert Baker, Nichole Drzewiecki, Christine Kaminski, Andrew Ochs

Group 10—D'WOK: Derek Ballard, Sarah Durand, Andrew Keeney, Megan Oliwa, Charles Welling

Group 12—The Fantastic Five: Chris Enourato, Steven Paris, Benjamin Whetzel

Group 13—Comm Gamers: Justin Kolodziej, Kristen Perfetto, Ryan White

Group 14—Five Foxy Flames: Chantal Biancheri, Jennifer Ferraro, Rachel Labaton, Brittany Pinion, Sheana Williams

Group 15—The Ski-Some: Joe Blalock, Sean Coveleski, Adam Lambruno, Jessica Poe

Group 16—Comm Junkies: Tavia Blount, Amanda Fischer, Adam Larrimore, Tara Potter, Cody Winters

Group 17—Four Busy People: David Lawson, Kayla Fisher, Daphne Pringle

Group 18—Variety Pack: Kevin Birkner, Evan Flynn, Matt Propst

Group 19—Communination: Kelli Brown, Matt Ford, Anne Lewis, Justin Pyles, Steve Young

Group 21—The Comm Ladies: Monique Burton, Scott Frye, Nelson Long, Donald Reese, Allison Sutherland

Group 22—The Jolly Roger Tenfour: Christopher Byrd, Andrew Garrison, Katie Minan, Aubrey Rothstein

Group 24—Old School Communicators: Jennifer Cain, Margaret Crandall, Nate Gladish, Ryan Lusk, Lauren Sarna

Group 28—The COMManders: Adam Castleman, Dan Melnik, Jake Segall

Group 29—The Little Rascals: Nathaniel Clay, Joey Greco, Chris Mahdavi, Robert Shearer, Evan Steadman

Group 30—Homegrown Mountaineers: Thomas Chandler, Lora Martin, Justin Miller, Cole Shaffer

Group 32—The Communicator Gators: Derek Combs, Brandon Coury, Vince McDermott, Shane Smith, Josh Waller

Group 35—The Phenomenals: Erica Conway, Justin Knight, Monica Hogge, Alastair Stansfield, Andrea McMillen

Group 39—Z Inc.: Zebulon Shively

Moreover, the case study in Appendix A is based on a case study written by Group 2: The Infamous Artists (Jessica Smith, Patrick McGraw, Grant Cupp, Nate Hoot, Mike Alfieri) as a COMM 112 course assignment at West Virginia University during the fall 2006 semester.

Fourth, we acknowledge the efforts of the reviewers who provided us with some excellent tips, suggestions, and ideas. These reviewers include Carolyn Clark, Salt Lake Community College; Chad Edwards, Western Michigan University; Ann Marie Jablonowski, Owens Community College; Curtis VanGeison, St. Charles Community College; Sally Vogl-Bauer, University of Wisconsin–Whitewater; and Shawn Wahl, Texas A&M University–Corpus Christi.

Fifth, we are indebted to our team at Sage Publications. Todd Armstrong believed in our ability to write this textbook and encouraged us to maintain our vision as we completed each chapter. Sarah Quesenberry guided us smoothly and effortlessly through the production process. Melinda Orman helped us find our active voice and refine our point of view. And although Katie Grim is no longer with Sage, she served as an invaluable source of support and guidance when we began this project. Without their collective involvement, this textbook would not have reached fruition.

And last, but certainly not least, we would like to thank our families and our friends who served, albeit unknowingly, as the inspiration for each case study. As small group communication researchers acknowledge, any group is only as good as its members. For that, we are grateful.

Components of Small Group Communication 1

After reading this chapter, you should be able to:

1. define small group communication,
2. identify and explain the three primary features of small group communication,
3. identify and explain the three secondary features of small group communication,
4. differentiate among the eight types of groups, and
5. explain the role ethical responsibility plays in the small group.

Case Study

It is the second day of COMM 112: Small Group Communication, and students are assigned to their work groups for the semester. This group consists of five members—David Cohen, Hassan Dedhia, Julie Miller, Shanika Bonvillian, and Joseph O'Day—whose first task is to develop a name, logo, and slogan for their group.

Photo 1.1 Being assigned to work in a small group is common in college courses.

Source: ©iStockphoto.com/ericsphotography.

David: I can't believe we're being made to start working in groups already. I mean, it's only the second day of class! How are we supposed to develop a name, logo, and slogan when we don't even know each other?

Julie: I think the purpose of the assignment is so we get to know each other. Remember, the name of the class is Small Group Communication, so it makes sense we would work in groups.

Hassan: I agree with Dave. It's only the second day of class! Usually when I work with people in a group I like to spend some time getting to know them before we start working together. I can't tell you how many groups I've been in where people don't get to know each other and they end up not doing the best job they could.

Shanika: Why don't we go around the group then and tell a little about our-selves? This way we can get to know each other, and that might help us start thinking about how to complete the assignment. Plus, we're all communication studies majors, so we may be more alike than we think. Joseph, would you like to start?

Joseph:	Not really. (awkward silence)
David:	Fine. I'll start. My name is Dave, I'm on the swim team, I don't work, and I have a girlfriend.
Hassan:	I'm Hassan, but my friends call me "Wizard." I work at Rockin' Rod's on the weekends, and I'm doing an internship with First American Savings & Loan, so I'll be really busy this semester. Plus, I'm a dee-jay at U-101.5, the campus radio station, and I work every night, so it's going to be tough for me to meet with you guys.
Julie:	Hi everyone. My name is Julie Miller, and I'm a fifth-year senior double majoring in communication studies and Spanish. I hope to go to graduate school next year in either comm. or Spanish—I haven't made up my mind yet. Eventually I hope to move to New York City and work for the United Nations as an interpreter, but that will probably depend on whether I get married to my boyfriend. He is from Indiana and doesn't like the thought of living in New York City, but I'm hoping I can change his mind (giggle). Anyway, I'm looking forward to this class and working in this group. I think we can do a great job, and I'm always looking for a challenge, so hopefully this class will be a great experience.
Shanika:	Well, I don't have much to add. My name is Shanika, and I'm also a fifth-year senior. I work at Payless ShoeSource at the mall, so if you ever need shoes, let me know and I can get you a discount.
Joseph:	My name is Joseph. Just so you know, I'm not a comm. major. I'm just taking this class because I needed a class. (another awkward silence)
Shanika:	It sounds like we all have a lot of things going on in our lives, so maybe we should look at our schedules and figure out a time when we can all meet and sort out this first assignment.
David:	If we meet at night, we could always meet at my house. I don't live too far from campus and my roommate is never home, so we'd have the place to ourselves.
Hassan:	If we're going to meet at night, it'd be easier if we met at the radio station. Like I said, I work every night. If you want to meet after 10 p.m., that's fine, but I'm unavailable until then.
Julie:	I think I'd be more comfortable meeting at the Student Center or the library. This way, we won't interrupt anyone's home life or job.

David:	You won't be interrupting anything at my house. I'm the only one there most of the time.
Hassan:	We won't be interrupting anything at the radio station either. As long as I have music playing, I can do what I want.
Shanika:	I don't care where we meet, just as long as we do it soon. This assignment is due next Monday! That's less than a week away. Joseph, what do you think?
Joseph:	I don't care, either. The sooner, the better.
Shanika:	Why don't we all write our e-mail addresses and phone numbers on a piece of paper and then make five copies? This way we won't have an excuse not to contact one another.
David:	If you want, I can photocopy it. My roommate works at Kinko's so if we ever need photocopies, I can do it.
Julie:	David, that's a good idea. You know, I think we're going to work well together.
Shanika:	Now I think we need to start thinking about some ideas on completing the assignment.
Hassan:	Why don't we all come up with ideas on our own and then get together and talk about them?
David:	Yeah, everyone should come up with three ideas, and we can choose the best one. Shanika, give me the paper, and I'll photocopy it and bring the copies to the meeting.
Shanika:	Okay. So when are we meeting?
Hassan:	Let's meet at the radio station Thursday night around 8 p.m. Does anyone have a problem with that?
Julie:	I guess that's okay, Wizard. I've always wanted to see what a radio station looks like anyway.
Hassan:	Joseph?
Joseph:	Whatever.
Hassan:	Dave?
David:	That's fine. If it gets too busy there, we can always go to my house.
Shanika:	Then it's settled. Thursday night at 8 p.m. at the radio station. See you then.

 s this case study demonstrates, working in a small group can be simultaneously exciting and frustrating. On one hand, working in a small group can be exciting when joint efforts are recognized and celebrated, when relationships with new people are formed, and when you can identify your contributions to making a small group endeavor successful. On the other hand, working in a small group can be frustrating due to the lack of cooperation that may exist among members, the possibility of the emergence of conflict, and the clash of personalities of group members. But regardless of the feelings you have about working (and communicating) in a small group, knowing about the small group communication process is beneficial.

The purpose of this chapter is to introduce you to small group communication. In this chapter, you will be provided with the advantages and disadvantages of working in a small group as well as a definition of small group communication. We then will identify and explain the three primary features and the three secondary features associated with small group communication. Once these features have been explained, we will explore the eight types of groups to which you may belong. Finally, we will examine the ethics associated with working in a small group.

Definition of Small Group Communication

Think back to the communication encounters in which you participated yesterday. Chances are you engaged in a variety of them: eating breakfast with your roommate, exchanging pleasantries with the clerk at the Daily Grind when you purchased your late-morning coffee, stopping by your favorite professor's office during her office hours, presenting a speech in your public-speaking class, spending time with your history study group preparing for an upcoming project, calling your dad to discuss your weekend trip home, e-mailing your romantic partner who attends another university, and yelling at the television when your team won in double overtime. Of these encounters, however, only one can be considered small group communication. Can you identify which encounter it is?

If you chose the encounter with the study group, you are correct. As you reflect again on these examples, you will note several characteristics that separate the time spent with the study group from the time spent in the other encounters. Once you've read this chapter, the characteristics will become even more apparent.

Before we offer a definition of small group communication, it is important to identify the advantages and disadvantages of working in a small group. Four advantages are associated with working in a small group. The first centers on the group's access to resources, which is considered to be the key advantage to working in groups (Baker & Campbell, 2004). In this sense, resources refer to time; money; member expertise, talent, or ability; or information. Successful groups take advantage of their access to resources. The second advantage is that group work provides members with a better understanding and retention of the concepts being examined by the group (Young & Henquinet, 2000). The third advantage is diversity in terms of group member opinion. The fourth advantage is creativity, which refers to the process by which group members engage in idea generation (Sunwolf, 2002).

Four disadvantages are associated with working in a group. The first is group member task coordination. As the number of group members increases, so does the ability for group members to coordinate, monitor, and regulate how the group task is accomplished. When group size increases, so too does the tendency for group communication to become less efficient as group members encounter more difficulty managing their relationships with each other (Bertcher & Maple, 1996) and less communication centers on the group task (Wheelan & McKeage, 1993). The second disadvantage is social loafing, which refers to the process by which individual member efforts decrease as the number of group members increases (Latane, Williams, & Harkins, 1979). The larger the group, the greater the likelihood that individual group members will become more lax in contributing to the group task.

The third disadvantage centers on conflict. Although conflict is inherent in group work (Fisher, 1970), excessive or destructive fighting and arguing among group members can occur. Conflict will be explored further in Chapter 11. The fourth disadvantage is coping with member misbehaviors. Examples of misbehaviors include missing group meetings, failing to meet deadlines, spending more time on interpersonal issues than task issues, and failing to respond to member requests. Although these misbehaviors may be minor, they can become problematic because they affect how the group eventually completes its task. Additionally, not all members will participate in group interaction. Some may feel their contributions are not welcomed by other members, some may

> **?** What are some additional advantages and disadvantages associated with working in your work group? Do the advantages outweigh the disadvantages? How?

figure it is easier to let other group members speak for them, some may feel like they have to fight for the chance to be heard by the group, or some may be apprehensive about communicating and therefore their contributions (or lack thereof) are never acknowledged by the group.

Now that you are aware of the advantages and disadvantages of working in a small group, let's turn our attention to the definition of small group communication. We define small group communication as three or more people working interdependently for the purpose of accomplishing a task. To further understand small group communication, we need to examine the three primary features of small group communication: group size, interdependence, and task.

Primary Features of Small Group Communication

Group Size

Although small group researchers have disagreed over exactly how many members equate to a group (Bertcher & Maple, 1996; Shaw, 1981; Simmel, 1902), the general consensus is that for a small group to exist, it must have a minimum of 3 members and no more than 15 members (Socha, 1997). John Cragan and David Wright (1999), two prominent researchers in the field of small group communication, identified the ideal small group size as five to seven members. Regardless of how many members a group comprises, it is important to consider that all members have an influence on each other. This leads us to the next characteristic of a small group, interdependence.

Interdependence

The concept of interdependence is most closely associated with systems theory, which states that all parts of a system work together to adapt to its environment. Because the parts are linked to one another, a change in one part affects, in some way, the other parts. The process by which a change in one part affects the other parts is called interdependence. In a small group, interdependence occurs when members coordinate their efforts to accomplish their task. When something happens to, or affects, one group member, it will impact the rest of the group members—that is, interdependence means that any group member's behavior influences both group members' task behaviors and their relational behaviors (Bertcher, 1994). Additionally, interdependence explains why a group can accomplish something collectively that individual members cannot accomplish alone (Henman, 2003). For example, suppose that Malik, a member of your history study group, does not attend the group's study session. His absence could affect the task behaviors of the group in numerous ways: If Malik has the only copy of the group's paper, your group now has to reconstruct the paper based on members' recollection of prior work. If Malik borrowed your class notes, you might have to borrow the notes from Mei-Len, another group member. If your group relies on Malik to question its decisions, his absence might cause the group to not examine its position. Malik's absence also could affect the relational behaviors of the group. For instance, when you ask Mei-Len to lend you her notes, she might hesitate based on her interpretation of Malik's behavior. Or if Malik is known to infuse humor into a tense group moment, his absence might cause conflict to escalate whereas his presence would cause conflict to subside. The bottom line is that regardless of how Malik's absence affects the rest of the group, his absence will affect, somehow, the ways in which group members complete the task and interact with each other.

Interdependence is a vital characteristic of a small group and should not be confused with independence (i.e., group members can work without ever having an effect on each other) or dependence (i.e., group members cannot function without being in the presence of each other). Rather, it is important to consider that a group's interdependence ultimately will have an impact on how the group accomplishes its task (sometimes referred to as an activity or goal), the primary reason why groups are formed.

Task

Without a task, a group need not exist. Often considered the purpose behind a group, a task is defined as an activity in which no externally correct decision exists and whose completion depends on member acceptance (Fisher, 1971). According to Ira Steiner (1972), small groups face additive tasks and conjunctive tasks. An additive task calls for group members to work individually on a task or one aspect of a task. Once all group members have completed their individual tasks, they then combine their efforts to create a final product. Groups that engage in an additive task often do not demonstrate interdependence until members combine their efforts. A conjunctive task requires group members to coordinate their efforts. Rather than work individually, group members work collectively to create a final product. This case necessitates interdependence from the moment a task is assigned to the moment of its accomplishment.

Regardless of whether a task is additive or conjunctive, consider the following: First, all members should participate in a group task. If a task is divisible or can be completed independently by group members, the nature of the task may need to be reevaluated. Second, group members may not fully comprehend the task assigned to them. Third, one member may have a vested interest in the group task, even though all group members should be working toward the same group goals. Not only should hidden agendas be discouraged; they should not be allowed. Fourth, after task completion, the group may terminate. Although this consideration may not apply to all groups, a group generally need not continue its existence if the purpose of the group centered on task accomplishment and this accomplishment was reached.

Secondary Features of Small Group Communication

In addition to group size, interdependence, and task, three secondary features of small group communication—norms, identity, and talk—need examining.

Norms

A **norm** is defined as "the limits of allowable behaviors of individual members of the group" (Bonney, 1974, p. 449). In other words, a norm is a guideline or rule designed to regulate the behaviors of group members (Fujishin, 2007). Norms can be one of three types: task, procedural, or social. A **task norm** enables the group to work toward task accomplishment. For instance, imagine a volunteer group engaging in brainstorming to select the best way to raise funds for a local charity. To accomplish this task—selecting the best way to raise funds for a local charity— the group may establish task norms such as asking members to hold their criti- cism until all ideas have been generated or requiring members to provide some support for the idea they are advocating. A **procedural norm** indicates the proce- dures the group will follow. One way the volunteer group can enact a procedural norm is by putting a time limit on the brainstorming session. A **social norm** gov- erns how group members engage in interpersonal communication. Examples of social norms include having the members of the volunteer group address each other by their first names and going out for coffee after the group meeting.

Keep in mind three considerations about norms. First, they can be developed in one of four ways (Feldman, 1984). Primarily developed through an explicit statement made by a group member, norms often transpire verbally (in either spoken or written form) and are agreed upon by the rest of the members. Norms also emerge based on a critical event in the group's history, the initial behaviors used by one member that make a lasting impression on the other group members, and members' experiences from previous group encounters. If you refer back to the case study, what norms has the group begun to develop? Which of the four ways of norm development explains the emergence of group norms for David, Hassan, Julie, Shanika, and Joseph?

?

Identify several examples of task, procedural, and social norms used in your work group. What sanctions exist for breaking these norms?

Second, a group might choose to impose a sanction on a group member if he or she violates a norm (Shaw, 1981). A sanction can be thought of as a punishment in response to a norm violation. Interestingly, the group also develops sanctions. For a sanction to be effective, the group must have both the power and the willingness to enforce it. Third, norms (and the possible accompanying sanctions) usually emerge after the second or third group meeting (Cragan & Wright, 1999). During the first meeting, most group members act on their best behavior because they are either unsure about the group task or concerned with the impressions they will make on other members. Once group members reduce their initial uncertainty about the task and each other, they let their guards down and group norms begin to develop.

Norms powerfully influence group member behavior. Developing a norm can determine not only how a group approaches its task and how group members communicate with each other but also how a group forges its identity.

Identity

Norms constitute one way a group establishes and maintains its identity (Olmsted & Hare, 1978). Identity refers to the psychological and/or physical boundaries that distinguish a group member from a non–group member. Psychological boundaries refer to the feelings experienced by group members based directly on their group membership. This psychological identity sometimes is referred to as "we-ness" and can result in both positive and negative feelings. Positive feelings include pride, cohesion, inclusion, and superiority. Negative feelings include disappointment, disgust, disapproval, and perhaps even embarrassment. Although these psychological boundaries are intangible, they play an important role in whether (and how) group members participate in group tasks, interact with one another, and perceive the group experience as enjoyable and worth their time.

Physical boundaries refer to the use of artifacts to indicate whether an individual belongs to a group. These boundaries include such things as clothing (e.g., wearing a sweatshirt or jacket emblazoned with the group's name or logo), seating arrangements in a social setting or the workplace (e.g., group members sitting next to each other in class when they are assigned a group project), and living arrangements (e.g., members of a fraternity sharing an apartment).

Photo 1.2   A uniform is one type of physical boundary that separates group members from non–group members.

Source: ©iStockphoto.com/LUGO.

Although the identity shared by group members acts as a powerful influence on them, group identity also can influence how nonmembers (i.e., people who do not belong to the group) react to group members. This influence is grouptyping. Grouptyping arises when a nonmember makes assumptions (either positive or negative) about a person based on the person's group memberships. These assumptions can be based on any number of factors: what nonmembers have heard about the group (i.e., the group's reputation), nonmembers' observations of group members, nonmembers' interactions with one member of the group, or the public display of artifacts by any group member. Suppose you decide to go study at the Student Center. As you scan the food court looking for a place to sit, you notice three available seats: one next to a student wearing a T-shirt with the letters of a sorority, one next to a student dressed in her ROTC uniform, and one next to a student wearing a Ben Roethlisberger football jersey. Which seat would you choose? If you made a judgment (whether positive or negative) about any of these three students based on their public display of artifacts announcing their group membership, you have engaged in grouptyping.

As you can guess, group identity produces ramifications for both group members and nonmembers. A group's identity will be reflected not only in how outsiders perceive the group but also in the types of talk in which group members participate.

Types of Talk

Small group communication researchers Lawrence Frey and Sunwolf (2005) posited communication is the essential defining feature of any small group. Group communication comprises four types of talk: problem-solving talk, role talk, consciousness-raising talk, and encounter talk (Cragan & Wright, 1999).

Problem-solving talk centers on accomplishing the group task. Because a group exists for the purpose of task accomplishment, members should participate in this type of talk. At the same time, it is essential to realize the bulk of a group's communication time should be spent on problem-solving talk. Although groups can use any number of discussion techniques to enhance problem-solving talk, the informal interaction of a group also can center on problem-solving talk.

Role talk centers on the specific role each group member plays in the group. Behind it is the idea that the role played by group members determines both the content and the relational aspect of their communication. In the case study provided at the beginning of this chapter, both David and Hassan struggle to establish themselves as the task leader. When David offers his house as a meeting place and Hassan suggests the group meet at the radio station, both are engaging in communication reflective of the task leader role. As you reread the exchange among the group members, what roles do Julie, Shanika, and Joseph play? You can identify these roles because group members' communication generally reflects the roles they desire to play.

Consciousness-raising talk centers on group identification and pride and is essential to group development, morale, and identity. Too much consciousness-raising talk is not productive, however. Although consciousness-raising talk enhances member satisfaction, when either a group's communication contains an inordinate amount of consciousness-raising talk or a group places greater emphasis on consciousness-raising talk than problem-solving talk, it can decrease a group's performance.

> **?** To what extent do the members of your work group engage in problem-solving talk? How often does your group engage in role talk, consciousness-raising talk, and encounter talk?

Encounter talk consists of interpersonal communication. Examples include self-disclosure, responsiveness, and empathy. When group members self-disclose to each other, respond to each other's needs, and listen to each other empathically, they develop a supportive communication climate. Furthermore, when group members feel satisfied with their group experience, they report greater feelings of closeness with their group members (Wheeless, Wheeless, & Dickson-Markman, 1982).

As such, all four types of talk contribute to effective small group communication. A group that engages in a balance of problem-solving talk, role talk, consciousness-raising talk, and encounter talk not only will accomplish its task effectively but also will act as a positive force behind whether its members enjoy the group experience. A group that fails to engage in one of these four types of talk or overemphasizes one type of talk runs the risk of hindering task accomplishment or alienating group members.

Types of Small Groups

Together, the small group communication process comprises three primary features and three secondary features. In any small group, size, interdependence, and task affect how its members communicate with each other. Norms, identity, and talk emerge from group member communication as well. These characteristics, however, are not restricted to just any one type of group.

Small group communication experts Isa Engleberg and Dianna Wynn (2003) have identified seven types of groups to which you can belong: primary, social, self-help, learning, service, work, and public. Another type of small group is the virtual group. As you read the definition of each of these eight groups, consider how the primary and the secondary features of small group communication apply to each group.

The first type of group is a primary group, which consists of members engaged in an intimate relationship. In this sense, intimacy centers on the use of several interpersonal communicative behaviors such as self-disclosure, empathy, trust, and perceived understanding. In a primary group, membership is based on sentiment (Olmsted & Hare, 1978). Two examples of a primary group are your family and your close circle of friends.

The second type of group is a social group. Unlike a primary group whose membership is composed of individuals in intimate relationships, a social group comprises members who share a common interest or engage in a common activity that binds them. Examples of a social group include membership in a fraternity or sorority, an intramural sports team, or an honor society such as Lambda Pi Eta, a national honorarium for students enrolled in communication studies courses. Although an intimate relationship can develop among members in a social group, the common interest or activity binds them.

The third type of group is a self-help group, whose membership comprises individuals who share a common problem or life situation (Meissen, Warren, & Kendall, 1996). Approximately 40% of the American population seeks help at some point from some type of a self-help group (Wuthnow, 1994). Examples of self-help groups include Alcoholics Anonymous and any number of support groups available on the Internet providing help for health, personal, or relationship issues. Greg Meissen and his colleagues (1996) found that college students are more likely to join self-help groups when dealing with such issues as a physical handicap, sexual assault, childhood abuse, AIDS, or drug abuse but are less likely to do so when dealing with such issues as relationship problems, sexual harassment, anxiety about school, or parental divorce. Once members have resolved the issue or solved the problem that influenced them to join the group, their membership in the group usually terminates.

The fourth type of group is a **learning group**. The purpose behind membership in a learning group is to enhance members' skills, abilities, or cognitive processes. In 2001, 47% of working adults joined a learning group to enhance job and language training (Snapshot, 2004). By belonging to a learning group, members hope to gain additional knowledge or improve a behavior. One example of a learning group is the group identified at the beginning of this chapter. Through membership in their classroom group, David, Hassan, Julie, Shanika, and Joseph should learn more about the small group communication process. Other examples of learning groups include enrolling in a yoga class, obtaining CPR certification, or taking a Lamaze class when you and your partner are expecting a child. Similar to membership in a self-help group, once members have acquired the needed skills, abilities, or cognitive processes (i.e., have mastered yoga, obtained their CPR certification, or experienced the birth of their child), they will no longer need to retain membership in the learning group.

The fifth type of group is a **service group**, composed largely of volunteers who donate their time, energy, and effort to help others in need of a particular service or who lack something that would help them lead a functional life. Although volunteers may belong to a service group for any number of reasons, a service group's task is to help someone less fortunate. A common service group found on many college campuses is Alpha Phi Omega. According to www.apo.org (n.d.), Alpha Phi Omega is a national, undergraduate fraternity dedicated to campus-based volunteerism. What are some examples of service groups on your college campus?

The sixth type of group is a **public group**, in which group members interact for the benefit of an audience. In most cases, little interaction occurs between the public group and the audience. At this point in your college career, you already may have participated in this type of group. One example of a public group is a **symposium**, in which each group member presents a speech on one aspect of a topic, whose theme unifies the group members in that each member is responsible for a subtopic. Another example is a **panel discussion**, when a group engages in a discussion about a topic. Usually, members of the panel provide the answers to questions posed by a moderator. The moderator may or may not be a member

Photo 1.3   Membership in a yoga class is one example of a learning group.

Source: ©iStockphoto.com/leezsnow.

of the group. If you have taken a public speaking course, you may have engaged in either a symposium or a panel discussion as one of the course requirements. Other examples of a public group include a governance board (e.g., the Student Government Association, your city council), a public forum, or some news programs on television (e.g., *Hardball* on MSNBC, *Crossfire* on CNN). These types will be discussed in greater detail in Appendix B.

The seventh type of group is a work group, which occurs within an organizational context. A work group's members complete a common task on behalf of an organization whose members take collective responsibility for the task (Keyton, 1993). Work groups are differentiated by the physical and intellectual abilities needed by group members, the amount of time the group dedicates to task completion, the task structure, the resistance group members encounter when attempting to complete the task, the degree to which task completion depends on technology, and the health risks assumed by group members as they engage in task completion (Devine, 2002). Take a moment and peruse the types of work groups listed in Table 1.1. To how many types of work groups have you belonged? What are some examples of each type?

Table 1.1   Types of Work Groups

Type	Purpose
Executive	Plan/direct
Command	Coordinate
Negotiation	Deal/persuade
Commission	Choose/investigate
Design	Create/develop
Advisory	Suggest/diagnose
Service	Provide/repair
Production	Assemble/build
Performance	Enact
Medical	Treat/heal
Response	Protect/rescue
Military	Protect/neutralize
Transportation	Haul
Sports	Compete/win

Source: From Devine, D. J. (2002). A review and integration of classification systems relevant to teams in organizations. *Group Dynamics: Theory, Research, and Practice, 6,* 291–310. Copyright © American Psychological Association.

The eighth type of group is a **virtual group**, composed of members who work interdependently on a task but from different physical locations via communication technology (Walther & Bunz, 2005). Unlike members of primary or social groups, members of virtual groups are less likely to exchange social-emotional information and their relationships may not develop as quickly or as fully (Krebs, Hobman, & Bordia, 2006). In some cases, virtual groups evolve into a **virtual community**, or a group that meets regularly in cyberspace for members to share their experiences, opinions, and knowledge on a particular topic or interest (Nicolopoulou, Kostomaj, & Campos, 2006). With the proliferation of technology and the Internet, membership in a variety of virtual groups and communities (Parker, 2003) is easily accessible.

Not all small groups can be classified neatly into one of these eight types, however. Other types of small groups, such as treatment groups and residential groups (Bertcher & Maple, 1996), exist. Also, one type of group may contain the characteristics of several of the eight types of groups. For instance, the Alpha Phi Omega Web site states membership in Alpha Phi Omega features three benefits: Membership allows members to develop their leadership skills (i.e., a learning group), experience friendship (i.e., a primary group), and engage in service activities (i.e., a service group). Although Alpha Phi Omega primarily fits the service group category, through group membership members also gain the benefits associated with a learning group and a social group.

Ethics of Small Group Membership

So far, we have provided the advantages and disadvantages of working in a small group, defined small group communication, identified and explained the primary and secondary features of small groups, and explored the eight types of groups to which you can belong. We have not yet discussed, however, the ethics associated with small group membership. Ethics, or the process of making judgments (e.g., good-bad/right-wrong/worthy-unworthy) about a person's behaviors or actions (Northouse, 2004; Seeger, 1997), surrounds the communication process (Jensen, 1997). In a small group, ethics is particularly important because as groups move through the decision-making or problem-solving process, several questions arise that must be addressed: For example, "Why are we doing this?" "Should we be doing this?" "What are the consequences (i.e., intended versus unintended, short- versus long-term) of doing this?" (Arnett, 1990; Minnick, 1980). At the same time, group members need to take into account how their verbal communication, nonverbal communication, and listening behaviors affect how they construct messages and how they interpret these messages. See Table 1.2 for ways to be an ethically responsible group member.

Many people's communicative behaviors reveal their sense of ethics. Examples of communicating in an unethical manner include deliberately lying, knowingly distorting or twisting the truth, using emotional appeals that cannot be supported, misrepresenting a position or stance on a topic, and pretending to be informed about a topic (Brown & Keller, 1994). To avoid communicating unethically, group members should follow four guidelines (Wallace, 1955): First, do not withhold information from group members. Second, be truthful and accurate when sharing information with group members.

> 66 *Ethically Speaking:* What are some ethical guidelines that your work group has adopted? How have these guidelines impacted how your group approaches a task? 99

Facts and opinions should be presented fairly, the use of propaganda should be avoided, and the appropriate

Table 1.2   Assuming Ethical Responsibility

To assume ethical responsibility, group members should:
1. be able to make up their minds without normative pressure to conform.
2. share the accountability of the task decisions and consequences.
3. communicate with each other as they would want other members to communicate with them.
4. self-disclose appropriately to share values and opinions in a spirit of openness and honesty.
5. be allowed to develop their potential as an individual and as a group member.
6. avoid attacking the competencies of other members.
7. engage in sound reasoning behaviors that reflect value.

Source: Reprinted by permission of Waveland Press, Inc. from R.l. Johannesen, *Ethics in human communication* (5th ed.). (Long Grove, IL: Waveland Press, Inc., 2002). All rights reserved.

vocabulary and language should be used when communicating with each other. Third, group members should reveal all sources of information and opinion by ensuring that the information does not contain rumor, gossip, or unsubstantiated fact. Moreover, group members should acknowledge any personal motivation they have when it comes to the group making a decision or solving a problem. Fourth, respect dissent by recognizing the diversity of argument and opinion that can exist among group members.

Perhaps the best method by which group members can embrace ethics is to adopt a code of ethical responsibility. Ethical responsibility requires group members to act in a way that not only promotes caring for both themselves and each other but also requires members to share equally in assuming responsibility for the consequences of their actions (Littlejohn & Jabusch, 1982). Ethics expert Richard Johannesen (2002) identified a host of ways in which group members can embrace ethical responsibility. By adopting a code of ethical responsibility, group members can establish a foundation for quality decision making and problem solving that considers the consequences of these decisions and problems.

A Final Note About Small Group Communication

After reading this book and completing this course, you will learn more about your own feelings about working in groups. Specifically, you will be able to identify the aspects of group work that intrigue, motivate, or perhaps even irritate you. You also may be able to determine whether any feelings of grouphate—feelings of dread that arise when faced with the possibility of having to work in a group (Sorensen, 1981)—are warranted or whether these feelings pertain to membership in a particular group. In such learning groups as classroom groups, grouphate can be particularly detrimental. Grouphate emerges in classroom groups for many reasons: Group members misbehave, fail to contribute equally to the task, receive the same grade regardless of their input, and experience personality clashes (Myers, Goodboy, & Members of COMM 612, 2004). Unfortunately, when students working in classroom groups experience grouphate, they report less learning, less group cohesion, less group consensus, less relational satisfaction, and fewer positive attitudes about group work (Keyton, Harmon, & Frey, 1996; Myers & Goodboy, 2005).

As researchers have noted, however, knowing how and being able to work effectively in a small group, both in and out of the classroom (Curtis, Winsor, & Stephens, 1989; Hawkins & Fillion, 1999; Wardrope & Bayless, 1999; Winsor, Curtis, & Stephens, 1997; Winter & Neal, 1995), has important ramifications. In fact, the results obtained from a national survey found that being able to work in a group is one of the most important competencies an employee can have (Echternacht & Wen, 1997). Because "membership in groups is almost inescapable" (Bonney, 1974, p. 445), being able to reflect on what you have learned as a member of a small group undoubtedly will help you become a viable partner in future academic, work, and community endeavors.

Conclusion

With the purpose of introducing you to small group communication, this chapter provided the advantages and disadvantages of working in a small group, defined small group communication, identified and explained the three primary features and the three secondary features associated with group communication, explored the eight types of groups to which you can belong, and examined the ethics associated with working in a small group. As you read the next chapter, consider how the features of small group communication contribute to the socialization process you experience when you join a group.

Discussion Questions

1. How would you define small group communication? In addition to the three primary features and the three secondary features of small group communication identified in this chapter, what additional features would you add? Why?

2. Review the advantages and disadvantages of group work. To what extent do these advantages and disadvantages depend on whether the group is a primary, social, self-help, learning, service, public, work, or virtual group?

3. Select two of the eight types of groups. For each group, generate examples of problem-solving talk, role talk, consciousness-raising talk, and encounter talk that have occurred. Is there a difference in the quantity of the types of talk between the two groups? Is there a difference in the quality of the types of talk between the two groups? How might you explain these differences?

4. Apply the three primary features and the three secondary features of small group communication to the case study provided at the beginning of this chapter. Based on this group's first interaction, how successful do you think the group will be?

5. How would the three primary features of small group communication and the three secondary features of small group communication apply to a virtual group?

References

Alpha Phi Omega. (n.d.). *About us.* Retrieved May 25, 2007, from http://www.apo.org/pages/show/About_Us

Arnett, R. C. (1990). The practical philosophy of communication ethics and free speech as the foundation for speech communication. *Communication Quarterly, 38,* 208–217.

Baker, D. F., & Campbell, C. M. (2004). When is there strength in numbers?: A study of undergraduate task groups. *College Teaching, 53,* 14–18.

Bertcher, H. J. (1994). *Group participation: Techniques for leaders and members* (2nd ed.). Thousand Oaks, CA: Sage.

Bertcher, H. J., & Maple, F. F. (1996). *Creating groups* (2nd ed.). Thousand Oaks, CA: Sage.

Bonney, W. C. (1974). The maturation of groups. *Small Group Behavior, 5,* 445–461.

Brown, C. T., & Keller, P. W. (1994). Ethics. In R. Anderson, K. N. Cissna, & R. C. Arnett (Eds.), *The reach of dialogue: Confirmation, voice, and community* (pp. 284–289). Cresskill, NJ: Hampton Press.

Cragan, J. F., & Wright, D. W. (1999). *Communication in small groups: Theory, process, skills* (5th ed.). Belmont, CA: Wadsworth.

Curtis, D. B., Winsor, J. L., & Stephens, R. D. (1989). National preferences in business and communication education. *Communication Education, 38,* 6–14.

Devine, D. J. (2002). A review and integration of classification systems relevant to teams in organizations. *Group Dynamics: Theory, Research, and Practice, 6,* 291–310.

Echternacht, L., & Wen, L-Y. M. (1997). The importance of workplace basics competencies (SCANS) as perceived by beginning-business teachers and experienced business teachers. *College Student Journal, 31,* 37–44.

Engleberg, I. N., & Wynn, D. R. (2003). *Working in groups: Communication principles and strategies* (3rd ed.). Boston: Houghton Mifflin.

Feldman, D. C. (1984). The development and emergence of group norms. *Academy of Management Review, 9,* 47–53.

Fisher, B. A. (1970). Decision emergence: Phases in group decision making. *Speech Monographs, 37,* 53–66.

Fisher, B. A. (1971). Communication research and the task-oriented group. *Journal of Communication, 21,* 136–149.

Frey, L. R., & Sunwolf. (2005). The communication perspective on group life. In S. A. Wheelan (Ed.), *The handbook of group research and practice* (pp. 158–186). Thousand Oaks, CA: Sage.

Fujishin, R. (2007). *Creating effective groups: The art of small group communication* (2nd ed.). Lanham, MD: Rowman & Littlefield.

Hawkins, K. W., & Fillion, B. P. (1999). Perceived communication skill needs for work groups. *Communication Research Reports, 16,* 167–174.

Henman, L. D. (2003). Groups as systems. In R. Y. Hirokawa, R. S. Cathcart, L. A. Samovar, & L. D. Henman (Eds.), *Small group communication theory & practice: An anthology* (8th ed., pp. 3–7). Los Angeles: Roxbury.

Jensen, J. V. (1997). *Ethical issues in the communication process.* Mahwah, NJ: Erlbaum.

Johannesen, R. L. (2002). *Ethics in human communication* (5th ed.). Prospect Heights, IL: Waveland Press.

Keyton, J. (1993). Group termination. *Small Group Research, 24,* 84–100.

Keyton, J. (1999). *Group communication: Process and analysis.* Mountain View, CA: Mayfield.

Keyton, J., Harmon, N., & Frey, L. R. (1996, November). *Grouphate: Implications for teaching group communication.* Paper presented at the annual meeting of the Speech Communication Association, San Diego, CA.

Krebs, S. A., Hobman, E. V., & Bordia, P. (2006). Virtual teams and group member dissimilarity: Consequences for the development of trust. *Small Group Research, 37,* 721–741.

Latane, B., Williams, K., & Harkins, S. (1979). Many hands make light the work: The causes and consequences of social loafing. *Journal of Personality and Social Psychology, 37,* 822–832.

Littlejohn, S. W., & Jabusch, D. M. (1982). Communication competence: Model and application. *Journal of Applied Communication Research, 10,* 29–37.

Meissen, G., Warren, M. L., & Kendall, M. (1996). An assessment of college student willingness to use self-help groups. *Journal of College Student Development, 37,* 448–456.

Minnick, W. C. (1980). A new look at the ethics of persuasion. *Southern Speech Communication Journal, 45,* 352–362.

Myers, S. A., Goodboy, A. K., & Members of COMM 612. (2004, April). *An investigation of grouphate in the small group communication course.* Paper presented at the annual meeting of the Central States Communication Association, Cleveland, OH.

Myers, S. A., & Goodboy, A. K. (2005). A study of grouphate in a course on small group communication. *Psychological Reports, 97,* 381–386.

Nicolopoulou, K., Kostomaj, M., & Campos, A. (2006). How to address group dynamics in virtual worlds. *AI & Society, 20,* 351–371.

Northouse, P. G. (2004). *Leadership: Theory and practice* (3rd ed.). Thousand Oaks, CA: Sage.

Olmsted, M. S., & Hare, A. P. (1978). *The small group* (2nd ed.) New York: Random House.

Parker, R. E. (2003). Distinguishing characteristics of virtual groups. In R. Y. Hirokawa, R. S. Cathcart, L. A. Samovar, & L. D. Henman (Eds.), *Small group communication theory and practice: An anthology* (8th ed., pp. 17–24). Los Angeles: Roxbury.

Seeger, M. W. (1997). *Ethics and organizational communication.* Cresskill, NJ: Hampton Press.

Shaw, M. E. (1981). *Group dynamics: The psychology of small group behavior* (3rd ed.). New York: McGraw-Hill.

Simmel, G. (1902). The number of members as determining the sociological form of the group. *American Journal of Sociology, 8,* 1–45, 158–196.

Snapshot. (2004, July 20). *USA Today,* p. D1.

Socha, T. J. (1997). Group communication across the life span. In L. R. Frey & J. K. Barge (Eds.), *Managing group life: Communicating in decision-making groups* (pp. 3–28). Boston: Houghton Mifflin.

Sorensen, S. M. (1981, May). *Grouphate.* Paper presented at the annual meeting of the International Communication Association, Minneapolis, MN.

Steiner, I. D. (1972). *Group process and productivity.* New York: Academic Press.

Sunwolf. (2002). Getting to "groupaha!": Provoking creative processes in task groups. In L. R. Frey (Ed.), *New directions in group communication* (pp. 203–217). Thousand Oaks, CA: Sage.

Wallace, K. R. (1955). An ethical basis of communication. *The Speech Teacher, 4,* 1–9.

Walther, J. B., & Bunz, U. (2005). The rules of virtual groups: Trust, liking, and performance in computer-mediated communication. *Journal of Communication, 55,* 828–846.

Wardrope, W. J., & Bayless, M. L. (1999). Content of the business communication course: An analysis of coverage. *Business Communication Quarterly, 62*(4), 33–40.

Wheelan, S. A., & McKeage, R. L. (1993). Developmental patterns in small and large groups. *Small Group Research, 24,* 60–83.

Wheeless, L. R., Wheeless, V. E., & Dickson-Markman, F. (1982). The relations among social and task perceptions in small groups. *Small Group Behavior, 12,* 373–384.

Winsor, J. L., Curtis, D. B., & Stephens, R. D. (1997). National preferences in business and communication education: A survey update. *Journal of the Association for Communication Administration, 3,* 170–179.

Winter, J. K., & Neal, J. C. (1995). Group writing: Student perceptions of the dynamics and efficiency of groups. *Business Communication Quarterly, 58*(2), 21–24.

Wright, K. B. (1999). Computer-mediated support groups: An examination of relationships among social support, perceived stress, and coping strategies. *Communication Quarterly, 47,* 402–414.

Wuthnow, D. S. (1994). *Sharing the journey: Support groups and America's new quest for community.* New York: Free Press.

Young, C. B., & Henquinet, J. A. (2000). A conceptual framework for designing group projects. *Journal of Education for Business, 76,* 56–60.

The Small Group Socialization Process | 2

After reading this chapter, you should be able to:

1. explain why individuals join groups,
2. define socialization from a communication perspective,
3. differentiate among the five phases of the Small Group Socialization Model,
4. describe the four outcomes of successful group socialization, and
5. identify and explain the socialization guidelines for newcomers and groups.

Case Study | Jason Erickson, Jamie Williams, Pat Simpson, Chris Walter, and Lei Zhong work in different departments at ASG Communication, Inc. While Jason and Lei are new hires, Jamie, Pat, and Chris joined the company more than two years ago. The company president asked this group to work on a project proposed by a new client, the March of Dimes.

As a not-for-profit organization, the March of Dimes depends on volunteers.
Its organizational goals include raising awareness about prevention of birth
defects, as well as raising money for health education and research of this health
issue. Besides this information, the group members knew no project details until
they met their appointed March of Dimes representative.

No different from most group members meeting for the first time,
Jason, Jamie, Pat, Chris, and Lei felt nervous about the project. Jamie and Pat
had not worked together on a project before. Jason and Lei had experienced
poor group relations at their prior employment organizations, where one or
two group members completed most of the work and thus carried the load
for the rest.

Michelle Lewis, promotions director for the March of Dimes, entered the
meeting room with lots of handouts and a prepared presentation explaining the
organization's mission and the multiple projects it needed the work group to
complete. The first project, a "walk- and run-a-thon event," would be held in the
summer, allowing the group just three weeks to design the event.

Jason: Let's get to know each other better. I think it will be important with all of these projects to bid on. Chances are we will be working long hours together.

Lei: We only have three weeks to come up with a plan. Who cares who we are? Let's talk about this project. That's what group members are supposed to be doing. I have responsibilities at home and have little time for socializing. My baby needs me.

Jamie: Come on, we have a few minutes. I think working on this project is great. My sister had a child with a birth defect, and the March of Dimes helped.

Chris: I agree with Lei. I work here all day and attend night school getting my master's degree. Let's just get to it. I can't spend extra time on this project.

Pat: Well, I see I'm going to have to take charge of this group. Who wants to do what?

Jamie: Look. We are all in this together, so lighten up. This project could be fun. Now, let's see what we know and what we need to know. Has anyone ever been involved in a "walk- and run-a-thon?"

A s the above case study demonstrates, employees endeavoring to begin group work sometimes find establishing how best to proceed with the task, as well as building relationships, difficult. Tension among members arises, too, when personal goals appear more important than group goals. This case study well exemplifies "getting started" in group work and relationship building, especially in a work setting.

This chapter purports to highlight the processes and practices of socialization of group members and the group as a whole. To do so, we will discuss ideas surrounding why we join groups and how group members come together to work on tasks and build relationships through successful socialization. We will define socialization from a communication perspective, present a five-phase model of group socialization, discuss positive outcomes of socialization, and offer guidelines for competencies that will help you and your group members become successful in completing tasks and building positive relationships.

Photo 2.2   Attraction theory explains why some members are motivated to join a group.

Source: ©iStockphoto.com/Yuri_Arcurs.

Why Individuals Join Groups

Individuals join groups for several reasons, including attraction to a particular group, wanting to satisfy interpersonal communication motives, and possessing a lack of volition. Let's begin with attraction theory.

Attraction Theory

Why do individuals join a specific company's work group, the company's bowling team, the Association for Women in Science, or the Public Relations Society of America? According to **attraction theory**, your answer can be traced to one of four reasons.

First, individuals may enjoy the company's products or services. Once an applicant becomes an employee, such group activities as bowling might interest him or her specifically. Suppose you bowled in college and excelled at it; chances are you will want to play on the team because you like the game. Second, a group's goals may attract individuals; for example, some join such professional groups as the Public Relations Society for America because they provide scholarships for students in need of financial aid. In this instance, members like participating in a group whose goals include humanitarian work. Third, just the idea of group membership may motivate a person to join. During college you may choose to pledge the fraternity to which your older brother belonged because you want to continue the family tradition. Fourth, individuals sometimes join groups because they like or feel a connection with one or more members. You might join a book club because your best friend is a member or you are physically attracted to and want to get to know a group member. Whatever the reason(s), attraction theory explains one reason why individuals join groups.

> **?** How does attraction theory explain why you have joined a group (or groups) at work?

Interpersonal Communication Motives

A second explanation behind individuals joining groups recalls the study of inter-personal communication motives, which addresses why people communicate in various contexts, such as groups. Researchers Rebecca Rubin and Matthew Martin (1998) argued that because communication is goal-directed, people often initiate and maintain interactions in order to satisfy their interpersonal needs. Why people interact, the means by which they interact, with whom they interact, and the content of the interactions all have been addressed by motives researchers who identify, simply, six interpersonal communication motives for communicating with people (Rubin, Perse, & Barbato, 1988; Schutz, 1966). These motives, or reasons, are detailed in Table 2.1.

Table 2.1   Interpersonal Communication Motives

Motive	Definition
Inclusion	Member is motivated to communicate to have a sense of belonging.
Affection	Member is motivated to communicate to feel liked and to like others.
Control	Member is motivated to communicate to have the power to manipulate the environment.
Escape	Member is motivated to communicate to avoid other activities or stressful situations.
Pleasure	Member is motivated to communicate to have fun.
Relaxation	Member is motivated to communicate to unwind and lower anxiety.

Source: Based on Rubin, R. B., Perse, E. M., & Barbato, C. A. (1988). Conceptualization and measurement of interpersonal communication motives. *Human Communication Research, 14,* 602–628.

The benefits of group work include the opportunity to meet one or all six interpersonal communication needs. Group members motivated to communicate for pleasure, affection, inclusion, and relaxation note greater satisfaction and cohesiveness with their group experiences while members motivated to communicate for control note lower satisfaction with their group experiences (Anderson & Martin, 1995). Additionally, members motivated to communicate for pleasure and affection attend and respond to their members whereas members motivated to communicate for control and escape neither attend nor respond to their members (Anderson & Martin, 1995). Members motivated to communicate for pleasure and affection report communicating more pleasurable and affectionate messages with their groups whereas members motivated to communicate for control interact more frequently than the other group members (Anderson & Martin, 2002).

As such, we may be motivated to communicate with others at different times and for different reasons. For example, when job hunting you might join a service group because it looks good on your resume rather than a social group because you need inclusion or affection.

Lack of Volition

A third reason some people join groups is simply that they have no choice. Once you enter the workforce, you likely will be asked to join committees or a task force at your workplace. Because organizations often rely on small groups to accomplish their mission, part of your job may require membership in several small groups.

The next section in this chapter discusses a different view of communicative processes whereby group members meet each other's needs by coming together to work in groups and build relationships. This focus turns to the processes and practices of socialization.

Small Group Socialization

A relatively new area of scholarly research, socialization in small groups provides a fresh topic for discussion in small group communication classes. The bulk of socialization research and literature fits the organizational communication context, which focuses on how employees assimilate and adjust to organizational life. Yet, from a different perspective, we can view organizations as small groups functioning as microsystems embedded within the macrosystem of organizational life. Thus, this perspective suggests socialization processes and practices also are present in small groups. Consider a major *Fortune* 500 organization, such as Ford

Motor Company, whose collective membership could not possibly solve all its problems and make all its decisions. In reality, a smaller number of members, such as a management team, assume the responsibility of working through the processes and practices of solving problems and making decisions.

> **?** When you think about your work group, what does the word *socialization* mean to you?

The remainder of this chapter specifies socialization in small groups and how group processes and practices affect the way members adjust and adapt to each other and group work. If the employees in the case study group had understood the need for member socialization, they might have gotten off to a better start than creating tension among themselves.

Definitions of Socialization

Several definitions of socialization exist. Group scholars Sheldon Stryker and Ann Statham (1985) suggested socialization occurs when newcomers become part of the group's patterns of activities. Social psychologists have defined socialization as occurring when group members create shared meaning about who will do what and how the group will operate (Mead, 1958) or when individuals learn enough to contribute skillfully and competently to the group (Dion, 1985). Each of these definitions emphasizes the role of the individual.

Taking a different perspective, social psychologists Richard Moreland and John Levine (1982) defined socialization as a reciprocal process of group members and the group as a whole coming together to meet each other's needs and accomplish goals. This type of definition suggests individuals actively participate in the socialization process rather than simply adjust and adapt to an existing group culture. Additionally, each group's culture changes when a member joins the group because she might influence the existing members to adopt new ways of communicating and functioning as a group. Thus, consider socialization as a process affecting both individual members and the group as a whole.

Taking a communication perspective, Carolyn Anderson and her colleagues (Anderson, Riddle, & Martin, 1999) posited that socialization comprises a two-way process of influence (e.g., I talk you into liking my idea, and you talk me into expanding that idea) and change whereby group members use verbal and nonverbal messages to create a new and unique group culture. The interaction among members allows them to establish rules and roles, make decisions and solve problems, and reach both individual and group goals. Furthermore, the interaction helps group members reduce their levels of uncertainty about how to complete tasks, get along with each other, and meet each other's interpersonal communication motives. Bruce Riddle, Carolyn Anderson, and Matthew Martin (2000) also created

Assessment Tool 2.1   Small Group Socialization Scale

Complete each item in regard to your experience thus far in your small group. Rate each item in relation to the following scale by filling in the blanks with what you consider an appropriate answer.

If you **strongly agree** with the statement, write **5** in the blank.

If you **agree** with the statement, write **4** in the blank.

If you **neither agree nor disagree** with the statement, write **3** in the blank.

If you **disagree** with the statement, write **2** in the blank.

If you **strongly disagree** with the statement, write **1** in the blank.

_____ 1. I understood what was appropriate dress for group meetings.

_____ 2. I understood the authority the group had for doing its work.

_____ 3. I did not see myself as an effective group member.*

_____ 4. I understood the "group talk" the group used to do its work.

_____ 5. I found someone in the group who could provide me with emotional support.

_____ 6. It was clear what was expected of me in this group.

_____ 7. I found someone in the group with whom I could talk about career plans.

_____ 8. It was not at all clear what was expected of me in this group.*

_____ 9. I depended on other group members for support in the group.

_____ 10. I found someone in the group who could help me adjust to the group.

_____ 11. I found someone in the group on whom I could depend for support.

_____ 12. I had no clear idea of what this group was to accomplish.*

_____ 13. I found someone in the group with whom I could discuss personal matters.

_____ 14. There was no one in the group on whom I could depend for support.*

Scoring:

Reverse score all items marked with an asterisk. (If you put a 5 for item 3, change this score to 1; if 4, change this score to 2; if 2, change this score to 4; if 1, change this score to 5.) Sum all items to create a general socialization outcome score. The higher the score, the more positive the socialization experience.

Source: From Riddle, B. L., Anderson, C. M., & Martin, M. M. (2000). Small Group Socialization Scale: Development and validity. *Small Group Research, 31,* 554–572. Thousand Oaks, CA: Sage.

a measurement scale for use in trying to understand the importance of socialization in small groups. Complete this scale to learn more about socialization.

To learn more about socialization, let's turn to a model of small group socialization that illustrates how socialization processes and practices function in groups.

Model of Small Group Socialization

In 1999, Carolyn Anderson and her colleagues introduced a model of small group socialization by using five phases to illustrate how communication influences socialization processes (see Figure 2.1). Phases are "different sub-periods within a total continuous period of interaction" (Bales & Strodtbeck, 1951, p. 485). As applied to group communication, each phase contains specific characteristics, either unique to that phase or appropriate across multiple phases. The phase-approach model helps group members understand how communication shapes socialization activities during the life span of groups. This model not only applies to members entering established groups; it also applies to zero history groups, such as the group illustrated in the case study.

Antecedent Phase

The first phase is the antecedent phase. In the case study, some members expressed beliefs and attitudes, both positive and negative, about group work based on personal experiences or experiences shared by others. Researchers seem to agree that whether you're entering an existing group or a new group matters not; what you bring to a group—beliefs, attitudes, and communicative and personality traits—will influence the group's culture and members. Group scholars Joann Keyton, Nicole Harmon, and Lawrence Frey (1996) posited some group members develop negative feelings toward group work because of poor experiences with it. Such members may approach current groups with less commitment and optimism than those who enjoy group work thanks to prior positive experiences. We also bring our age, race, and sex to the group composition. Biases against how people look or their origins can impede socialization of group members, resulting in some feeling unwelcome or unwanted.

Anticipatory Phase

The second phase is the anticipatory phase, in which individuals decide what they expect from group membership as well as each group member. At the group level,

Figure 2.1 Group Socialization Model: Individual Member

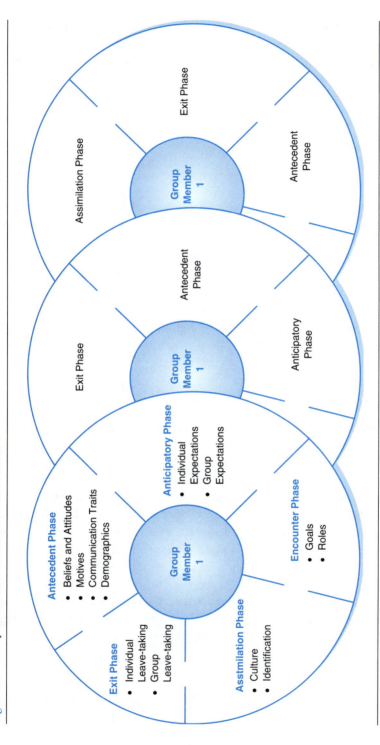

Antecedent Phase
- Beliefs and Attitudes
- Motives
- Communication Traits
- Demographics

Anticipatory Phase
- Individual Expectations
- Group Expectations

Encounter Phase
- Goals
- Roles

Assimilation Phase
- Culture
- Identification

Exit Phase
- Individual Leave-taking
- Group Leave-taking

Group Member 1

Assimilation Phase

Exit Phase

Antecedent Phase

Exit Phase

Antecedent Phase

Anticipatory Phase

Source: From Frey, L.R., Gouran, D.S., & Poole, M.S. (1999). *The handbook of group communication theory and research.* Thousand Oaks, CA: Sage.

Note: The model illustrates that in a group, individual members move through temporally and developmentally distinct socialization phases in a nonlinear cycle. Simultaneously, individuals belong to other groups likely to be in different phases of socialization processes.

existing groups form expectations about new group members. Equally, members of a zero history group (i.e., a group whose members never worked together before) harbor preconceived expectations for the group. Some researchers think the closer members come to meeting their and the group's expectations, the greater the likelihood of successful socialization (Van Maanen, 1976). According to scholar Meryl Reis Louis (1980), the group experience can prove stressful if expectations are unrealistic or not met upon entering the group. For example, in the case study, if Jason wants to spend time getting to know the group's members and Lei wants to solely focus on the task, they clearly project different expectations toward the group, the members, and the task.

Encounter Phase

During the third phase, called the encounter phase, individuals usually come together for the first time, either face-to-face or through other media (e.g., a computer software program or teleconferencing), and begin the process of establishing group goals and roles. Group scholar Dennis Gouran (1994) defined goals as what people want to achieve from joining groups, working in groups, and building relationships. One key to successful socialization in this phase is achieving the right balance among personal, group, task, and relational goals. To balance potential conflicts among the various goals, group members communicate by sharing, requesting, and receiving information. Furthermore, the members discuss acceptable behaviors and practices to assist them and the group with balancing group goal conflicts. Researchers have found members who achieve an acceptable balance among the various goals strengthen their commitment to the group and its members.

In addition, establishing roles and orienting members to their roles factor into the encounter phase. It is important to establish one critical activity in this phase: the adjustment and accommodation between individual members and the group over desirable role choices and appropriate role behaviors. Examples include negotiation among the members for the role of leader. In the case study, Jamie exhibits leadership behavior by directing communication to the task as well as attending to relational tensions by asking group members to "lighten up." As role positions and behaviors become established in this phase, expect them to continue as the members and group move to the next phase.

Assimilation Phase

In the fourth phase, the assimilation phase, new members accept the established group culture and begin to identify with the group and its members. As applied to groups, culture encompasses members creating a unique group and using communicative behaviors exclusive to their group to make sense of what they do (Swogger, 1981). These behaviors might include rites and rituals—for example, the group members in the case study meeting in the lobby coffee shop instead of in Lei's office. Sometimes, however, group members find themselves adopting the established culture but also trying to change it as the group moves through the process of task work and maintaining relationships. Researcher Richard Moreland (1985) offered that how long it takes to establish a group's culture affects how long it will take for successful assimilation of each member.

Identification contributes necessarily to successful assimilation of members into groups. Oftentimes, group members refer to assimilation as "we-ness" or the feeling of "group-ness." Continually accomplishing tasks and building relationships allows individual members and the group to communicate while creating and re-creating their identity. Successful assimilation occurs when each member sees his values and interests coinciding with those of the group. Problems arise when a group member finds he cannot accept other members' attempts to change the group's course of direction.

> **?** At what point did you realize you had reached the assimilation stage of socialization in a current or prior work group? How long did it take for you to reach this stage?

In such instances, the member experiences a break in the feeling of "we-ness" and may be forced to leave the group. The case study challenges Lei and Chris to take the time to help establish a group culture and identity during the assimilation phase.

Exit Phase

The fifth phase is the **exit phase**. Members exit learning, work, and social groups, and the groups themselves may end. In the case study, the group gets three weeks to complete the project, after which the group ends. On the other hand, if you quit your job, you leave the group, but the group remains as part of the organization. Group scholars are beginning to focus on group endings and individual leave-taking effects as key factors in the exit phase because they are thought to influence attitudes about future groups and behaviors in them (Sinclair-James & Stohl, 1997).

Scholar Joann Keyton (1993) offered that when groups end, members should meet one last time to evaluate their work, celebrate a job well done, and say goodbye. This is good advice—one reason stems from the fact that all members of successful groups experience the tensions associated with disbanding a successful group and sustaining the friendships built in them. In some cases, when group conflict is high, a final meeting can defuse emotions and force the members to reflect on the positive points of their group experience.

When individuals voluntarily leave an existing group, such as a work team, they form impressions and attitudes about their experience and add it to their library of experiences (Anderson et al., 1999). After a poor experience, an individual may struggle to identify with another work team and be less receptive to future socialization processes. Leave-taking, when a member quits or drops out, can affect groups positively or negatively. One positive example describes the established members welcoming to their group a new individual who brings a needed expertise to share. A negative leave-taking might force established members to spend time socializing a new member and confronting the process of change.

In summary, the model of small group socialization illustrates in five phases how group members bring competencies, attitudes, and beliefs to each group to which they belong (Anderson et al., 1999). Socialization processes begin in anticipating the group and its members. Once members come together, their unique communicative interactions help them establish ground rules and norms in building an identity. When the members feel comfortable with the group and each other, they engage in the assimilation phase, which binds and helps them make sense of their collective task. After completion, group members must confront life without that group membership, and when individuals leave the group, their exit affects how they confront life without that group experience. The next section explores the outcomes of successful or unsuccessful small group socialization.

Outcomes of Socialization

A large body of small group research focuses on task and relational outcome factors as measures of successful (or unsuccessful) small groups and member relationships. Similarly, successful groups benefit from positive socialization outcomes, which describe how members and the group as a whole feel about how they cooperated and succeeded in completing goals. Four group outcomes relate to group socialization: cohesion, consensus, communication satisfaction, and loneliness.

Cohesion

Although various definitions of cohesion exist, Dorwin Cartwright (1968) discussed cohesion from a member's perspective. He defined cohesion as a member reaching an acceptable level of desire to stay in the group. Furthermore, he identified such factors as attraction among group members, evaluation of the group's chances for success, and identification with the group as ways to view and measure cohesion. Subsequently, group scholars continue to expand ideas associated with cohesion; some researchers suggest that cohesion can result from the task, the relationships, or a blending of both. At the group level, groups can be perceived as cohesive by displaying their "we-ness," such as by all members wearing the same shirts. As for the relationship between cohesiveness and socialization, two studies have reported that members who perceive their socialization processes as positive also perceive their groups as cohesive (Anderson & Martin, 2001; Riddle et al., 2000).

Consensus

On occasion groups reach agreement on decision-making tasks or group goals through a process known as consensus. Consensus means all group members agree with and commit to the decision (DeStephen & Hirokawa, 1988). Consensus takes preference over majority rule (e.g., "Three members win against two members") and compromise (e.g., "I don't like arguing, so I'll give in") because groups reaching consensus often reach cohesion. In general, group scholars Sunwolf and David Seibold (1999) suggested members reaching consensus feel better about and want to remain in their groups. Because consensus closely relates to cohesion, Riddle et al. (2000) predicted consensus also would relate to positive socialization practices—a supported prediction. Plausibly, this finding results from socialization processes and practices creating an atmosphere where members feel comfortable communicating with the group and each other and thus successfully navigate decision-making processes that permit full member participation.

Communication Satisfaction

Communication scholar Michael Hecht (1978) offered what now holds sway among the popular definitions of communication satisfaction, describing it as a "felt experience," or when people experience feelings of satisfaction or dissatisfaction with the communication that takes place interpersonally. As applied to the group setting, scholars have suggested communication satisfaction describes members who walk away from group meetings or from the group feeling positively fulfilled from the experience (Anderson & Martin, 1995; Anderson, Martin, & Riddle, 2001).

In a review of the group satisfaction literature, Richard Heslin and Dexter Dunphy (1964) reported satisfaction can be viewed from three dimensions:

1. how members see consensus in their group concerning each member's role,

2. judgments of the group's progress toward reaching goals,

3. freedom to participate in group interaction.

Notice these factors also relate to concepts illustrated in the model of small group socialization. To support these ideas, researchers have found in three studies

Photo 2.3   When group members experience loneliness, they also may experience negative feelings toward the group task and their group members.

Source: ©iStockphoto.com/aldomurillo.

that members' reports of positive socialization experiences positively correlate with members' reports of satisfaction with the communication in their group (Anderson & Martin, 2001; Anderson et al., 2001; Riddle et al., 2000).

Loneliness

Not all group experiences are positive. The same holds true for socialization experiences in groups. Stephen Worchel (1994) described loneliness in the group setting as a powerlessness some members feel from not being able or allowed to participate in the group's process (e.g., not feeling free to contribute ideas or opinions). Furthermore, Jon Hess (1993), a professor of communication studies at the University of Dayton, suggested loneliness results from socialization practices that include only the task dimension and fail to attend to the relational dimension of group work. According to Joann Keyton (2000), the relational side of group work is as important as the task; in fact, the two dimensions are interdependent.

Loneliness may be an understudied factor in groups because it is hard to imagine a person feeling lonely in a small group. Carolyn Anderson and Matthew Martin (1995) reported group members experience loneliness as a result of dissatisfaction with the communicative processes and practices in the group. In effect, loneliness closely relates to negative perceptions of cohesion, consensus, and communication satisfaction in the group.

In another study, Bruce Riddle and his coauthors (2000) found support for the speculation that positive socialization processes and practices result in members not feeling lonely. Their results make sense. Remember, people join and work in groups to meet needs associated with inclusion, affection, and control (Schutz, 1966). Furthermore, people also have needs associated with motives for communicating in groups. When these types of needs are not met through positive socialization processes and practices,

> ❝ *Ethically Speaking:* Should employees be trained in how to engage in positive socialization processes and practices in groups so that no member experiences loneliness? Why? ❞

newcomers or members in newly formed groups often experience frustration, isolation, and feelings of alienation in the group. Loneliness, then, may lead to negative feelings about groups or a member's exit.

Socialization Guidelines

In the final section of this chapter, we offer socialization guidelines as ideas for the successful socialization of members to help ensure success, from the perspective of both the new member and the group. Although not exhaustive, the ideas presented provide a basic foundation for groups and group members to consider as they confront and move through socialization processes and practices.

New Member Socialization

Some group scholars suggest four guidelines for successful new member socialization. In this instance, individuals become successfully socialized into an existing group, such as when a new member joins a company's public relations staff, a department club, or a bowling team. Table 2.2 defines these guidelines.

The bottom line requires that your attitudes and behaviors fit with the attitudes and beliefs already established by the group. For example, if the group has agreed that meetings start on time, arriving late for a meeting violates the group's norm concerning members' behaviors. This violation will cause tensions in the group as members decide how to apply a sanction to your actions. Further, group members expect you as a newcomer to learn all you can about your role by gathering information, asking questions, and seeking feedback from other members.

Table 2.2   Socialization Guidelines

As a new member, you should:
1. embrace the values, norms, and behaviors established in the group,
2. acquire the skills and knowledge needed to assume appropriate roles,
3. learn what is and what is not important,
4. move from a non-performing member to a contributing member.
As a group member, you should:
1. recruit individuals who will fit in and contribute to the attainment of group goals,
2. initiate new members in formal orientation sessions or individually in work group,
3. include the new group member in group activities,
4. engage in a mentoring relationship with the new member.

John Van Maanen (1976) offered that sometimes new members get frustrated because they do not have the information they need to perform their role, they receive conflicting information, or they have too much information thrown at them too fast or too soon. Nonetheless, new members' obligations include acquiring the skills they need to perform.

Robin Lester (1987) suggested also that new members often worry too much about failure and evaluation. In this case, they may attempt to overextend and burn themselves out. Ideally, new members should seek advice from established members as to the priority of factors important to a group's success. Lastly, established members and the new member eventually should feel comfortable working together to reach task goals (McComb, 1995). Of course, this comfort also includes a positive relational climate for cooperation (Keyton, 2000). The goal requires each member to work at helping the group balance the tensions associated with task and member relationships.

In summary, consider the four guidelines when a new member joins an established group. Also, when you find yourself entering a zero history group, these guidelines serve as a basis for discussion in helping each member share ideas associated with adjusting and adapting to each other in building group goals.

Group Socialization

At the group level, members may want to consider the recommended guidelines for the group as a whole to practice in striving for successful socialization of new members. These guidelines, defined in Table 2.2, concern recruitment, initiation, inclusion, and mentorship.

According to scholars Richard Moreland and John Levine (1984), the group searches for individuals who will fit and "contribute to the attainment of group goals" (p. 182). Perhaps simultaneously, the prospective member looks for groups to fill personal needs. When each party commits to the relationship, prospective members become new members. Successful recruitment requires clear group goals, appropriate steps for investigating potential members, and a determination of whether the group can meet individual needs of potential members.

Preparing the new member for entry into the work group is important. For example, Gareth Jones (1986) established that in organizational groups, initiation may comprise formal tactics, such as orientation sessions where new members "go through common learning experiences designed to produce standardized responses to [a] situation" (p. 264). In such cases, not only do the new members learn about the benefits associated with organizational membership; they also may hear speeches by leaders who echo the mission and goals of the organization. One benefit of this method is all new members receive the same training. Yet, in the case of smaller group settings or informal social groups, individualized socialization practices uniquely offer a new member the opportunity to learn "the ropes" from various members and perspectives. This type of exposure allows the new member to interact by asking questions and receiving feedback interpersonally in less formal settings.

As we discussed earlier in this chapter concerning motives for communication, inclusion is key (Schutz, 1966). Group members ensure the inclusion of new members in established group activities. For example, if, once a month after meetings, the group meets for dinner to socialize, it should communicate in such a manner that a new member feels not only encouraged to attend but welcome.

Group members need to consider mentoring the newcomer. Although the mentor-protégé relationship primarily remains a topic of organizational communication and research (Noe, 1988), the mentoring concept applies to groups. We conceptualize **mentoring** as an interpersonal relationship between an experienced member and an inexperienced member whereby the experienced member facilitates the professional and social development of the new member. In this sense, the mentor acts as a sounding board for the new member when she seeks advice and feedback concerning her performance.

A Final Note About the Small Group Socialization Process

Although group member socialization can assist both the new member and the group in maximizing the potential toward task accomplishment, one downside to socialization exists: For optimal socialization to occur, group members must establish trust all around. Trust, as conceptualized by Richard Moreland and John Levine (2002), involves group members' willingness to "take a chance" on each other. Without trust, new members likely will fail to gain acceptance by established group members and established members will remain wary of new members. As such, a lack of trust may explain why some group members never fully socialize, perceive their socialization experience as negative, or simply remain uncommitted to the group task.

Conclusion

This chapter endeavored to highlight the processes and practices of socialization of group members and the group as a whole. In this chapter, we discussed ideas surrounding why we join groups and how group members come together to work on tasks and build relationships through successful socialization. We defined socialization from a communication perspective, presented a five-phase model of group socialization, discussed positive outcomes of socialization, and offered guidelines for competencies to help you and your group members become successful in completing tasks and building positive relationships. The next chapter focuses on what members bring to the group in the form of communication and personality traits. Keep in mind how member communication and personality traits might influence small group member socialization.

Discussion Questions

1. Attraction theory states people join groups because they like the group's activities and/or goals, the group itself, or one or more of its members. The work group members in the case study joined the group because their job required it. Does this make a difference? Why?

2. For each phase of the model of small group socialization, generate a list of other factors that might pertain to successful socialization. How would the members in the case study have benefited from knowledge of the importance of successful socialization processes and practices?

3. Would such demographic characteristics as age, race, and sex make a difference as work groups move through the five phases of socialization? Do members experience more positive socialization experiences in same-sex or opposite-sex groups? Why?

4. Suppose you were asked to train a dysfunctional group in communication. Which ideas in this chapter would you include in the training? Why?

5. Choose a group to which you currently belong. Identify five ways you and your group members could create a positive socialization experience for a new member.

References

Anderson, C. M., & Martin, M. M. (1995). The effects of communication motives, interaction involvement, and loneliness on satisfaction: A model of small groups. *Small Group* Research, *26,* 118–137.

Anderson, C. M., & Martin, M. M. (2001, November). *Communication traits and cohesion as predictors of socialization in task groups.* Paper presented at the annual meeting of the National Communication Association, Atlanta, GA.

Anderson, C. M., & Martin, M. M. (2002). Communication motives (state vs. trait?) and task group outcomes. *Communication Research Reports, 19,* 269–282.

Anderson, C. M., Martin, M. M., & Riddle, B. L. (2001). Attitudes, style and socialization as predictors of satisfaction and commitment in workgroups. *Communication Research Reports, 18,* 241–254.

Anderson, C. M., Riddle, B. L., & Martin, M. M. (1999). Socialization processes in groups. In L. R. Frey (Ed.), D. S. Gouran, & M. S. Poole (Assoc. Eds.), *The handbook of group communication theory & research* (pp. 139–163). Thousand Oaks, CA: Sage.

Bales, R. F., & Strodtbeck, F. L. (1951). Phases in group problem-solving. *Journal of Abnormal and Social Psychology, 46,* 485–495.

Cartwright, D. (1968). The nature of group cohesiveness. In D. Cartwright & A. Zander (Eds.), *Group dynamics: Research and theory* (3rd ed., pp. 91–109). New York: Harper & Row.

DeStephen, R., & Hirokawa, R. (1988). Small group consensus: Stability of group support of the decision, task process, and group relationships. *Small Group Behavior, 19,* 227–239.

Dion, K. K. (1985). Socialization in adulthood. In G. Lindzey & E. Aronson (Eds.), *Handbook of social psychology: Special fields and applications* (Vol. 2, pp. 123–147). New York: Random House.

Gouran, D. S. (1994). The future of small group communication research: Revitalization or continued good health? *Communication Studies, 45,* 29–39.

Hecht, M. L. (1978). The conceptualization and measurement of interpersonal communication satisfaction. *Human Communication Research, 4,* 253–264.

Heslin, R., & Dunphy, D. (1964). Three dimensions of member satisfaction in small groups. *Human Relations, 17,* 99–112.

Hess, J. A. (1993). Assimilating newcomers into an organization: A cultural perspective. *Journal of Applied Communication Research, 21,* 189–210.

Jones, G. R. (1986). Socialization tactics, self-efficacy, and newcomers' adjustments to organizations. *Academy of Management Journal, 29,* 262–279.

Keyton, J. (1993). Group termination: Completing the study of group development. *Small Group Research, 24,* 84–100.

Keyton, J. (2000). Introduction: The relational side of groups. *Small Group Research, 31,* 387–396.

Keyton, J., Harmon, N., & Frey, L. R. (1996, November). *Grouphate: Implications for teaching group communication.* Paper presented at the annual meeting of the Speech Communication Association, San Diego, CA.

Lester, R. E. (1987). Organizational culture, uncertainty reduction, and the socialization of new organizational members. In S. Thomas (Ed.), *Studies in communication* (Vol. 3, pp. 105–113). Norwood, NJ: Ablex.

Louis, M. R. (1980). Surprise and sense making: What newcomers experience in entering unfamiliar organizational settings. *Administrative Science Quarterly, 25,* 226–251.

McComb, M. (1995). Becoming a travelers aid volunteer: Communication in socialization and training. *Communication Studies, 46,* 297–316.

Mead, G. H. (1958). *The social psychology of George Herbert Mead* (A. Strauss, Ed.). Chicago: University of Chicago Press.

Moreland, R. L. (1985). Social categorization and the assimilation of "new" group members. *Journal of Personality and Social Psychology, 48,* 1173–1190.

Moreland, R. L., & Levine, J. M. (1982). Socialization in small groups: Temporal changes in individual-group relations. In L. Berkowitz (Ed.), *Advances in experimental social psychology* (Vol. 15, pp. 137–192). New York: Academic Press.

Moreland, R. L., & Levine, J. M. (1984). Role transition in small groups. In V. L. Allen & E. Van de Vliert (Eds.), *Role transitions: Exploration and explanations* (pp. 181–195). New York: Plenum.

Moreland, R. L., & Levine, J. M. (2002). Socialization and trust in work groups. *Group Processes & Intergroup Relations, 5,* 185–201.

Noe, R. A. (1988). Women and mentoring: A review and research agenda. *Academy of Management Review, 13,* 65–78.

Riddle, B. L., Anderson, C. M., & Martin, M. M. (2000). Small Group Socialization Scale: Development and validity. *Small Group Research, 31,* 554–572.

Rubin, R. B., & Martin, M. M. (1998). Interpersonal communication motives. In J. C. McCroskey, J. A. Daly, M. M. Martin, & M. J. Beatty (Eds.), *Communication and personality: Trait perspectives* (pp. 287–308). Cresskill, NJ: Hampton Press.

Rubin, R. B., Perse, E. M., & Barbato, C. A. (1988). Conceptualization and measurement of interpersonal communication motives. *Human Communication Research, 14,* 602–628.

Schutz, W. C. (1966). *The interpersonal underworld.* Palo Alto, CA: Science and Behavior Books.

Sinclair-James, L., & Stohl, C. (1997). Group endings and new beginnings. In L. R. Frey & J. K. Barge (Eds.), *Managing group life: Communicating in decision-making groups* (pp. 308–334). Boston: Houghton Mifflin.

Stryker, S., & Stratham, A. (1985). Symbolic interaction and role theory. In G. Lindzey & E. Aronson (Eds.), *Handbook of social psychology: Theory and method* (Vol. 1, pp. 311–378). New York: Random House.

Sunwolf, & Seibold, D. R. (1999). The impact of formal procedures on group processes, members, and task outcomes. In L. R. Frey (Ed.), D. S. Gouran, & M. S. Poole (Assoc. Eds.), *The handbook of communication theory & research* (pp. 395–432). Thousand Oaks, CA: Sage.

Swogger, G. (1981). Human communication and group experiences. In J. E. Durkin (Ed.), *Living groups: Group psychotherapy and general system theory* (pp. 63–78). New York: Brunner/Mazel.

Van Maanen, J. (1976). Breaking in: Socializing to work. In R. Dubin (Ed.), *Handbook of work, organization and society* (pp. 67–130). Chicago: Rand McNally.

Worchel, S. (1994). You can go home again: Returning group research to the group context with an eye on developmental issues. *Small Group Research, 25,* 205–223.

Small Group Member Communication and Personality Traits

3

After reading this chapter, you should be able to:

1. differentiate between a communication trait and a personality trait,
2. identify and define the four communication traits discussed in this chapter,
3. identify and define the three personality traits discussed in this chapter,
4. explain how communication and personality traits impact group work, and
5. develop a profile of the ideal group member based on traits.

Case Study

Abdul arrives home after attending a committee meeting on loss prevention at Aim, a department store where he has worked as a shift supervisor for the past two years. His wife, Ashley, is waiting for him and the dinner he was supposed to bring home.

Photo 3.1 Working in a small group allows members to communicate through a variety of verbal and nonverbal behaviors.

Source: ©iStockphoto.com/aldomurillo.

Ashley:	Hey, where were you?
Abdul:	(mumbles something as he hangs up his coat)
Ashley:	I've told you a hundred times, I can't understand you when you mumble. Where's the food? I'm starving.
Abdul:	I forgot the food. My committee meeting with my loss prevention group lasted twice as long as I planned.
Ashley:	Why did the meeting last so long?
Abdul:	Because my group members are driving me crazy.
Ashley:	How so?
Abdul:	Well, there's James who just sits there, never saying a word. When anyone asks him a specific question, he just nods his head and says as little as possible. He talks so softly, I can't hear what he is saying. When

I was talking to him, I tried to make eye contact with him but he kept looking away. He's so nervous. He makes me feel uncomfortable.

Ashley: Is everyone else quiet?

Abdul: I wish. There's this guy Vinnie who has something to say about everything. When I told him I disagreed with him, he told me I was stupid and lacked his personal experiences and that I should keep my mouth shut. It took all my self-control not to yell at him. During the meeting, I think he insulted everyone at least twice.

Ashley: Did anyone say anything to him?

Abdul: Well, there is this other member, Sachiko. She talks a lot, too, and often disagrees with what is being said, but I like her because she always stays on topic. She has a way of talking to you where she disagrees with you but doesn't put you down at the same time. She allows everyone to make their points and really seems to care about what others have to say. I like her the best and hope she becomes the leader of the group. She tried to tell Vinnie that we needed to stay constructive and develop a solution, but he just rolled his eyes.

Ashley: What do you think the other group members think about you?

Abdul: They probably think that I don't want to be there, and they're right. A couple of times they would get off track, talking about their personal lives and what they were going to do after work, and I had to interrupt their gabbing to remind them that we needed to stay focused on the task at hand. I'm not there to make friends. I just want us to prepare our loss prevention plan, delegate the work responsibilities, and meet with the manager next week. I have better things to do than spend time with this particular work group, and I don't need any more friends.

Ashley: (sarcastically) With that attitude, I bet you're the most popular person in the group.

Abdul: Okay, okay, okay. I guess I could have a better attitude about my group. I just get frustrated when I have to work with others, especially when the other people don't communicate like I do.

Ashley: (a little less sarcastically) With a little effort, you'll get along fine with your group. Maybe someday they will learn to love and appreciate you as much as I do.

Abdul: Very funny. What's for dinner?

Ashley: You were supposed to bring dinner home from Cha-Cha's, remember?

Abdul: Oh yeah.

Ashley: Grab your coat. You're driving, and you're paying.

I n this case study, Abdul describes his group members, and we read, in the brief descriptions, how the group members' communication behaviors differ. Some group members are quiet and reserved while others are loud and outgoing. Some discuss an issue constructively while others attack the person with whom they are speaking instead of focusing on the topic being discussed. Some members talk to demonstrate control while other members think before they speak.

This chapter aims to explore the communication and personality traits group members possess. To do so, we will define the term *trait* and differentiate between a communication trait and a personality trait. We then will examine four prevalent communication traits and three prevalent personality traits. Finally, we will summarize the research conducted on these communication and personality traits in the small group.

Definition and Differentiation of Traits

Think of traits as relatively enduring behaviors that people tend to use consistently across their life span. For instance, if Abdul possesses the assertiveness trait, he would be expected to assert himself across different situations and contexts—not to say that the specific situation would not influence his behavior (i.e., Abdul might project more assertiveness toward his loss prevention group than he would toward his wife). However, a person high in trait assertiveness would display it more often in more situations than a person low in trait assertiveness. Trait researchers do not deny that the situation influences how a person behaves; they just believe that traits play a significant role in why and how people communicate.

A communication trait is defined as an individual's consistencies and differences in message-sending and -receiving behaviors (Infante & Rancer, 1996), and a personality trait is defined as an individual's psychological makeup comprising attitudes, values, beliefs, experiences, and behaviors. Communication traits differ from personality traits in that communication traits focus specifically on how people use verbal and nonverbal messages to stimulate meaning in receivers' minds (Infante, Rancer, & Womack, 2003). In a way, communication traits can be considered a subset of a person's personality traits.

This chapter will introduce you to several communication and personality traits. Because communication is vital to the small group communication process, we will focus first on communication traits.

Communication Traits

Although a person possesses many communication traits (Frey, 1997; Haslett & Ruebush, 1999; Keyton & Frey, 2002), we will focus on four communication traits known to influence how group members communicate: communication apprehension, communicator style, argumentativeness, and verbal aggressiveness.

Communication Apprehension

Arguably the most researched communication trait, communication apprehension describes "an individual's level of fear or anxiety associated with either real or anticipated communication with another person or persons" (McCroskey, 1977, p. 78). Generally, an individual ranks high, moderate, or low in communication apprehension. An individual who is high in communication apprehension almost always feels apprehensive about communicating with other people whereas an individual who is low in communication apprehension hardly ever feels apprehensive about communicating with other people. An individual who is moderate in communication apprehension falls somewhere between being highly fearful and not being fearful at all, and tends to be more flexible in dealing with communication apprehension on a daily basis.

According to James McCroskey (1984), communication apprehension can emerge in four forms: trait, context-based, audience-based, and situational. Trait apprehension refers to a relatively enduring level of apprehension across a variety of situations. People who are high in trait communication apprehension feel anxious about communicating across all situations. Whether communication involves talking during a job interview, participating in a class discussion, or giving a public speech in the community, a person with high trait communication apprehension usually will experience anxiety and apprehension. On the other hand, a person who is low in trait communication apprehension will feel comfortable in most situations and not experience any discomfort or anxiety.

Context-based apprehension, a form of apprehension tied to a specific context (i.e., small group, meetings, interpersonal, public speaking), is based on the idea that people sometimes feel comfortable talking in one context and anxious in another. Some people feel completely comfortable talking to almost anyone face-to-face but experience a great deal of anxiety when giving a public speech. Other people may experience no anxiety when giving a formal presentation in front of a crowd but a great deal of apprehension when attempting to communicate in a small group.

Audience-based apprehension is linked to communicating with a specific audience. Some people, though low in trait communication apprehension, may experience apprehension when it comes to communicating, for example, with their superiors at work. In the case study, Abdul might not worry about communicating in groups most of the time, but if he is attracted to or annoyed with someone in the group, he might experience some apprehension when communicating with that person in the group setting.

A person experiences situational apprehension when communicating with a given person in a particular situation. For instance, Sachiko might not normally feel apprehension about communicating with her group, but if everyone in the group has completed the group assignment except her, she might experience some apprehension about confronting her group with the news of her unpreparedness. Note that almost everyone, including you, will experience situational apprehension at one time or another.

A person with communication apprehension will experience internal anxiety and discomfort (McCroskey & Beatty, 1998), which may or may not manifest itself in external signs of nervousness or apprehensiveness about communicating with others. These external signs include the physiological (e.g., sweating, increased heart rate, blushing) and the interactive. Based on the research conducted on communication apprehension, communication researchers James McCroskey, John Daly, and Gail Sorensen (1976) compiled a profile of the highly apprehensive person and the minimally apprehensive person. For instance, highly communication-apprehensive individuals often act aloof, prefer to work alone, get easily annoyed, withdraw, and dislike interaction whereas minimally communication-apprehensive individuals are calm, self-assured, ego-involved, decisive, and relaxed. Though not exhaustive, this profile provides an idea about feeling, thought, and behavior differences in highly and minimally communication-apprehensive individuals.

> 66 *Ethically Speaking:* How acceptable is it for group members to attribute their group participation or involvement (or lack thereof) to their communication apprehension? 99

Ultimately, the only way to identify people as high-communication apprehensives is if they admit to being apprehensive. Complete the Personal Report of Communication Apprehension scale developed by communication scholar James C. McCroskey to identify your trait communication apprehension and your apprehension in four contexts: small group settings, meetings, interpersonal settings, and public speaking settings.

Assessment Tool 3.1   Personal Report of Communication Apprehension

This questionnaire contains statements about communicating with other people. Indicate the extent to which each statement applies to you personally according to the following scale.

If you **strongly agree** with the statement, write **1** in the blank.

If you **agree** with the statement, write **2** in the blank.

If you **are undecided** about the statement, write **3** in the blank.

If you **disagree** with the statement, write **4** in the blank.

If you **strongly disagree** with the statement, write **5** in the blank.

_____ 1. I dislike participating in group discussions.

_____ 2. Generally, I am comfortable while participating in group discussions.

_____ 3. I am tense and nervous while participating in group discussions.

_____ 4. I like to get involved in group discussions.

_____ 5. Engaging in a group discussion with new people makes me tense and nervous.

_____ 6. I am calm and relaxed while participating in group discussions.

_____ 7. Generally, I am nervous when I have to participate in a meeting.

_____ 8. Usually, I am calm and relaxed while participating in meetings.

_____ 9. I am very calm and relaxed when called on to express an opinion at a meeting.

_____10. I am afraid to express myself at meetings.

_____11. Communicating at meetings usually makes me uncomfortable.

_____12. I am very relaxed when answering questions at a meeting.

_____13. While participating in a conversation with a new acquaintance, I feel very nervous.

_____14. I have no fear of speaking up in conversations.

_____15. Ordinarily I am very tense and nervous in conversations.

_____16. While conversing with a new acquaintance, I feel very relaxed.

_____17. Ordinarily I am very calm and relaxed in conversations.

_____18. I'm afraid to speak up in conversations.

_____19. I have no fear of giving a speech.

_____20. Certain parts of my body feel very tense and rigid while I am giving a speech.

_____21. I feel relaxed while giving a speech.

_____22. My thoughts become confused and jumbled when I am giving a speech.

_____23. I face the prospect of giving a speech with confidence.

_____24. While giving a speech, I get so nervous I forget facts I really know.

(Continued)

(Continued)

Scoring:

1. Take a base score of **18**. To this score, add your scores for items 2, 4, and 6. Subtract your scores for items 1, 3, and 5. This is your **small group** communication apprehension score.

2. Take a base score of **18**. To this score, add your scores for items 8, 9, and 12. Subtract your scores for items 7, 10, and 11. This is your **meetings** communication apprehension score.

3. Take a base score of **18**. To this score, add your scores for items 14, 16, and 17. Subtract your scores for items 13, 15, and 18. This is your **interpersonal** communication apprehension score.

4. Take a base score of **18**. To this score, add your scores for items 19, 21, and 23. Subtract your scores for items 20, 22, and 24. This is your **public speaking** communication apprehension score.

5. To compute your trait communication apprehension score, add the score from each step.

A score (in step 5) between 80 and 120 indicates you are **high** in communication apprehension.

A score (in step 5) between 51 and 79 indicates you are **moderate** in communication apprehension.

A score (in step 5) between 24 and 50 indicates you are **low** in communication apprehension.

Source: Reprinted with permission of James C. McCroskey.

It is important to consider, though, that if an individual exhibits high communication apprehension, she will not necessarily be quiet. Some highly communication-apprehensive individuals talk too much from nervousness, and some minimally communication-apprehensive individuals hardly talk at all because they simply are not interested in communicating.

Communicator Style

Communicator style describes the way an individual uses verbal and nonverbal communicative behaviors to indicate how literally others should take a message (Norton, 1978, 1986). According to communication scholar Robert Norton (1978, 1983), an individual's communicator style comprises any combination of 10 communicative attributes: friendly, impression leaving, relaxed, contentious, attentive, precise, animated, dramatic, open, and dominant. Based on Norton's (1978, 1983)

Assessment Tool 3.2   Communicator Style Measure

This questionnaire contains statements about your communicative behaviors. Indicate how often each statement is true for you personally according to the following scale.

If the statement is **almost always true**, write **5** in the blank.

If the statement is **often true**, write **4** in the blank.

If the statement is **occasionally true**, write **3** in the blank.

If the statement is **rarely true**, write **2** in the blank.

If the statement is **almost never true**, write **1** in the blank.

_____ 1. I am comfortable with all varieties of people.

_____ 2. I laugh easily.

_____ 3. I readily express admiration for others.

_____ 4. What I say usually leaves an impression on people.

_____ 5. I leave people with an impression of me that they definitely tend to remember.

_____ 6. To be friendly, I verbally acknowledge others' contributions.

_____ 7. I am a very good communicator.

_____ 8. I have some nervous mannerisms in my speech.

_____ 9. I am a very relaxed communicator.

_____10. When I disagree with others, I am very quick to challenge them.

_____11. I can always repeat back to a person exactly what he or she meant.

_____12. The sound of my voice is very easy to recognize.

_____13. I am a very precise communicator.

_____14. I leave a definite impression on people.

_____15. The rhythm or flow of my speech is sometimes affected by nervousness.

_____16. Under pressure, I come across as a relaxed speaker.

_____17. My eyes reflect exactly what I am feeling when I communicate.

_____18. I dramatize a lot.

_____19. I always find it very easy to communicate on a one-to-one basis with people I do not know very well.

_____20. Usually, I deliberately react in such a way that people know I am listening to them.

_____21. Usually, I do not tell people much about myself until I get to know them well.

_____22. I tell jokes, anecdotes, and stories when I communicate.

(Continued)

(Continued)

_____23. I tend to constantly gesture when I communicate.

_____24. I am an extremely open communicator.

_____25. I am a vocally loud communicator.

_____26. In a small group of people I do not know very well, I am a very good communicator.

_____27. In arguments or differences of opinion, I insist upon very precise definitions.

_____28. In most situations, I speak very frequently.

_____29. I find it extremely easy to maintain a conversation with a member of the opposite sex.

_____30. I like to be strictly accurate when I communicate.

_____31. Because I have a loud voice, I can easily break into a conversation.

_____32. Often I physically and vocally act out when I communicate.

_____33. I have an assertive voice.

_____34. I readily reveal personal things about myself.

_____35. I am dominant in conversations.

_____36. I am very argumentative.

_____37. Once I get wound up in a heated discussion, I have a hard time stopping myself.

_____38. I am an extremely friendly communicator.

_____39. I really like to listen very carefully to people.

_____40. I insist that other people document or present some kind of proof for what they are arguing.

_____41. I try to take charge of things when I am with people.

_____42. It bothers me to drop an argument that is not resolved.

_____43. In most situations I tend to come on strong.

_____44. I am very expressive nonverbally.

_____45. The way I say something usually leaves an impression on people.

_____46. Whenever I communicate, I tend to be very encouraging to people.

_____47. I actively use a lot of facial expressions when I communicate.

_____48. I verbally exaggerate to emphasize a point.

_____49. I am an extremely attentive communicator.

_____50. As a rule, I openly express my feelings and emotions.

Scoring:

Reverse score items 8, 15, and 21. (If you put a 5 for item 8, change this score to 1; if 4, change this score to 2; if 2, change this score to 4; if 1, change this score to 5.)

1. Add your scores for items 3, 6, 38, and 46. This is your **friendly** score.

2. Add your scores for items 4, 5, 14, and 45. This is your **impression leaving** score.

3. Add your scores for items 8, 9, 15, and 16. This is your **relaxed** score.

4. Add your scores for items 10, 36, 37, and 42. This is your **contentious** score.

5. Add your scores for items 11, 20, 39, and 49. This is your **attentive** score.

6. Add your scores for items 13, 27, 30, and 40. This is your **precise** score.

7. Add your scores for items 17, 23, 44, and 47. This is your **animated** score.

8. Add your scores for items 18, 22, 32, and 48. This is your **dramatic** score.

9. Add your scores for items 21, 24, 34, and 50. This is your **open** score.

10. Add your scores for items 28, 35, 41, and 43. This is your **dominant** score.

Source: Reprinted by permission of Blackwell Publishing from Norton, R. W. (1978). Foundations of a communicator style construct. *Human Communication Research, 4,* 99–112.

work, Scott Myers, Matthew Martin, and Timothy Mottet (2000) offered the following definitions. *Friendly* people, generally considered kind and caring, recognize others in a positive way. The *impression leaving* communicate using a memorable style. *Relaxed* communicators appear anxiety-free, calm, and at ease when engaged in interactions with others. *Contentious* individuals like to argue and may seem belligerent at times. *Attentive* communicators, concerned with understanding others, listen effectively. *Precise* communicators try to be strictly accurate, using well-defined arguments and specific proof or evidence to clarify their positions. *Animated* communicators use eye contact, facial expressions, gestures, body movement, and posture to exaggerate content. *Dramatic* communicators use stylistic devices (e.g., exaggerations, rhythm, stories) to underscore content. *Open* communicators are straightforward and do not have problems directly communicating their thoughts or emotions. *Dominant* communicators "take charge" of the situation by talking louder, longer, and more frequently than others. Generally, an individual will use several attributes at the same time (Norton, 1983), which creates an individual's communicator style, or cluster. For example, a dominant person also may be animated, dramatic, and/or impression leaving, and an attentive person also may be friendly and relaxed (Norton, 1978). If you complete the Communicator Style Measure, you should be able to identify your communicator style.

Despite arguments that some attributes appear preferable over other attributes, note there is no preferred cluster of communicator style attributes per se. Yet researchers have found that organizational employees prefer their superiors to use the relaxed, friendly, and attentive attributes (Infante & Gorden, 1991); college students prefer their professors to use the friendly, relaxed, dramatic, and impression leaving attributes (Nussbaum, 1992); charismatic leaders use the attentive, relaxed, friendly, and dominant attributes (Holladay & Coombs, 1994); and strong public speakers use the dominant, animated, open, friendly, dramatic, and attentive attributes (Holladay & Coombs, 1993).

Photo 3.2 A group member who communicates using the dramatic, animated, and impression leaving attributes will not likely be forgotten.

Source: ©iStockphoto.com/mammamaart.

Argumentativeness

Argumentativeness comprises an individual's ability to defend his position on a controversial issue while simultaneously attempting to refute another person's position on the same issue (Infante & Rancer, 1982). From this definition, an argumentative individual rationally discusses a topic and does not engage in personal attacks against others. People high in argumentativeness are more likely to initiate an argument and less likely to back away from an argument than people low in argumentativeness.

Of the 10 communicator style attributes, which attributes (or cluster) would you find desirable in a group member? Why?

Highly argumentative individuals feel more motivated to argue (Rancer & Infante, 1985), have a greater number of positive beliefs about arguing (Rancer, Baukus, & Infante, 1985), and perceive an argument as more enjoyable (Rancer, Kosberg, & Baukus, 1992) than minimally argumentative individuals. Highly argumentative people also often grow more involved in interactions, and those with whom they interact perceive them as more credible than minimally argumentative people (Onyekwere, Rubin, & Infante, 1991). To determine your level of argumentativeness, complete the Argumentativeness Scale.

According to argumentativeness experts Dominic Infante and Andrew Rancer (1996), engaging in argumentativeness offers many benefits. When people argue, they learn more, become less egocentric, realize how others think and why, and become aware of information previously unknown to them. Argumentative

Assessment Tool 3.3   Argumentativeness Scale

This questionnaire contains statements about controversial issues. Indicate how often each statement is true for you personally according to the following scale.

If the statement is **almost always true**, write **5** in the blank.

If the statement is **often true**, write **4** in the blank.

If the statement is **occasionally true**, write **3** in the blank.

If the statement is **rarely true**, write **2** in the blank.

If the statement is **almost never true**, write **1** in the blank.

_____ 1. While in an argument, I worry that the person I am arguing with will form a negative impression of me.

_____ 2. Arguing over controversial issues improves my intelligence.

_____ 3. I enjoy avoiding arguments.

_____ 4. I am energetic and enthusiastic when I argue.

_____ 5. Once I finish an argument, I promise myself that I will not get into another argument.

_____ 6. Arguing with a person creates more problems than it solves.

_____ 7. I have a pleasant, good feeling when I win a point in an argument.

_____ 8. When I finish arguing with someone, I feel nervous and upset.

_____ 9. I enjoy a good argument over a controversial issue.

_____10. I get an unpleasant feeling when I realize I am about to get into an argument.

_____11. I enjoy defending my point of view on an issue.

_____12. I am happy when I keep an argument from happening.

_____13. I do not like to miss the opportunity to argue over a controversial issue.

_____14. I prefer being with people who rarely disagree with me.

_____15. I consider an argument to be an exciting intellectual challenge.

_____16. I find myself unable to think of effective points during an argument.

_____17. I feel refreshed and satisfied after an argument on a controversial issue.

_____18. I have the ability to do well in an argument.

_____19. I try to avoid getting into arguments.

_____20. I feel excitement when I expect that a conversation I am in is leading to an argument.

Scoring:

1. Add your scores for items 2, 4, 7, 9, 11, 13, 15, 17, 18, and 20.
2. Add 60 to the sum obtained in step 1.

(Continued)

(Continued)

3. Add your scores for items 1, 3, 5, 6, 8, 10, 12, 14, 16, and 19.
4. Subtract the sum obtained in step 3 from the total obtained in step 2. This is your argumentativeness score.

A score (in step 4) between 73 and 100 indicates you are **high** in argumentativeness.

A score (in step 4) between 56 and 72 indicates you are **moderate** in argumentativeness.

A score (in step 4) between 20 and 55 indicates you are **low** in argumentativeness.

Source: Infante, D. A., & Rancer, A. S. (1982). A conceptualization and measure of argumentativeness. *Journal of Personality Assessment, 46,* 72–80. Reproduced with permission of Lawrence Erlbaum Associates, Inc.

individuals also improve their abilities in perspective taking, which is important when individuals attempt to influence others. Additionally, researchers have found that people enjoy communicating with argumentative individuals, including coworkers, superiors, and professors (Infante & Gorden, 1985, 1989; Myers & Knox, 2000). Argumentativeness, however, sports a downside: When extremely argumentative individuals invest highly or put a personal stake in the issue, communicating with them presents a challenge (Frantz & Seburn, 2003).

Verbal Aggressiveness

Although argumentativeness falls into the category of constructive communication traits, verbal aggressiveness fits in with destructive communication traits. Verbal aggressiveness, or the tendency for an individual to attack the self-concept of another individual for the purpose of inflicting psychological harm (Infante & Wigley, 1986), is a form of symbolic aggression. From this definition, a verbally aggressive individual does not attack the topic or the issue; rather, a verbally aggressive individual attacks some attribute of a person (Infante, 1987; Kinney, 1994). These attributes are listed in Table 3.1. People displaying high verbal aggressiveness use these messages more frequently than people displaying low verbal aggressiveness (Infante, Riddle, Horvath, & Tumlin, 1992), and they believe the use of these verbally aggressive messages is justified (Martin, Anderson, & Horvath, 1996). To determine your level of verbal aggressiveness, complete the Verbal Aggressiveness Scale.

At times, the situation can increase the likelihood of a person communicating in a verbally aggressive manner (Wigley, 1998). When the discussion topic particularly interests someone and the impact or consequence of winning the discussion is high, a person may more likely resort to using a verbally aggressive message.

Table 3.1   Types of Verbally Aggressive Messages

1. Making derogatory comments about a group member's character or competence
2. Making derogatory comments about a group member's background or physical appearance
3. Making derogatory comments about a group member's friends or romantic partner
4. Making derogatory comments about a group member's group memberships
5. Ridiculing or making fun of how a group member communicates
6. Swearing at a group member
7. Using sarcasm to belittle a group member
8. Teasing a group member
9. Threatening to physically or psychologically harm a group member

Source: Based on Infante, D. A. (1987). Aggressiveness. In J. C. McCroskey & J. A. Daly (Eds.), *Personality and interpersonal communication* (pp. 157–192). Thousand Oaks, CA: Sage.

Assessment Tool 3.4   Verbal Aggressiveness Scale

This questionnaire is concerned with how we try to get people to comply with our wishes. For each statement, please indicate the extent to which you feel it is true for you in your attempts to influence others.

If the statement is **almost always true**, write **5** in the blank.

If the statement is **often true**, write **4** in the blank.

If the statement is **occasionally true**, write **3** in the blank.

If the statement is **rarely true**, write **2** in the blank.

If the statement is **almost never true**, write **1** in the blank.

_____ 1. I am extremely careful to avoid attacking individuals' intelligence when I attack their ideas.

_____ 2. When individuals are very stubborn, I use insults to soften the stubbornness.

_____ 3. I try very hard to avoid having other people feel bad about themselves when I try to influence them.

_____ 4. When people refuse to do a task I know is important, without good reason, I tell them that they are unreasonable.

_____ 5. When other people do things I regard as stupid, I try to be extremely gentle with them.

_____ 6. If individuals I am trying to influence really deserve it, I attack their character.

(Continued)

(Continued)

_____ 7. When people behave in ways that are in very poor taste, I insult them in order to shock them into proper behavior.

_____ 8. I try to make people feel good about themselves even when their ideas are stupid.

_____ 9. When people simply will not budge on a matter of importance, I lose my temper and say rather strong things to them.

_____10. When people criticize my shortcomings, I take it in good humor and do not try to get back at them.

_____11. When individuals insult me, I get a lot of pleasure out of really telling them off.

_____12. When I dislike individuals greatly, I try not to show it in what I say or how I say it.

_____13. I like poking fun at people who do things that are very stupid in order to stimulate their intelligence.

_____14. When I attack others' ideas, I try not to damage their self-concept.

_____15. When I try to influence people, I make a great effort not to offend them.

_____16. When people do things that are mean or cruel, I attack their character in order to help correct their behavior.

_____17. I refuse to participate in arguments when they involve personal attacks.

_____18. When nothing seems to work in trying to influence others, I yell and scream in order to get some movement from them.

_____19. When I am not able to refute others' positions, I try to make them feel defensive in order to weaken their positions.

_____20. When an argument shifts to personal attacks, I try very hard to change the subject.

Scoring:

1. Add your scores for items 2, 4, 6, 7, 9, 11, 13, 16, 18, and 19.

2. Add your scores for items 1, 3, 5, 8, 10, 12, 14, 15, 17, and 20.

3. Subtract the sum obtained in step 2 from 60.

4. Add the sum obtained in step 1 to the score obtained in step 3. This is your verbal aggressiveness score.

A score (in step 4) between 59 and 100 indicates you are **high** in verbal aggressiveness.

A score (in step 4) between 39 and 58 indicates you are **moderate** in verbal aggressiveness.

A score (in step 4) between 20 and 38 indicates you are **low** in verbal aggressiveness.

Source: From "Verbal Aggressiveness: An Interpersonal Model and Measure," by D. A. Infante & C. J. Wigley, III, 1986, *Communication Quarterly, 53,* pp. 61–69. Reproduced with permission of Routledge Publishing, Inc.

Other times—especially when they are reciprocating a verbally aggressive message to a prior hurtful message (Martin et al., 1996)—people believe the use of verbal aggression is justified. However, research indicates that responding to one verbally aggressive message with another makes the situation worse, not better (Sutter & Martin, 1998). Verbal aggressiveness also stems from frustration; in fact, individuals sometimes use verbally aggressive messages because they are frustrated they do not know how to argue constructively (Infante, 1988).

No known positive outcomes to using verbally aggressive messages exist (Infante & Rancer, 1996), primarily because verbally aggressive people seem less likable (Myers & Johnson, 2003) and less agreeable (Blickle, Habasch, & Senft, 1998). This is not a big surprise, given that people in general dislike being the target of verbal aggressiveness. For example, employees produce less work under a verbally aggressive supervisor (Infante & Gorden, 1985), siblings emerge less satisfied from interactions with a verbally aggressive sibling (Martin, Anderson, Burant, & Weber, 1997), and college students learn less from verbally aggressive professors (Myers & Knox, 2000). For the most part, people do not appreciate receiving a verbally aggressive message and will do whatever it takes to avoid spending time with a verbally aggressive person.

Now that we have examined four communication traits likely to be exhibited by group members, let's examine three prevalent personality traits exhibited by group members as well.

> **?** In your work group, what topics of discussion lead group members to engage in verbal aggressiveness? In what situations is a group member's use of verbal aggressiveness justified?

Personality Traits

Similar to communication traits, a person can possess numerous personality traits (Davies, 1994). In this section, we will focus on three personality traits—Machiavellianism, self-monitoring, and self-esteem—known to influence group member communication.

Machiavellianism

Machiavellianism, a concept based on the 16th-century writings of Niccolò Machiavelli who offered advice on how to influence people and exert power over others, refers to an individual's ability to manipulate a situation in order to

Photo 3.3   A group member high in self-monitoring pays attention to her behavior in a group setting.

Source: ©iStockphoto.com/Yuri_Arcurs.

influence and control it for his own purposes (Davies, 1994). People high in Machiavellianism (high Machs) not only manipulate and persuade other people more than people low in Machiavellianism (low Machs); they often defeat others' persuasions (Christie & Geis, 1970). People high in this personality trait will go to great lengths to reach success. Generally, high Machs view interactions as social competitions. These individuals often are ideologically neutral, involve little emotion in their interpersonal relationships, and will shift commitment when doing so promotes personal gain (Mudrack & Mason, 1995).

Self-Monitoring

Self-monitoring is the extent to which a person pays attention to the social requirements of a situation and, striving for appropriateness and effectiveness, adapts her verbal and nonverbal behaviors (Snyder, 1987). Although most people modify their communication at one time or another depending on the context, some people modify their behaviors much more regularly. High self-monitors, for example, pay close attention to others' reactions to them and control how they present themselves in social interactions. Low self-monitors, on the other hand, concern themselves less with how others react to them and typically express what they think and feel regardless of the communicative situation (Kent & Moss, 1990).

Communication scholar John Daly (2002) offered two general findings about the research conducted on self-monitoring. First, high self-monitors are more conversationally sensitive and flexible in their behaviors than low self-monitors. Adapting their behavior allows high self-monitors, considered helpful by their peers (Flynn, Reagans, Amanatullah, & Ames, 2006), to be more interpersonally effective. Second, low self-monitors behave more consistently and maintain more trusting friendships than high self-monitors. Low self-monitors communicate more honestly, often not worrying about the impression they make on other people.

Self-Esteem

Self-esteem describes a person's overall self-worth. People with high self-esteem feel good about and praise themselves whereas people with low self-esteem do not. Self-esteem cannot be given or appointed to someone. Although we can commend our friends and their accomplishments, individuals must recognize their level of self-esteem. At the same time, an individual's perception of self usually is based on his social interactions and conversations with others (Glauser, 1984), and thus, not surprisingly, individuals with high self-esteem feel more comfortable and confident with whom they interact compared to individuals with low self-esteem.

Communication and Personality Traits in the Small Group

So how do these communication and personality traits surface in the small group? Based on the research conducted to date, we can draw the following conclusions:

1. Group members who are unwilling to communicate interact less (Burgoon, 1977). At the same time, apprehensive group members avoid expressing disagreement with each other and more likely will make irrelevant comments (McCroskey & Richmond, 1992). Highly apprehensive members also attend fewer group meetings and report less group cohesiveness (C. M. Anderson & Martin, 1995). Additionally, these members experience more difficulty attempting to socialize with group members and becoming assimilated into the group when it first forms. Highly apprehensive members also less likely will be selected by their group members as the leader than moderately and minimally apprehensive

members (Limon & LaFrance, 2005), and highly apprehensive members rate lower in social and task attractiveness than minimally apprehensive members (Hawkins & Stewart, 1991).

2. A link exists between a group member's communication apprehension and communicator style in the small group. Thomas Porter (1982) found that group members judge highly communication-apprehensive individuals as less relaxed and dominant than individuals with low communication apprehension.

3. Highly argumentative group members prove likelier than minimally argumentative members to be rated more influential in the group (Shultz, 1982) and to be nominated as the group leader (Limon & LaFrance, 2005; Shultz, 1982). Highly argumentative members also report greater satisfaction with their group experiences and a greater level of cohesiveness with their groups (C. M. Anderson & Martin, 1999). Conversely, highly verbally aggressive members report lower satisfaction, lower levels of group consensus, and lower levels of cohesiveness than less verbally aggressive members (C. M. Anderson & Martin, 1999).

4. Furthermore, highly argumentative group members rate themselves higher on several personality traits than minimally argumentative group members. Argumentativeness researchers Nancy and Stephen Schullery (2002) reported that self-perceived argumentativeness correlates positively with being a reliable worker, exhibiting leadership, engaging effectively in brainstorming, and enjoying small group work. At the same time, group members high in argumentativeness report that they are neither shy nor want to avoid conflict.

> **?** Identify your level of communication apprehension, your communicator style cluster, your level of argumentativeness, and your level of verbal aggressiveness. How do these four communication traits affect your participation in your work group? How do these four communication traits affect your attitude toward your work group?

5. A group member's level of Machiavellianism influences group interaction (Bochner & Bochner, 1972). Although high Machs participate frequently in group interaction (Bochner, DiSalvo, & Jonas, 1975), they disagree more often than low Machs (Bochner & Bochner, 1972). High Machs often communicate very skillfully and serve several task-related functions, such as asking questions, offering suggestions, and giving directions (Hacker & Gaitz, 1970). Incidentally, if their own interests coincide with the best interests of the group, the group may benefit from high Machs' behavior. However, high Machs almost always put their self-interests ahead of the group's.

6. High self-monitors are more active, talkative, and likely to emerge as leaders than low self-monitors (Ellis, Adamson, Deszca, & Cawsey, 1988; Ellis & Cronshaw, 1992), perhaps because low self-monitors more often present their true selves when

interacting in groups. High self-monitors, on the contrary, often display the part of themselves that is socially expected by members and effective in accomplishing the group's task. They also tend to speak faster than low self-monitors (Dabbs, Evans, Hopper, & Purvis, 1980), conform more than low self-monitors in group situations (Rarick, Soldow, & Geizer, 1976), and are viewed by group members as providing a valuable contribution to the group process (Kent & Moss, 1990).

7. A group member with low self-esteem is more susceptible to group member influence. In a group setting, members with low self-esteem will comply or agree with other members instead of disagreeing or presenting a dissenting voice. Chances are, if they disagree, they will downplay their disagreement to the group, hoping to avoid projecting a negative image (Cohen & Sheposh, 1977). Moreover, members with low self-esteem less likely will assume a leadership role in groups (Kwal & Fleshler, 1975), which may explain why members with low self-esteem rate the group experience less favorably than members with high self-esteem (Crocker & Schwartz, 1985).

A Final Note About Small Group Member Traits

Paraphrasing L. R. Anderson (1978), Joann Keyton and Lawrence Frey (2002) asserted that "groups often are only as good as the members that make them up" (p. 99). This statement underscores the importance of recognizing a group member's communication and personality traits' impact on a group. Developing an understanding of the influence of members' communication and personality traits helps explain not only the manner in which members communicate but also members' predispositions toward group work (Keyton & Frey, 2002); the emergence of such outcomes as cohesion, consensus, and satisfaction (C. M. Anderson & Martin, 1999); and the compatibility of group members. More importantly, developing an understanding of communication and personality traits influences the impressions you make about group members. In the case study, had he realized that James was exhibiting the characteristics of a person high in communication apprehension, Abdul likely would have perceived James more favorably, which ultimately would exert a positive influence on future group meetings.

Conclusion

This chapter explored the communication and personality traits possessed by group members. In doing so, we defined the term *trait* and differentiated between a communication trait and a personality trait. We then examined four prevalent communication traits and three prevalent personality traits. Finally, we summarized the research conducted on these communication and personality traits in the small group. As you read the next chapter, consider how your own communication and personality traits reflect the diversity represented by small group members.

Discussion Questions

1. Refer to the case study presented at the beginning of the chapter. For each group member (i.e., Abdul, James, Vinnie, and Sachiko), identify a communication trait from this chapter that each member displays.

2. Suppose a group member feels apprehensive about communicating in your classroom group. What can the group do to make the member more comfortable? Compile a list of recommendations your group can implement.

3. Both argumentativeness, a constructive trait, and verbal aggressiveness, a destructive trait, are considered aggressive communication traits. In what group situations would argumentativeness be considered destructive? In what group situations would verbal aggressiveness be considered constructive?

4. Chapter 9 will discuss the characteristics of effective leadership. Based on your experience, which communication and personality traits do you associate with strong leadership? Which communication and personality traits do you associate with weak leadership?

5. How are a group member's communication and personality traits conveyed when working in a virtual group? To what extent does technology enhance or restrict the impressions group members make about each other in terms of their communication and personality traits?

References

Anderson, C. M., & Martin, M. M. (1995). The effects of communication motives, interaction involvement, and loneliness on satisfaction: A model of small groups. *Small Group Research, 26,* 118–137.

Anderson, C. M., & Martin, M. M. (1999). How argumentativeness and verbal aggressiveness affect cohesion, consensus, and satisfaction in small groups. *Communication Reports, 12,* 21–31.

Anderson, L. R. (1978). Groups would do better without humans. *Personality and Social Psychology Bulletin, 4,* 557–558.

Blickle, G., Habasch, A., & Senft, W. (1998). Verbal aggressiveness: Conceptualization and measurement a decade later. *Psychological Reports, 82,* 287–298.

Bochner, A. P., & Bochner, B. (1972). A multivariate investigation of Machiavellianism and task structure in four-man groups. *Speech Monographs, 39,* 277–285.

Bochner, A. P., DiSalvo, V., & Jonas, V. (1975). A computer-assisted analysis of small group process: An investigation of two Machiavellian groups. *Small Group Behavior, 6,* 197–203.

Burgoon, J. K. (1977). Unwillingness to communicate as a predictor of small group discussion behaviors and evaluations. *Central States Speech Journal, 28,* 122–133.

Christie, R., & Geis, F. L. (1970). *Studies in Machiavellianism.* New York: Academic Press.

Cohen, P. A., & Sheposh, J. P. (1977). Audience and level of esteem as determinants of risk taking. *Personality and Social Psychology Bulletin, 3,* 119–122.

Crocker, J., & Schwartz, I. (1985). Prejudice and ingroup favoritism in a minimal intergroup situation: Effects of self-esteem. *Personality and Social Psychology Bulletin, 11,* 379–386.

Dabbs, J. M., Jr., Evans, M. S., Hopper, C. H., & Purvis, J. A. (1980). Self-monitors in conversation: What do they monitor? *Journal of Personality and Social Psychology, 39,* 278–284.

Daly, J. A. (2002). Personality and interpersonal communication. In M. L. Knapp & J. A. Daly (Eds.), *Handbook of interpersonal communication* (3rd ed., pp. 133–180). Thousand Oaks, CA: Sage.

Davies, M. F. (1994). Personality and social characteristics. In A. P. Hare, H. H. Blumberg, M. F. Davies, & M. V. Kent (Eds.), *Small group research: A handbook* (pp. 41–78). Norwood, NJ: Ablex.

Ellis, R. J., Adamson, R. S., Deszca, G., & Cawsey, T. F. (1988). Self-monitoring and leadership emergence. *Small Group Behavior, 19,* 312–324.

Ellis, R. J., & Cronshaw, S. F. (1992). Self-monitoring and leadership emergence: A test of moderator effects. *Small Group Research, 23,* 113–131.

Flynn, F. J., Reagans, R. E., Amanatullah, E. T., & Ames, D. R. (2006). Helping one's way to the top: Self-monitors achieve status by helping others and knowing who helps whom. *Journal of Personality and Social Psychology, 91,* 1123–1137.

Frantz, C. M., & Seburn, M. (2003). Are argumentative people better or worse at seeing both sides? *Journal of Social and Personal Relationships, 20,* 565–573.

Frey, L. R. (1997). Individuals in groups. In L. R. Frey & J. K. Barge (Eds.), *Managing group life: Communicating in decision-making groups* (pp. 52–79). Boston: Houghton Mifflin.

Glauser, M. J. (1984). Self-esteem and communication tendencies: An analysis of four self-esteem/verbal dominance personality types. *Psychological Record, 34,* 115–131.

Hacker, S. L., & Gaitz, C. M. (1970). Interaction and performance correlates of Machiavellianism. *Sociological Quarterly, 11,* 94–102.

Haslett, B. B., & Ruebush, J. (1999). What differences do individual differences in groups make? The effects of individuals, culture, and group composition. In L. R. Frey (Ed.), D. S. Gouran, & M. S. Poole (Assoc. Eds.), *The handbook of group communication theory & research* (pp. 115–138). Thousand Oaks, CA: Sage.

Hawkins, K., & Stewart, R. A. (1991). Effects of communication apprehension on perceptions of leadership and intragroup attraction in small task-oriented groups. *Southern Communication Journal, 57,* 1–10.

Holladay, S. J., & Coombs, W. T. (1993). Communicating visions: An exploration of the role of delivery in the creation of leader charisma. *Management Communication Quarterly, 6,* 405–427.

Holladay, S. J., & Coombs, W. T. (1994). Speaking of visions and visions being spoken: An exploration of the effects of content and delivery on perceptions of leader charisma. *Management Communication Quarterly, 8,* 165–189.

Infante, D. A. (1987). Aggressiveness. In J. C. McCroskey & J. A. Daly (Eds.), *Personality and interpersonal communication* (pp. 157–192). Newbury Park, CA: Sage.

Infante, D. A. (1988). *Arguing constructively.* Prospect Heights, IL: Waveland Press.

Infante, D. A., & Gorden, W. I. (1985). Superiors' argumentativeness and verbal aggressiveness as predictors of subordinates' satisfaction. *Human Communication Research, 12,* 117–125.

Infante, D. A., & Gorden, W. I. (1989). Argumentativeness and affirming communicator style as predictors of satisfaction/dissatisfaction with subordinates. *Communication Quarterly, 37,* 81–90.

Infante, D. A., & Gorden, W. I. (1991). How employees see the boss: Test of an argumentative and affirming model of supervisors' communicative behavior. *Western Journal of Speech Communication, 55,* 294–304.

Infante, D. A., & Rancer, A. S. (1982). A conceptualization and measure of argumentativeness. *Journal of Personality Assessment, 46,* 72–80.

Infante, D. A., & Rancer, A. S. (1996). Argumentativeness and verbal aggressiveness: A review of recent theory and research. In B. R. Burleson (Ed.), *Communication yearbook* (Vol. 19, pp. 319–351). Thousand Oaks, CA: Sage.

Infante, D. A., Rancer, A. S., & Womack, D. F. (2003). *Building communication theory* (4th ed.). Prospect Heights, IL: Waveland Press.

Infante, D. A., Riddle, B. L., Horvath, C. W., & Tumlin, S. A. (1992). Verbal aggressiveness: Messages and reasons. *Communication Quarterly, 40,* 116–126.

Infante, D. A., & Wigley, C. J., III. (1986). Verbal aggressiveness: An interpersonal model and measure. *Communication Monographs, 53,* 61–69.

Kent, R. L., & Moss, S. E. (1990). Self-monitoring as a predictor of leader emergence. *Psychological Reports, 66,* 875–881.

Keyton, J., & Frey, L. R. (2002). The state of traits: Predispositions and group communication. In L. R. Frey (Ed.), *New directions in group communication* (pp. 99–120). Thousand Oaks, CA: Sage.

Kinney, T. A. (1994). An inductively derived typology of verbal aggression and its association to distress. *Human Communication Research, 21,* 183–222.

Kwal, T., & Fleshler, H. (1975). The influence of self-esteem on emergent leadership patterns. *Speech Teacher, 22,* 100–106.

Limon, M. S., & LaFrance, B. H. (2005). Communication traits and leader emergence: Examining the impact of argumentativeness, communication apprehension, and verbal aggressiveness in work groups. *Southern Communication Journal, 70,* 123–133.

Martin, M. M., Anderson, C. M., Burant, P. A., & Weber, K. (1997). Verbal aggression in sibling relationships. *Communication Quarterly, 45,* 304–317.

Martin, M. M., Anderson, C. M., & Horvath, C. W. (1996). Feelings about verbal aggression: Justifications for sending and hurt from receiving verbally aggressive messages. *Communication Research Reports, 13,* 19–26.

McCroskey, J. C. (1977). Oral communication apprehension: A summary of recent theory and research. *Human Communication Research, 4,* 78–96.

McCroskey, J. C. (1984). The communication apprehension perspective. In J. A. Daly & J. C. McCroskey (Eds.), *Avoiding communication: Shyness, reticence, and communication apprehension* (pp. 13–38). Beverly Hills, CA: Sage.

McCroskey, J. C., & Beatty, M. J. (1998). Communication apprehension. In J. C. McCroskey, J. A. Daly, M. M. Martin, & M. J. Beatty (Eds.), *Communication and personality: Trait perspectives* (pp. 215–232). Cresskill, NJ: Hampton Press.

McCroskey, J. C., Daly, J. A., & Sorensen, G. (1976). Personality correlates of communication apprehension: A research note. *Human Communication Research, 2,* 376–380.

McCroskey, J. C., & Richmond, V. P. (1992). Communication apprehension and small group communication. In R. S. Cathcart & L. A. Samovar (Eds.), *Small group communication: A reader* (6th ed., pp. 361–374). Dubuque, IA: William C. Brown.

Mudrack, P. E., & Mason, E. S. (1995). Extending the Machiavellianism construct: A brief measure and some unexplored relationships. *Journal of Social Behavior and Personality, 10,* 187–200.

Myers, S. A., & Johnson, A. D. (2003). Verbal aggression and liking in interpersonal relationships. *Communication Research Reports, 20,* 90–96.

Myers, S. A., & Knox, R. L. (2000). Perceived instructor argumentativeness and verbal aggressiveness and student outcomes. *Communication Research Reports, 17,* 299–309.

Myers, S. A., Martin, M. M., & Mottet, T. P. (2000). The relationship between student communication motives and perceived instructor communicator style. *Communication Research Reports, 17,* 161–170.

Norton, R. W. (1978). Foundation of a communicator style construct. *Human Communication Research, 4,* 99–112.

Norton, R W. (1983). *Communicator style: Theory, applications, and measures.* Beverly Hills, CA: Sage.

Norton, R. W. (1986). Communicator style in teaching: Giving good form to content. In J. M. Civikly (Ed.), *New directions for teaching and learning, no. 26: Communicating in college classrooms* (pp. 33–40). San Francisco: Jossey-Bass.

Nussbaum, J. F. (1992). Communicator style and teacher influence. In V. P. Richmond & J. C. McCroskey (Eds.), *Power in the classroom: Communication, control, and concern* (pp. 145–158). Hillsdale, NJ: Erlbaum.

Onyekwere, E. O., Rubin, R. B., & Infante, D. A. (1991). Interpersonal perception and communication satisfaction as a function of argumentativeness and ego-involvement. *Communication Quarterly, 39,* 35–47.

Porter, D. T. (1982). Communicator style perceptions as a function of communication apprehension. *Communication Quarterly, 30,* 237–244.

Rancer, A. S., Baukus, R. A., & Infante, D. A. (1985). Relations between argumentativeness and belief structures about arguing. *Communication Education, 34,* 37–47.

Rancer, A. S., & Infante, D. A. (1985). Relations between motivation to argue and the argumentativeness of adversaries. *Communication Quarterly, 33,* 209–218.

Rancer, A. S., Kosberg, R. L., & Baukus, R A. (1992). Beliefs about arguing as predictors of trait argumentativeness: Implications for training in argument and conflict management. *Communication Education, 41,* 375–387.

Rarick, D. L., Soldow, G. F., & Geizer, R. S. (1976). Self-monitoring as a mediator of conformity. *Central States Speech Journal, 27,* 267–271.

Schullery, N. M., & Schullery, S. E. (2002). Relationships between group skills, temperament, and argumentativeness. *Communication Research Reports, 19,* 246–257.

Schultz, B. (1982). Argumentativeness: Its effects in group decision-making and its role in leadership perception. *Communication Quarterly, 30,* 368–375.

Sutter, D. L., & Martin, M. M. (1998). Verbal aggression during disengagement of dating relationships. *Communication Research Reports, 15,* 318–326.

Snyder, M. (1987). *Public appearances, private realities: The psychology of self-monitoring.* New York: W. H. Freeman.

Wigley, C. J., III. (1998). Verbal aggressiveness. In J. C. McCroskey, J. A. Daly, M. M. Martin, & M. J. Beatty (Eds.), *Communication and personality: Trait perspectives* (pp. 191–214). Cresskill, NJ: Hampton Press.

Diversity Among Small Group Members 4

After reading this chapter, you should be able to:

1. explain how diversity impacts a small group,
2. identify and describe the four dimensions of culture,
3. differentiate between sex and gender,
4. identify and describe the four learning styles, and
5. explain how members' communication traits impact group performance.

Case Study

At 1 p.m. the servers who work the breakfast shift at the Lunch Bucket, a local restaurant, meet to discuss how to increase weekend sales. The weekend servers include Lupe, a retired factory worker originally from Mexico; Heidi, a mother of two, a native of Finland, and a United States resident for 20 years; Gene, a single father of three who has worked at the Lunch Bucket for 35 years; Gyeong-Ho, a student originally from Seoul, Korea, enrolled in the hospitality program at the community college; and Teon, a senior from

Photo 4.1 Diversity is an issue that must be embraced by group members.

Source: Mel Stuart/Westend61/Jupiterimages.

Chicago who is finishing his undergraduate degree in landscape architecture at State University. Mrs. Perry, whose brother-in-law owns the Lunch Bucket, supervises.

Mrs. Perry:	Good afternoon, folks. I appreciate everyone taking the time to meet today so we can discuss how to increase our shift sales on the weekends. If we don't develop a way to get more people into the restaurant on the weekend, we may have to cut hours, and since the five of you work every weekend, this could affect your pay.
Heidi:	I've worked here for 20 years. If anyone should have their hours cut, it should be Gyeong-Ho or Teon since they have worked here only for a short time.
Gene:	Well, I've worked here for 35 years, so if anyone is going to have his hours cut, it shouldn't be me. I've got three kids to feed, and, frankly, I don't like the idea that my hours could get cut after all the time I've put into working here. Plus, my regulars wouldn't like it if I wasn't here to serve them.

Mrs. Perry:	I'm not saying that we will cut your hours; I'm just letting all of you know that unless business picks up, we may be forced to cut back.
Lupe:	How can you say that business is slow? Every Sunday it seems that I'm in the weeds at least four to five times each shift. And I still haven't finished my side work, so I have to stay and do that after this meeting.
Teon:	Me, too. And even though I don't have any kids or haven't worked here for decades, I need this job so I can get through school. So does Gyeong-Ho, right?
Gyeong-Ho:	Yes, but since I have not worked here as long as Gene and Heidi, I will leave the decision to Mrs. Perry.
Heidi:	If our hours aren't based on seniority, then they should at least be based on performance. I always receive "excellents" on my yearly reviews, and I've been named Outstanding Server three years in a row by *Dining Out* magazine. Since this award is voted on by the readers, it doesn't make sense for my hours to be cut. If anyone should have her hours cut, it should be Lupe because she is the slowest.
Lupe:	I can't help it if I take time to get to know our customers. Some of these folks are like my second family, like Ida who just celebrated her 94th birthday and Bob and Shirlette who invited me to their 50th anniversary party.
Teon:	That's the problem, Lupe. We're not here to get to know the customers; we're here to get them in and out so we can serve more people and make more money.
Gene:	I agree with Lupe. Perhaps if you tried to get to know the regulars, Teon, they would ask for your section and you would make more money.
Mrs. Perry:	I think we're getting off topic. Perhaps this meeting wasn't the best idea. Does anyone have a suggestion for how we can increase sales? Gyeong-Ho?
Gyeong-Ho:	Whatever you think, Mrs. Perry.
Mrs. Perry:	Fine. What I think is that this meeting officially has ended. Let's meet next week to discuss this again. And Lupe, finish your side work before the meeting starts.

In this case study, the members experience diversity issues that affect their communication, even though the members may not know it. As they discuss their impending reduction in work hours, each member communicates in a way that reflects his or her diverse background. Heidi and Gene articulate why they should receive preferential treatment, Lupe defends her performance, Teon offers arguments and refutes members' statements, and Gyeong-Ho says little. Interestingly, these differences in communication can be attributed to the diversity of the group members.

This chapter purports to identify how diversity affects communication in small groups. To do this, we will define diversity and the associated positive and negative outcomes. We then will focus on three components (i.e., cultural, demographic, and cognitive) of group diversity. First, we will examine how cultural diversity differs based on the dimensions of power distance, uncertainty avoidance, individualism-collectivism, and time orientation. Second, we will differentiate between sex and gender (a type of demographic diversity) and explore how they affect communication in small groups. Third, we will discuss learning styles (a type of cognitive diversity) and illustrate how they can affect task accomplishment in the small group. Finally, we will examine how the communication traits of group members reflect the cultural, demographic, and cognitive diversity often encountered in a small group.

Definition and Outcomes of Diversity

Diversity describes the joining of individuals who differ in cultural, demographic, and cognitive backgrounds (Harris & Sherblom, 2005; Neuliep, 2006). These differences include race, age, ethnicity, education level, gender, sexual orientation, sex, social class, and socioeconomic status. Groups comprising members similar in cultural, demographic, and cognitive backgrounds are considered homogeneous; groups comprising members who differ in cultural, demographic, and cognitive backgrounds are considered heterogeneous (Oetzel, Meares, & Fukumoto, 2003). Although the members of the group in the case study may appear different from the members of the groups to which you have belonged thus far, diversity is becoming more prominent in the workplace, the community, and our schools.

> **?** Reflect on your work group. How diverse is your work group in terms of group members' demographic, cultural, and cognitive backgrounds?

Because diversity is unavoidable and only will continue to increase throughout your life span, learning about these differences is necessary to make communication more effective in small groups. A prevalent theme in today's workplace and academia centers on "value in diversity" (Neuliep, 2006) and emphasizes the positive effects of diversity in small groups, suggesting belonging to a diverse group offers more advantages than belonging to a homogeneous group (McLeod, Lobel, & Cox, 1996). A popular reason behind this idea upholds that diverse, as opposed to homogeneous, members of a small group bring more options to the group (Kirchmeyer, 1993). In the case study, Lupe and Heidi can bring their experiences from Mexico and Finland, respectively; Gene can bring his experiences as a single parent; and Gyeong-Ho and Teon can bring their experiences from urban life to the group meeting. The idea suggests that diverse members—more creative, adaptable, and innovative because of their unique experiences (Zenger & Lawrence, 1989)—may solve problems more efficiently. A homogeneous group composed of members with similar backgrounds and experiences may not be as imaginative and therefore not as efficient in problem solving. Diverse groups present another advantage in the high degree of task cohesion (Keyton, 1999; McLeod et al., 1996). If you recall from Chapter 2, cohesion occurs when a member reaches an acceptable level of desire to stay in the group. Members with different backgrounds achieve an acceptable level of desire to accomplish the group's goal and work well together to complete the task. Although this advantage suggests that the group members from the case study will complete their task in an effective manner, what do you think?

Not all outcomes of diverse groups are positive, however. Unfortunately, members who believe they represent the minority in a small group likely will participate less (Kirchmeyer, 1993). This means that any group member who perceives herself as "outnumbered" by other group members due to differences in demographic, cultural, and cognitive backgrounds may not feel inclined to communicate in the group. This lack of communication prevents group members from getting to know one another better, which may explain why members of diverse groups have less affect (i.e., emotion and caring) for one another than members of homogeneous groups (McLeod et al., 1996), and contributes to the slow development of social cohesion (Keyton, 1999).

Group members who support the "value in diversity" theme believe any group can overcome these negative outcomes. To do so, group members first must understand the components of their communicative practices (McLeod et al., 1996; Neuliep, 2006). The first component is cultural diversity.

> 66 *Ethically Speaking:* Should a group be required to adopt a "value in diversity" theme? What are the group benefits for doing so? What are the group costs for doing so? 99

Cultural Diversity

Cultural diversity comprises "the sum total of beliefs, values, attitudes, meanings, perceptions, customs, practices, language, and other artifacts of social life that are learned, shared, and passed on by a group of people" (Hirokawa, Cathcart, Samovar, & Henman, 2003, p. 215). In other words, cultural diversity embraces the various behaviors and perceptions perpetuated by a group of individuals. According to anthropologist Edward Hall (1976), culture influences all aspects of our communication, yet most cultural members are unaware of the four dimensions of culture—power distance, uncertainty avoidance, individualism-collectivism, and time orientation (see Table 4.1)—that distinguish one culture from another.

Power Distance

The first dimension of culture, power distance, refers to the inequality that exists between a less powerful person and a more powerful person (Hofstede, 2001). Distinguishing areas of inequality include wealth; social status; privilege; and cognitive, mental (e.g., mental illness), and physical (e.g., disabilities) characteristics. Differences in power distance often are referred to as a high-power-distance culture or a low-power-distance culture. In a high-power-distance culture, individuals with less power do not dispute the control other individuals have over them. For instance, in the case study, Gyeong-Ho does not contradict Heidi's position that his hours should be cut, even though he needs the job as much as she does.

Table 4.1   Dimensions of Culture

Dimension	Definition
Power distance	The inequality that exists between a less powerful person and a more powerful person
Uncertainty avoidance	The amount of stress that a culture associates with an unknown future
Individualism-collectivism	Whether attention is focused on the group or the individual
Time orientation	How quickly a culture assumes important aspects of life (e.g., relationships, careers) should develop

Source: Based on Hofstede, G. (2001). *Culture's consequences: Comparing values, behaviors, institutions, and organizations across nations* (3rd ed.). Thousand Oaks, CA: Sage.

A low-power-distance culture stresses equality among all individuals (Hofstede, 2001). Powerful individuals, such as a professor or a manager, presumably will lead democratically and include all members in decision making.

In a small group, problems can occur when members differ in their cultural preferences of power distance. A low-power-distance leader will not understand why a high-power-distance group member does not contribute or appears apprehensive in a group meeting; a high-power-distance leader will be offended when a low-power-distance member engages in argumentativeness. Although group members need not necessarily be homogeneous in their collective preference for power distance, they should articulate their preferences to avoid confusion, misunderstanding, or hurt feelings.

Uncertainty Avoidance

The second dimension of culture, uncertainty avoidance, refers to the amount of stress that a culture associates with an unknown future (Hofstede, 2001). Uncertainty can stem from the behavior of group members, individuals outside the group, and the environment (Hofstede, 2001). Cultures differ in will to accept these uncertainties and how much stress accepting them will cause. Cultures unaccepting of uncertainty are considered high in uncertainty avoidance; cultures accepting of uncertainty are considered low in uncertainty avoidance. Individuals in high-uncertainty cultures try to avoid human error as much as possible by implementing technology, instituting rigid rules, and stressing efficiency and task orientation. Individuals in low-uncertainty cultures, though more creative and relationally oriented, may experience issues with punctuality and precision.

A group composed of high- and low-uncertainty-avoidant members can encounter problems when accomplishing a task. A high-uncertainty-avoidant member will attempt to ensure efficient use of time, but by behaving rigidly, he will be less concerned with members communicating for relational purposes. Mrs. Perry demonstrates this notion by dismissing the servers when they fail to focus on the task. A member low in uncertainty more likely will develop creative solutions that, never before used, present greater potential for failure. Members should voice their opinions, affected by their uncertainty avoidance preference, in group discussions, during which high- and low-uncertainty-avoidant members can reach a satisfying compromise (Hofstede, 2001).

Individualism-Collectivism

The third dimension of culture, individualism-collectivism, refers to whether attention is focused on the group or the individual (Hofstede, 2001). A culture that values the individual over the group, termed individualistic, rewards competitiveness and tends to have a history of being an industrial society (Hofstede, 2001; Porter & Samovar, 2003). The United States exemplifies an individualistic culture that emphasizes the individual over the group, as evidenced by how Americans distinguish individuals from society for being the smartest, the toughest, the fastest, and the most determined. Heidi attempts to do this when she lists the reasons why Mrs. Perry should not reduce her hours. Not surprisingly, individualistic cultures pressure members to perform under the guise of guilt (Hofstede, 2001).

A culture that values the group over the individual is termed **collectivistic**. Members of collectivistic cultures, such as Mexico and North Korea, desire to remain in the same groups over a long period of time. By maintaining long-term memberships in groups, individuals grow more accustomed to the group norms and have a better chance at establishing group harmony. Group harmony beats any individual achievement; in fact, an individual achievement actually might embarrass a member of a collectivistic culture. Not surprisingly, collectivistic cultures pressure members to perform well under the threat of shaming the group (Hofstede, 2001).

In a small group, the difference between collectivism and individualism can confuse members (Porter & Samovar, 2003). Although all members want to accomplish the group task, individualistic members desire personal recognition, which may disturb collectivistic members who find these personal recognitions disruptive to the group harmony. Leaders must pay attention to this cultural dimension when motivating members. The threat of letting down the group would not be as effective with an individualistic member as it would with a collectivistic member; the threat of not receiving an individual award would not be as effective with a collectivistic member as it would with an individualistic member.

Time Orientation

The fourth dimension of culture, **time orientation**, refers to how quickly a culture assumes important aspects of life (e.g., relationships, careers) should develop (Hofstede, 2001). Cultures that believe in focusing work and thoughts on the future are considered long-term oriented whereas cultures that believe in focusing work and thoughts on the present are considered short-term oriented. In sum, cultures emphasize either the future (i.e., long-term oriented) or the present (i.e., short-term oriented).

Long- and short-term-oriented cultures differ in two primary ways: The first relates to how the culture views family, social relations, and work; the second relates to how the members think. Long-term-oriented cultures value creativity as well as relationships and careers that build slowly over time. Short-term-oriented cultures value analytic thinking and quick solutions to problems that provide immediate results. This difference appears in the exchange between Lupe and Teon as they discuss the purpose of their jobs as servers.

Even in classroom groups with rigid time constraints, preferences for how to conduct group meetings will differ based on this dimension. Long-term-oriented group members will place more value on developing the most innovative solution to a problem and on spending considerable time developing relationships with group members. Short-term-oriented group members will not see the value in building relationships, particularly if they believe the group will terminate after task accomplishment.

Because these four dimensions of culture (i.e., power distance, uncertainty avoidance, individualism-collectivism, and time orientation) affect the communication that occurs in small groups, group members must address them. Though not necessarily obvious, these cultural dimensions influence the ways group members develop ideas, make decisions, and implement solutions (Hofstede, 2001). As such, members should discuss these differences openly and focus on reducing the dominance of certain ideas and opinions (Kirchmeyer, 1993).

As should be evident at this point, groups need not feature homogeneity to ensure success; however, groups should not ignore the cultural diversity that affects them. In the next section, we will discuss demographic diversity, of which one type contains sex and gender.

Demographic Diversity: Sex and Gender

Sex and *gender* are two words that people often use synonymously, as are *male* and *masculine* and *female* and *feminine*. These terms, however, represent two different constructs: Sex (i.e., male, female) refers to the biological difference between men and women as evidenced by an individual's external genitalia and internal sexual organs whereas gender (i.e., masculinity, femininity) refers to the social beliefs and values associated with being male or female (Reich & Wood, 2003).

In a small group, sex differences exist in how group members communicate. Men use more instrumental, or task-related, communication as group members than women (Reich & Wood, 2003). Men also interrupt and reroute group conversations (i.e., move conversations in different directions than initially intended) more often than women (Anderson & Leaper, 1998) and tend to direct the communication toward themselves (Reich & Wood, 2003). Conversely, female group members typically focus more on expressive, or relationally oriented, communication. When female members participate in group interactions, they spend more time justifying their opinions and decisions, tend to agree with group members more often than men (Turner, Dindia, & Pearson, 1995), and contribute less to group discussions than men (Johnson & Schulman, 1989; Kirchmeyer, 1993). These differences may explain the perception that female group members have less power than male group members (Haslett & Ruebush, 1999), although groups that devote more time to relationally oriented communication more likely will dismiss this perception (Shimanoff & Jenkins, 2003). In addition, when a small group contains more men than women, women emerge less satisfied with the discussions that occur in the group (Johnson & Schulman, 1989).

> In your work group, have you noticed differences in how male and female group members communicate? If so, are these differences attributed to group member sex or other influences, such as group member personality, group member ability, or role talk?

When it comes to group leadership, very few sex differences exist (Powell, 1993; Shimanoff & Jenkins, 2003; Wilkins & Andersen, 1991). Group members express equal satisfaction with both male and female leaders (Powell, 1993) and report that male and female leaders produce equal effects (Shimanoff & Jenkins, 2003). Any differences that do exist are minimal (Eagly & Karau, 1991). Although men and women do not display distinct preferences in how to exert leadership, women tend to lead more democratically and collaboratively than men and men tend to lead more autocratically than women (Eagly & Karau, 1991; Wilkins & Andersen, 1991)—perhaps because group members expect women to be responsive and relationally oriented (Duran & Carveth, 1990; Shimanoff & Jenkins, 2003). As such, this expectation may explain why women who do lead more autocratically are perceived less favorably (Eagly & Karau, 1991).

Gender generally divides into two categories: masculinity and femininity (Bem, 1974; Wheeless & Dierks-Stewart, 1981). Masculine individuals possess high levels of masculine behavior and low levels of feminine behavior whereas feminine individuals possess high levels of feminine behavior and low levels of masculine behavior. Based on this social construction, masculinity and femininity each associate with particular behaviors (Bem, 1974; Wheeless & Dierks-Stewart, 1981), including those listed in Table 4.2. Wealth and status gauge masculine individuals' achievement; competition motivates masculine individuals, who resolve conflict by actively fighting or reacting with complete disregard (Hofstede, 2001; Rahim, 1983). Relationships gauge achievement for feminine individuals, who, motivated by cooperation, resolve conflict through negotiation and problem solving (Hofstede, 2001; Rahim, 1983).

Although males are often masculine and females are often feminine, this notion is not absolute. Feminine men exist, as do masculine women. Gender can be divided further into two additional categories: androgyny and undifferentiated (Bem, 1974). Androgynous individuals possess high levels of both masculine and feminine behaviors and undifferentiated individuals possess low levels of both

Table 4.2   Masculine and Feminine Behaviors

Masculine behaviors	*Feminine behaviors*
Acts as a leader	Gentle
Has leadership abilities	Tender
Dominant	Understanding
Aggressive	Warm
Willing to take a stand	Sensitive to needs of others
Forceful	Compassionate
Assertive	Sincere
Strong personality	Helpful
Competitive	Eager to soothe hurtful feelings
Independent	Friendly

Source: Wheeless, V. E., & Dierks-Stewart, K. (1981). The psychometric properties of the Bem Sex-Role Inventory: Questions concerning reliability and validity. *Communication Quarterly, 29,* 173–186.

masculine and feminine behaviors. Of the four gender categories, androgynous individuals may communicate the most competently because they can enact behaviors, either masculine or feminine, that most appropriately fit the situation.

Most likely, the small groups to which you belong will not be homogeneous in regard to group member sex and gender. Members need to avoid making assumptions about each other based on their sex and gender. For example, not all female leaders will emphasize relationally oriented communication, and not all male leaders will engage in authoritarian leadership. We now will address cognitive diversity, of which one type is learning styles.

Cognitive Diversity: Learning Styles

Learning styles refer to individuals' preferences for acquiring information in a learning environment and influence how individuals listen to and present information, all of which is important in any small group (Kolb, 1984). Although an

Photo 4.2   Like students, group members bring their learning styles to any group task.

Source: ©iStockphoto.com/Yuri_Arcurs.

individual's learning style can be accessed in several ways, one well-established way of assessing learning styles is based on David Kolb's experiential learning theory (de Jesus, Almeida, & Watts, 2004). According to Kolb, an individual's learning style falls into one of four categories: the converger, the diverger, the assimilator, and the accommodator. These four learning styles differ in their general orientation toward learning and their preferred methods of instruction (Little, 2004).

A converger, or a group member who learns through a combination of thinking and doing (Kolb, 1984), prefers tasks that require problem solving, deductive reasoning, and practical application; these learners tend to be unemotional and would rather work alone than with a group (de Jesus et al., 2004; Evans, Forney, & Guido-DiBrito, 1998). They learn best by tinkering and experimenting (Dwyer, 1998).

A diverger, or a group member who learns through a combination of watching and feeling (Kolb, 1984), prefers tasks that require imagination and brainstorming; these learners tend to be emotional and would rather work with other people than alone (Evans et al., 1998). Divergers learn best by listening and sharing (Dwyer, 1998).

An **assimilator**, or a group member who learns through a combination of thinking and watching (Kolb, 1984), prefers tasks that require abstract thinking, inductive reasoning, and logic; they do not care if the task produces a practical result and would rather work alone than with a group (Evans et al., 1998). Assimilators learn best by critiquing ideas (Dwyer, 1998).

An **accommodator**, or a group member who learns through a combination of feeling and doing (Kolb, 1984), prefers tasks that require action, risk taking, and trial-and-error methods. They rely on their group members to help accomplish the task, and they like teaching their group members; however, they

> **?** Which learning style do you possess? How does this style help your work group? How does this learning style hinder your work group?

can become impatient if their group members are not equally enthusiastic and motivated (Evans et al., 1998). Accommodators learn best by exploring (Dwyer, 1998).

To aid in the innovation of task accomplishment, it is advantageous for a group to have members who possess each of these four learning styles. Each style has a weakness, however; convergers make hasty decisions, divergers struggle to reach any decision at all, assimilators encounter problems creating a practical solution, and accommodators find difficulty completing the task in a timely manner (Evans et al., 1998). Nonetheless, the diversity of these learning styles can help a group consider alternative perspectives as the group makes a decision or solves a problem.

Communication Traits as a Reflection of Diversity

Additionally, it is important to realize that the communicative traits of group members reflect the cultural and demographic diversity you will encounter in a small group. For example, American college students demonstrate less communication apprehension than Australian, Puerto Rican, and Micronesian college students (Burroughs, Marie, & McCroskey, 2003; Sallinen-Kuparinen, McCroskey, & Richmond, 1991; Watson, Monroe, Fayer, & Aloise, 1988); American college students show more argumentative traits than Japanese college students (Prunty, Klopf, & Ishii, 1990) but less than Finnish college students (Klopf, Thompson, & Sallinen-Kuparinen, 1991); and American college students act less argumentative and verbally aggressive than Australian college students (Avtgis & Rancer, 2002).

Men and women also differ in their communication traits. Specifically, women express more communication apprehension than men, although fewer differences show in younger men and women (Donovan & MacIntyre, 2004), and men reveal both more argumentative and more verbally aggressive traits than women (Kinney, Smith, & Donzella, 2001; Nicotera & Rancer, 1994). Men and women tend to use the 10 communicator style attributes in a relatively similar manner; however, men generally use the precise attribute more than women, and women use the animated attribute more than men (Montgomery & Norton, 1981). Furthermore, masculine individuals have been found to be more argumentative than feminine, androgynous, and undifferentiated individuals (Rancer & Dierks-Stewart, 1985), and feminine individuals do not consider themselves verbally aggressive (Kinney et al., 2001).

A Final Note About Diversity Among Small Group Members

In work groups, diversity is not limited to culture, demographic (e.g., sex and gender), or cognitive (e.g., learning style) diversity. Diversity also can emerge in the forms of informational diversity and value diversity (Jehn, Northcraft, & Neale, 1999). **Informational diversity** refers to differences among group members based on their education, work experience, group experience, and expertise; **value diversity** refers to differences among group members in terms of what they consider as their group's goals, mission, and purpose (Jehn et al., 1999). Other examples of diversity include members' ages, attitudes, beliefs, and values. Regardless of how you define diversity, you essentially must resist engaging in **ethnocentrism**, or the tendency for individuals to use the values, attitudes, and behaviors of their ingroup as the basis for judging and evaluating another group's values, attitudes, and behaviors (Neuliep, 2002). Although ethnocentrism provides group members with a sense of cultural "we-ness," it also can act as a barrier to communication within culturally, demographically, or cognitively diverse groups (Hinkle, 2006), which never fares well.

Conclusion

This chapter explained how diversity affects communication in small groups. To do this, we defined diversity and identified the positive and negative outcomes associated with it. We then focused on three components of group diversity: We examined how cultural diversity differs based on the dimensions of power distance, uncertainty avoidance, individualism-collectivism, and time orientation; we differentiated between sex and gender (a type of demographic diversity) and explored how sex and gender affect communication in small groups; and we discussed learning styles (a type of cognitive diversity) and illustrated how they can affect task accomplishment in the small group. Finally, we examined how the communicative traits of group members reflect the cultural, demographic, and cognitive diversity you will encounter in a small group. As you reflect on the role diversity plays in the small groups to which you belong, consider how diversity can affect the rate at which group development occurs.

Discussion Questions

1. Does your work group possess an individualistic orientation or a collectivistic orientation? What are some examples of this orientation? How is this orientation influenced by the organization's culture or your group's supervisor?

2. In a small group, what are the repercussions of leaders who do not lead the way they are expected to based on their culture, sex, or gender?

3. To be the most effective, it has been suggested that groups should have members who are diverse in their learning styles. Do you agree with this statement? Is it easier or more difficult to work with members who share the same learning style? Why?

4. Is diversity an issue that a virtual group would need to address? Why?

5. What are some other forms of diversity that exist in small groups? Do these forms differ based on the type of small group (i.e., primary, social, self-help, learning, service, public, work, or virtual) to which you belong?

References

Anderson, K., & Leaper, C. (1998). Meta-analysis of gender effects on conversational interruption: Who, what, when, where, and how. *Sex Roles, 39,* 225–252.

Avtgis, T. A., & Rancer, A. S. (2002). Aggressive communication across cultures: A comparison of aggressive communication among United States, New Zealand, and Australia. *Journal of Intercultural Communication Research, 31,* 191–200.

Bem, S. L. (1974). The measurement of psychological androgyny. *Journal of Consulting and Clinical Psychology, 42,* 155–162.

Burroughs, N. F., Marie, V., & McCroskey, J. C. (2003). Relationships of self-perceived communication competence and communication apprehension with willingness to communicate: A comparison with first and second languages in Micronesia. *Communication Research Reports, 20,* 230–239.

de Jesus, H. P., Alemeida, P., & Watts, M. (2004). Questioning styles and students' learning: Four case studies. *Educational Psychology, 24,* 531–548.

Donovan, L. A., & MacIntyre, P. D. (2004). Age and sex differences in willingness to communicate, communication apprehension, and self-perceived competence. *Communication Research Reports, 21,* 420–427.

Duran, R. L., & Carveth, R. A. (1990). The effects of gender-role expectations upon perceptions of communicative competence. *Communication Research Reports, 7,* 25–33.

Dwyer, K. K. (1998). Communication apprehension and learning style preference: Correlations and implications for teaching. *Communication Education, 47,* 137–150.

Eagly, A. H., & Karau, S. J. (1991). Gender and the emergence of leaders: A meta-analysis. *Journal of Personality and Social Psychology, 60,* 685–710.

Evans, N. J., Forney, D. S., & Guido-DiBrito, F. (1998). *Student development in college: Theory, research, and practice.* San Francisco: Jossey-Bass.

Hall, E. T. (1976). *Beyond culture.* Garden City, NY: Doubleday.

Harris, T. E., & Sherblom, J. C. (2005). *Small group and team communication.* Boston: Allyn & Bacon.

Haslett, B. B., & Ruebush, J. (1999). What differences do individual differences in groups make? The effects of individuals, culture, and group composition. In L. R. Frey (Ed.), D. S. Gouran, & M. S. Poole (Assoc. Eds.), *The handbook of group communication theory and research* (pp. 115–138). Thousand Oaks, CA: Sage.

Hinkle, L. L. (2006). Brief reading: Diversity in the small group. In S. A. Myers (Ed.), *An introduction to small group communication* (pp. 177–183). Littleton, MA: Tapestry Press.

Hirokawa, R. Y., Cathcart, R. S., Samovar, L. A., & Henman, L. D. (Eds.). (2003). *Small group communication theory and practice: An anthology* (8th ed.). Los Angeles: Roxbury.

Hofstede, G. (2001). *Culture's consequences: Comparing values, behaviors, institutions, and organizations across nations* (3rd ed.). Thousand Oaks, CA: Sage.

Jehn, K. A., Northcraft, G. B., & Neale, M. A. (1999). Why differences make a difference: A field study of diversity, conflict, and performance in groups. *Administrative Science Quarterly, 44,* 741–763.

Johnson, R. A., & Schulman, G. I. (1989). Gender-role composition and role entrapment in decision-making groups. *Gender and Society, 3,* 355–372.

Keyton, J. (1999). Relational communication in groups. In L. R. Frey (Ed.), D. S. Gouran, & M. S. Poole (Assoc. Eds.), *The handbook of group communication theory and research* (pp. 192–224). Thousand Oaks, CA: Sage.

Kinney, T. A., Smith, B. A., & Donzella, B. (2001). The influence of sex, gender, self-discrepancies, and self-awareness on anger and verbal aggressiveness among U.S. college students. *Journal of Social Psychology, 141,* 245–275.

Kirchmeyer, C. (1993). Multicultural task groups: An account of the low contribution level of minorities. *Small Group Research, 24,* 127–148.

Klopf, D. W., Thompson, C., & Sallinen-Kuparinen, A. (1991). Argumentativeness among selected Finnish and American college students. *Psychological Reports, 68,* 161–162.

Kolb, D. A. (1984). *Experiential learning: Experience as the source of learning and development.* Englewood Cliffs, NJ: Prentice Hall.

Little, L. (2004). Kolb's learning styles for leaders. *Administrator, 23*(8), 8.

McLeod, P. L., Lobel, S. A., & Cox, T. H. (1996). Ethnic diversity and creativity in small groups. *Small Group Research, 27,* 248–264.

Montgomery, B. M., & Norton, R. W. (1981). Sex differences and similarities in communicator style. *Communication Monographs, 48,* 121–132.

Neuliep, J. W. (2002). Assessing the reliability and validity of the generalized ethnocentrism scale. *Journal of Intercultural Communication Research, 31,* 201–215.

Neuliep, J. W. (2006). *Intercultural communication: A contextual approach* (3rd ed.). Thousand Oaks, CA: Sage.

Nicotera, A. M., & Rancer, A. S. (1994). The influence of sex on self-perceptions and social stereotyping of aggressive communication predispositions. *Western Journal of Communication, 58,* 283–307.

Oetzel, J. G., Meares, M., & Fukumoto, A. (2003). Cross-cultural and intercultural work group communication. In R. Y. Hirokawa, R. S. Cathcart, L. A. Samovar, & L. D. Henman (Eds.), *Small group communication theory and practice: An anthology* (8th ed., pp. 239–252). Los Angeles: Roxbury.

Porter, R. E., & Samovar, L. A. (2003). Communication in the multicultural group. In R. Y. Hirokawa, R. S. Cathcart, L. A. Samovar, & L. D. Henman (Eds.), *Small group communication theory and practice: An anthology* (8th ed., pp. 230–238). Los Angeles: Roxbury.

Powell, G. (1993). *Women and men in management.* Newbury Park, CA: Sage.

Prunty, A. M., Klopf, D. W., & Ishii, S. (1990). Argumentativeness: Japanese and American tendencies to approach and avoid conflict. *Communication Research Reports, 7,* 75–79.

Rahim, M. A. (1983). A measure of styles of handling interpersonal conflict. *Academy of Management Journal, 26,* 368–376.

Rancer, A. S., & Dierks-Stewart, K. J. (1985). The influence of sex and sex-role orientation on trait argumentativeness. *Journal of Personality Assessment, 1,* 69–70.

Reich, N. M., & Wood, J. T. (2003). Sex, gender, and communication in small groups. In R. Y. Hirokawa, R. S. Cathcart, L. A. Samovar, & L. D. Henman (Eds.), *Small group communication theory and practice: An anthology* (8th ed., pp. 218–229). Los Angeles: Roxbury.

Sallinen-Kuparinen, A., McCroskey, J. C., & Richmond, V. P. (1991). Willingness to communicate, communication apprehension, introversion, and self-reported communication competence: Finnish and American comparisons. *Communication Research Reports, 8,* 55–64.

Shimanoff, S. B., & Jenkins, M. M. (2003). Leadership and gender: Challenging assumptions and recognizing resources. In R. Y. Hirokawa, R. S. Cathcart, L. A. Samovar, & L. D. Henman (Eds.), *Small group communication theory and practice: An anthology* (8th ed., pp. 184–198). Los Angeles: Roxbury.

Turner, L. H., Dindia, K., & Pearson, J. C. (1995). An investigation of female/male verbal behaviors in same-sex and mixed-sex conversation. *Communication Reports, 8,* 86–96.

Watson, A. K., Monroe, E. E., Fayer, J. M., & Aloise, M. E. (1988). Communication apprehension in Puerto Rican and U.S. mainland children. *Communication Research Reports, 2,* 161–168.

Wheeless, V. E., & Dierks-Stewart, K. (1981). The psychometric properties of the Bem Sex-Role Inventory: Questions concerning reliability and validity. *Communication Quarterly, 29,* 173–186.

Wilkins, B. M., & Andersen, P. A. (1991). Gender differences and similarities in management communication: A meta-analysis. *Management Communication Quarterly, 5,* 6–35.

Zenger, T. R., & Lawrence, B. S. (1989). Organizational demography: The differential effects of age and tenure distributions on technical communication. *Academy of Management Journal, 32,* 353–376.

Models of Small Group Development | 5

After reading this chapter, you should be able to:

1. explain the importance of studying group communication from a life span approach,

2. explain how group history and maturity affect group development,

3. identify and explain the five stages of Tuckman's model of group development,

4. explain the premise behind Gersick's model of group development, and

5. identify and explain the three tracks of Poole's model of group development.

Case Study

At the beginning of the spring semester, roommates Chad, Mark, and Kevin sit in their living room, playing a game on the PlayStation 2 and discussing their spring break plans. A fourth roommate, Dan, is in his bedroom e-mailing his girlfriend, Tawny. Chad, Mark, Kevin, and Dan

Photo 5.1   Playing video games is one way group members move through the developmental process of relationship building.

Source: Wang Leng/Asia Images/Jupiterimages.

live together while enrolled at the business school obtaining their master's degrees in business administration.

Chad: Spring break is only two months away. We need to figure out where we're going so we can make some reservations. Any ideas, guys?

Mark: We could go back to Cancun. We had a good time there last year. Remember what happened to Dan?

Kevin: Yeah, that was funny. Too bad Dan can't go with us this year, but that's what happens when you get engaged. All of the fun ends.

Chad: That's not true. I'm engaged, and I still have fun. Dan's problem is that Tawny doesn't trust him. And after what happened last year, who can blame her?

Mark: Let's focus on our spring break plans and not those two. They cause enough problems around here. This is why I don't have a girlfriend. I want to go to Cancun and get crazy with a lot of women!

Kevin: You don't have as much fun as you used to. You don't even act the same anymore. Ever since you met Nancy this past summer, you seem to have become this whole other person. You pretend like you don't have a past and that you've never done anything "bad."

Chad: Hey, man, priorities change as you grow older.

Kevin: Older? You're 27.

Mark: How about if I go to Cancun by myself and let you two girls stay home and watch *Oprah?* Let's get back to talking about spring break and women!

Chad: If we're not going to Cancun, what about Acapulco?

Kevin: Hey, spring break isn't for two months. Why do we have to decide today where we're going?

Chad: We don't, but because last year we waited until the middle of the semester to make our reservations, I thought we should jump on it sooner. And since you're the one who is always complaining that you don't have any money, it's cheaper if we book now.

Kevin: Watch it, buddy. I don't have any money because I'm paying for school myself. Not all of us have rich parents who throw money our way whenever we want it.

Mark: Give it a rest. You two argue over the same things all the time. After living together for two years, you'd think you would be able to talk about something else. Focus on where we're going. And since Dan won't be coming with us, maybe we should see if Sam wants to come. We'll need four to get the best room rate.

Chad: I don't know about him.

Kevin: Why not? You lived with the kid your sophomore year, and he's always stopping by here.

Chad: He's always checking me out.

Kevin: (laughs) He is not. We've already discussed this, remember? You're not his type. (laughs again)

Chad: And you are?

Kevin: You just don't like it that he thinks you've become an idiot since you met Nancy. Besides, you were friends with him before he came out, so let it go.

Mark: Like I said before, let's talk about spring break, women, and Cancun!

A s this case study demonstrates, one aspect of group work centers on how well members work together to meet the goals of completing the task and maintaining relationships. Some scholars view the process of how groups develop through the lens of a **life span approach**, which means groups have a beginning, a growing stage, and an ending (Socha, 1997). Using this approach, we can investigate communication in small groups as members proceed through phases that lead to group output. Other scholars view the process of how groups develop through the exploration of events that result in a shift in group focus, which means groups experience multiple events (some of which happen simultaneously) that impact their developmental process (Chidambaram & Bostrom, 1996). Using this approach, we can investigate communication in small groups as members confront and deal with issues as they arise.

This chapter endeavors to highlight important concepts researchers have found appropriate when analyzing communication and group development. We will discuss how a group's history and maturity factor into thinking about how prior group experiences and specific task situations influence how members work together. Next, we will examine three models of group development that illustrate various approaches to thinking about the issues and tensions small groups encounter as they move through the developmental process of task work and the building of relationships from group formation to goal completion. Finally, we will identify five characteristics of a developed group.

Group Development

Two factors influence group development: group history and group maturity.

History

Group members build a history of working together, as well as the methods and motivation behind their move through group development. Communication scholar Thomas Socha (1997) suggested when we think about communication and group development, we should consider that communication changes not only across the life span of a specific group but also across the life span of each group to which we belong. As members of multiple groups throughout our lives, we bring ever-changing levels of expertise, cognitive abilities, and social skills to each group experience. Furthermore, even if we participate in groups facing different tasks or activities with people we know or have worked with before, the members still must redefine themselves as part of a new group with its own unique developmental process. Just as no two groups comprise the same mix of individuals or strive for the same task or goal, no two groups develop and move through the process of group work the same way. Lee Gardenswartz and Anita Rowe (1994) claimed the challenges of group work include the understanding that "disparate people can come together to achieve work-related goals of varying complexity, importance, and impact" (p. 145). Successful groups just don't happen; instead they comprise the proper blend of human dynamics, abilities, and skills to confront and complete the task.

Maturity

Not only do groups develop a history; they also mature as they move toward goal achievement. Maturity, marked by the fact that all group members are task oriented and work cooperatively toward furthering the group goal (Bonney, 1974), refers to the ability and willingness a group possesses as it moves through the developmental process (Hersey, Blanchard, & Johnson, 2000). Ability describes a group's collective knowledge, skills, and experience whereas willingness refers to a group's collective motivation and confidence. When groups are mature (i.e., both able and willing), they are more active and more organized and do not need extensive encouragement to work on a task (Krayer & Fiechtner, 1984). In college classrooms, mature groups meet more often, express more satisfaction with the group experience, and perform better than immature groups (Krayer, 1988).

> **?** Refer to your work group. How has your group's history influenced group development? How has your group's maturity influenced group development?

Developmental Models

Although several models of group development exist (Bales & Strodtbeck, 1951; Caple, 1978; Fisher, 1970; Near, 1978; Wheelan & Hochberger, 1996; Worchel,

1994), in this section we will examine three unique models of group development: Bruce Tuckman's five-phase model of group development, Connie Gersick's model of punctuated equilibrium, and Marshall Scott Poole's multiple-sequence model.

Tuckman's Five-Phase Model

Bruce Tuckman (1965) introduced a four-phase linear model of group development and then later added another phase (Tuckman & Jensen, 1977). **Tuckman's five-phase model** provides a popular contribution to understanding group development and the discussion process. The five phases, referred to as the forming, storming, norming, performing, and adjourning stages, cover group structure (i.e., relationship patterns) and task behavior (i.e., what the group is working on).

Forming. In the forming phase, group members meet the group process with their own reasons for joining the group. According to Joann Keyton (1999), individuals face such issues as inclusion and dependency (e.g., "What ideas will the members like?" and "What will I be asked to do?"). During this phase, no reason yet advises group members to completely trust each other. Group discussion takes on an exploratory nature as members try to find their place, confirm their perceptions about other members, and decide what they will agree to do. The discussion in this phase more than likely is superficial.

Social politeness theory suggests when individuals join groups they operate under a norm of being polite to others. Remember, the members think not yet in terms of "we"; rather, they think in terms of "I." In this phase, members exhibit

Table 5.1   Tuckman's Five-Phase Model

Phase	Description
Forming	Members come to the group concerned about individual goals.
Storming	Members develop relationships and the group process begins.
Norming	Members work together on the task and attempt to get along.
Performing	Members ready task for output and evaluation by an external audience.
Adjourning	Members reach the end of their involvement together and/or have finished their task.

Source: Based on Tuckman, B. W., & Jensen, M. A. C. (1977). Stages of small-group development revisited. *Group & Organization Studies, 2,* 419–427.

(not too strong, pushy, or abrasive) verbal and nonverbal behaviors. Because members are not committed to each other, they draw upon prior group experiences to determine if they will meet their expectations in the group.

Storming. In the storming phase, group members begin to actively participate by sharing ideas and talents. Group scholar Ernest Bormann (1989) labeled group discussion and members' behaviors during this phase as primary tensions and secondary tensions. Primary tensions reflect the anxiety members feel about being in the group and the uncertainty surrounding the roles they will play. Additionally, the group has not yet established norms, and members may worry status differences exist that will result in conflicts. To reduce primary tension, group members may work actively toward learning more about each other. When members share information about themselves, they feel more comfortable and thus engage in more laughter and less silence, disagreement, and interruptions (Booth-Butterfield, Booth-Butterfield, & Koester, 1988).

After working through the primary tensions, secondary tensions emerge as members seek to influence others, develop norms and roles, and explore the issues surrounding the task. Bormann (1989) stated these tensions result from differences of opinion, disagreements about how to approach the task, power struggles, and/or personality differences. Small amounts of conflict may occur in this phase and usually center on procedural matters as members disagree on ways to approach the task. Group scholars Steven Beebe and John Masterson (2003) suggested even the most cohesive groups engage in some form of conflict.

Norming. In the norming phase, the group and its members work together on the task and attempt to get along. In this phase, trust begins to develop, and acceptance starts to emerge (Keyton, 1999). Tuckman believed this phase reflects group cohesiveness. Cohesive groups commit to working on the goal and task as a collective unit—a commitment sometimes referred to as the "glue" that holds the group together. Cohesiveness increases with group discussion that facilitates role taking and norm stabilizing. The degree of cohesiveness continues to build as the productivity of the group increases and the group achieves consensus on decisions it needs to make (Beebe & Masterson, 2003). At the same time, group members' trust, commitment to the group, and willingness to cooperate increases in this phase (Wheelan, Davidson, & Tilin, 2003).

Conformity and deviance can affect the development of cohesion (Pavitt & Curtis, 1994). Conformity occurs when a group member agrees with the group's decision because the majority of the group members agrees. Conformity succeeds when a group member "conforms in beliefs as well as in behaviors" (Pavitt & Curtis, 1994, p. 179)—that is, the member supports the group decision, even though she might have chosen a different option. If the member cannot live with the decision but goes along with it anyway, conformity still occurs, but it then is considered unsuccessful.

Photo 5.2   In the performing phase, a group often is evaluated by an external audience.

Source: Getty Images/Taxi/Getty Images.

Deviance occurs when a group member disagrees with the group's decision, even though the majority of the group members, who may view this member as rebelling against the group's norms (Scheerhorn & Geist, 1997), agrees. Deviance proves positive when a member forces the group to rethink its discussion procedures, such as when a member plays the devil's advocate role. The movie *12 Angry Men* provides a classic example of getting members to change their minds. A single juror refused to go along with the "guilty" plea the majority wanted, and one by one, the lone juror convinced the other jurors to change their minds. On the other hand, deviance proves negative when a member refuses to listen to valid arguments or reason and holds on to his position. This stance creates a barrier to movement through the norming phase.

A note of caution: Groups would be wise not to fall into the trap of thinking that because they are cohesive, they do not have to follow the steps to making good decisions based on rational thinking. They still must follow the principles surrounding sound decision making and problem solving, as discussed in Chapter 7.

Performing. In the performing phase, the task is readied for output and evaluation by an external audience. Considered the stage at which members produce the most work (Chidambaram & Bostrom, 1996), members focus their energy on task accomplishment and goal achievement (Wheelan et al., 2003). At this point, trust should be established so the group will succeed in goal achievement to the best of members' abilities. Joann Keyton (1999) suggested during the performing phase, "group members are so tightly integrated with the team they find it diffi-cult to distinguish themselves from the group" (p. 362). The established relation-ship structure of the group allows for solving of interpersonal conflicts, and constructive attempts are made to complete the task (Pavitt & Curtis, 1994). Lee Gardenswartz and Anita Rowe (1994) described the performing phase in group life as growth from infancy (i.e., forming phase) to maturity (i.e., performing phase), manifested by group pride in accomplishments and a "willingness to do what it takes to keep doing the job" (p. 196).

Adjourning. In the adjourning phase, the group reaches the end of its involvement. Sometimes the adjourning phase depends on the time frame given to the group; at other times, the adjourning phase simply occurs when the group finishes its task. Regardless of how the group arrives at this phase, group members may express mixed feelings. Some group members may feel happy the group has ended, some may mourn the loss of being involved in an interesting task and forming interpersonal relationships, and some may attempt to keep the group intact (Lewis, 1978; Rose, 1989). Lucinda Sinclair-James and Cynthia Stohl (1997) stated cohesive group endings are less traumatic for members if they expect to see each other or work together again. Members who like each other will stay in touch through e-mail, tele-phone, or other forms of communica-tion. Thus, when the group adjourns, the socioemotional dimension changes, and the relationships among group members move to different levels of intimacy.

> **?** How does Tuckman's five-phase model apply to your work group?

Tuckman's five-phase model of group development appeals to many due to its easy-to-identify-with sequential nature. Because many college classroom groups progress through the five phases (Runkel, Lawrence, Oldfield, Rider, & Clark, 1971), you likely can identify how this model surfaced in your previous classroom group experiences.

Gersick's Punctuated Equilibrium Model

Not convinced that all groups develop in a sequential manner, Connie Gersick (1988) developed a model of group development to address this position. In Gersick's punctuated equilibrium model, she asserted that groups progress through a period of inertia punctuated by a period of concentrated change (Chidambaram & Bostrom, 1996). In her model, group development occurs around the defining characteristic of time. Unlike sequential models of group development, Gersick argued that groups follow temporal periods of development she labeled as phases.

According to Gersick (1988), group development starts with the first meeting of the group members. During this meeting, members set the precedent for how the group will approach task accomplishment. Group members' behaviors during this initial meeting implicitly guide the group's behavior for an indefinite amount of time, labeled phase one, during which little work is accomplished (Arrow, Poole, Henry, Wheelan, & Moreland, 2004). Rather, group members attempt to make sense of the task in light of their own experiences, viewpoints, and biases. They spend time attempting to diagnose the issue rather than trying to make a decision or solve a problem.

Phase one lasts until the group approaches the midpoint of its allotted time to complete the task (Gersick, 1989). This midpoint, which Gersick labeled as transition, occurs when the group members realize they have used (or wasted, depending on their point of view) half of their time and now must determine how to accomplish the task. The transition, considered the group's "wake-up call," results in a sudden burst of activity devoted to the task (Gersick, 1989). In the case study, for example, Chad references a transition when discussing how the room-mates planned their spring break trip the year before. At the transition point, members engage in a variety of behaviors: They drop old work patterns and habits, make an effort to start working more diligently, may or may not adopt new perspectives, and may or may not contact a stakeholder to determine whether they are proceeding in the right direction. (A stakeholder is a person external to the group who has a vested interest in the task.) Most importantly, they realize they need to seriously focus on completing the task, and this transition provides a basis for their work pattern in phase two (Gersick, 1988, 1989).

Once the group experiences its transition, its members enter phase two. Unlike in phase one, group members accomplish much more work in phase two (Arrow et al., 2004), although they lack the urgency to finish their task. Not until the final group meeting, or what Gersick (1989) labeled as completion, must the group absolutely finish the task. During this time, group members put the finishing touches on their task, hypothesize about how outsiders will view their task, and express their feelings about the task and each other (Gersick, 1988).

> **Ethically Speaking:** How acceptable is it for group members to work less diligently and wait for the midpoint transition to occur before mustering energy to finish the task? How do these types of behaviors affect productivity?

Although Gersick's model of punctuated equilibrium hasn't received as much attention from researchers as Tuckman's five-phase model of group development, Gersick's model, excitingly, explains why so many groups tend to wait until the last minute to finish a task. One important point to consider: Although Gersick's model seems to imply that group members avoid working on the task, this is not true. Rather, members work more diligently at the transition and completion points than they do during phases one and two.

Poole's Multiple-Sequence Model

Marshall Scott Poole (1981, 1983a, 1983b), a communication professor at the University of Illinois, developed another exciting model of group development, derived from the traditional phase model approach. Poole asserted groups do not always follow a rigid, phase-like approach when accomplishing a group task. Rather, he believed groups engage in three types of activity tracks that do not necessarily follow in a logical sequence. As described in Table 5.2, these three activity tracks include task process activities, relational activities, and topical focus.

According to Poole, in an ideal group experience, the group will move forward on all three tracks to successfully complete its goals. At any point, a group will alternate among the three activity tracks. Switching from one activity track to another, known as a breakpoint (Poole & Roth, 1989), helps the group develop consensus (Fisher & Stutman, 1987). Poole (1983b) identified three breakpoints a group may use: normal, delay, and disruption. A normal breakpoint occurs when a group shifts focus or examines another aspect of a task. This breakpoint does not disrupt or impede task accomplishment. A delay breakpoint occurs when a

Table 5.2   Poole's Multiple-Sequence Model

Activity Track	Description
Task process	Members analyze the task by using various decision-making and problem-solving procedures, engage in critical analysis of the positive and negative consequences of the alternative, or evaluate the implementation of a solution(s).
Relational	Members engage in behaviors that promote member relationships and might determine how to handle conflict.
Topical focus	Members concern themselves with the major issues or themes that emerge at any given point in the group's work that become agenda items.

Source: Based on Poole, M. S. (1983b). Decision development in small groups III: A multiple sequence model of group decision development. *Communication Monographs, 50,* 321–341.

group decides to reexamine a position or needs to repeat some part of a task—that is, when the group must adapt to a new contingency or focus strongly on comprehending the issue (Poole & Doelger, 1986). A **disruption breakpoint** occurs when conflict forces the group to stop working or failure forces the group to reevaluate its position. Whenever a breakpoint occurs, group members need to be flexible enough to address the breakpoint and then get back on track. In the case study, which breakpoint do the roommates use?

Poole believed in examining each track separately when conducting research or analyzing a specific group's development because the speed and rate of movement may differ from group to group. Ideally, group members' competent communicative behaviors enable groups to move along on each track in a timely and appropriate manner.

> **?** How does your work group use breakpoints? Do these breakpoints aid in developing consensus?

Characteristics of Group Development

Regardless of the developmental path a group takes, five characteristics, as detailed in question form below, reflect group development (Chidambaram & Bostrom, 1996):

1. *How cohesive is the group?* Cohesion experts Albert Carron and Lawrence Brawley (2000) proposed that in any group, members will develop task cohesion (needed for group performance) and social cohesion (needed for member relationships) but not at the same rate or with the same intensity. Cohesion also may develop as a result of pride in group membership (Street & Anthony, 1997). Carron and Brawley asserted as a group moves through any developmental process (i.e., stage, phase, track), the cohesiveness that accompanies the group's development must be appropriate given the stage, phase, or track at which the group is located or engaged.

2. *How does the group handle conflict?* In Chapter 11, you will learn more about conflict and how to handle conflict in a small group. One important consideration in handling conflict involves recognizing that conflict, inherent in any group's developmental process (Fisher, 1970), should not be taken personally. Group communication expert Roger Pace (1990) found that depersonalizing conflict is essential for effective group conflict management. **Depersonalizing conflict** occurs when group members recognize that conflict forms part of the small group

Photo 5.3 Group members should recognize that conflict is inherent in their group's developmental process.

Source: ©iStockphoto.com/Yuri_Arcurs.

process and thus do not attribute conflict to a specific group member. When group members depersonalize conflict, they report greater levels of cohesion and consensus (Pace, 1990).

3. *How does the group balance its task and socioemotional needs?* According to small group communication researcher Joann Keyton (1997), each time a group member communicates, he or she contributes to "the task or social reality of the group, not to both" (p. 240). This means a group must pay attention to how its members communicate so that their interaction includes both task-orientation and socioemotional orientation. In Chapter 8, we will discuss how members should engage in role flexibility. By being flexible in how you act and what you say, you can fulfill any role your group needs at any particular time.

> **?** How do the members of your work group balance its task and socioemotional needs? How difficult is it to meet both needs?

4. *How does the group communicate?* Susan Wheelan and her associates (2003) reported that, with every year of existence, group members engage in less

"pseudo-work" talk (i.e., comments or stories about topics not related to the group task) or disagreements about group procedures and goals. Moreover, they found the members of developed groups consider themselves more effective and productive in how they communicate about the task.

5. *How involved is the group with its task?* Group member involvement with any task is crucial. As groups begin to move through the developmental process, members make a decision about the group's ability to perform (Baker, 2001). This early decision about group performance affects not only how a group accomplishes a task but also whether group members believe they can accomplish a task. This belief in the group's ability—sometimes referred to as **group efficacy**—is important for members to possess. With group efficacy present, members work together more willingly as a group, report greater learning, and require less supervision to complete their tasks (Pescosolido, 2003).

So how do these five characteristics reflect group development? The answer is simple. Fully developed groups include members who are cohesive and able to depersonalize conflict, strike a balance between the group's task and socioemotional needs, engage in effective communication, and possess group efficacy. Yet, of the five characteristics, none is more important than the other. As you look ahead, consider how these five characteristics reflect the developmental process of the groups to which you currently belong.

A Final Note About Small Group Development

In this chapter, we presented three distinct models of group development. Communication researcher Kenneth Cissna (1984) commented that "every group is like all groups in some respects, like some—or perhaps even most—groups in some respects, and like no groups in other respects" (p. 25). Rather than focusing on which model of group development is the most superior, consider that each model explains, to some degree, the ways the groups to which you belong develop.

Conclusion

This chapter aimed to highlight important concepts researchers have found appropriate when analyzing communication and group development. We discussed how a group's history and maturity level factor into thinking about how prior group experiences and specific task situations influence how members work together. We also examined three models of group development and identified five characteristics of a developed group. As you read the next chapter, consider how a group accomplishes its tasks may depend on the stage, phase, or track at which the group is located within its developmental process.

Discussion Questions

1. Identify the advantages and disadvantages of studying group development from a life span approach.

2. For each phase of Tuckman's five-phase model (i.e., forming, storming, norming, performing, and adjourning), compile a list of the communication skills you believe are essential for group members to use.

3. Identify a group to which you previously belonged. At what point did adjourning occur? What was your emotional reaction to the adjournment? What behaviors did group members use in this stage?

4. Use Poole's three activity tracks to analyze the movie *The Breakfast Club*. How did this small group follow each track? Which track did this group follow the most? How might other types of groups differ in their activity patterns?

5. Choose a group to which you previously belonged. Of the three models of development, which model best explains the group's development? Why?

References

Arrow, H., Poole, M. S., Henry, K. B., Wheelan, S., & Moreland, R. (2004). Time, change, and development: The temporal perspective on groups. *Small Group Research, 35,* 73–105.

Baker, D. F. (2001). The development of collective efficacy in small task groups. *Small Group Research, 32,* 451–474.

Bales, R. F., & Strodtbeck, F. L. (1951). Phases in group problem-solving. *Journal of Abnormal and Social Psychology, 46,* 485–495.

Beebe, S. A., & Masterson, J. T. (2003). *Communicating in small groups: Principles and practices* (7th ed.). Boston: Allyn & Bacon.

Bonney, W. C. (1974). The maturation of groups. *Small Group Behavior, 5,* 445–461.

Booth-Butterfield, M., Booth-Butterfield, S., & Koester, J. (1988). The function of uncertainty reduction in alleviating primary tension in small groups. *Communication Research Reports, 5,* 146–153.

Bormann, E. G. (1989). *Discussion and group methods: Theory and practice* (3rd ed.). New York: Harper & Row.

Caple, R. B. (1978). The sequential stages of group development. *Small Group Behavior, 9,* 470–476.

Carron, A. V., & Brawley, L. B. (2000). Cohesion: Conceptual and measurement issues. *Small Group Research, 31,* 89–106.

Chidambaram, L., & Bostrom, R. P. (1996). Group development (I): A review and synthesis of development models. *Group Decision and Negotiation, 6,* 159–187.

Cissna, K. N. (1984). Phases in group development: The negative evidence. *Small Group Behavior, 15,* 3–32.

Fisher, B. A. (1970). Decision emergence: Phases in group decision-making. *Speech Monographs, 37,* 53–66.

Fisher, B. A., & Stutman, R. K. (1987). An assessment of group trajectories: Analyzing developmental breakpoints. *Communication Quarterly, 35,* 105–124.

Gardenswartz, L., & Rowe, A. (1994). *Diverse teams at work: Capitalizing on the power of diversity.* Chicago: Irwin Press.

Gersick, C. J. G. (1988). Time and transition in work teams: Toward a new model of group development. *Academy of Management Journal, 31,* 9–41.

Gersick, C. J. G. (1989). Marking time: Predictable transitions in task groups. *Academy of Management Journal, 32,* 274–309.

Hersey, P., Blanchard, K. H., & Johnson, D. E. (2000). *Management of organizational behavior: Leading human resources* (8th ed.). Englewood Cliffs, NJ: Prentice Hall.

Keyton, J. (1997). Coding communication in decision-making groups. In L. R. Frey & J. K. Barge (Eds.), *Managing group life: Communicating in decision-making groups* (pp. 234–269). Boston: Houghton Mifflin.

Keyton, J. (1999). *Group communication: Process and analysis.* Mountain View, CA: Mayfield.

Krayer, K. J. (1988). Exploring group maturity in the classroom: Differences in behavioral, affective, and performance outcomes between mature and immature groups. *Small Group Behavior, 19,* 259–272.

Krayer, K. J., & Fiechtner, S. B. (1984). Measuring group maturity: The development of a process-oriented variable for small group communication research. *Southern Speech Communication Journal, 50,* 78–92.

Lewis, B. F. (1978). An examination of the final phase of a group development theory. *Small Group Behavior, 9,* 507–517.

Near, J. P. (1978). Comparison of developmental patterns in groups. *Small Group Behavior, 9,* 493–506.

Pace, R. C. (1990). Personalized and depersonalized conflict in small group discussions: An examination of differentiation. *Small Group Research, 21,* 79–96.

Pavitt, C., & Curtis, E. (1994). *Small group discussion: A theoretical approach* (2nd ed). Scottsdale, AZ: Gorsuch Scarisbrick.

Pescosolido, A. T. (2003). Group efficacy and group effectiveness: The effects of group efficacy over time on group performance and development. *Small Group Research, 34,* 20–42.

Poole, M. S. (1981). Decision development in small groups I: A comparison of two models. *Communication Monographs, 48,* 1–24.

Poole, M. S. (1983a). Decision development in small groups II: A study of multiple sequences in decision making. *Communication Monographs, 50,* 206–232.

Poole, M. S. (1983b). Decision development in small groups III: A multiple sequence model of group decision development. *Communication Monographs, 50,* 321–341.

Poole, M. S., & Doelger, J. A. (1986). Developmental processes in group decision-making. In R. Y. Hirokawa & M. S. Poole (Eds.), *Communication and group decision-making* (pp. 35–61). Beverly Hills, CA: Sage.

Poole, M. S., & Roth, J. (1989). Decision development in small groups IV: A typology of group decision paths. *Human Communication Research, 15,* 323–356.

Rose, S. R. (1989). Members leaving groups: Theoretical and practical considerations. *Small Group Behavior, 20,* 524–535.

Runkel, P. J., Lawrence, M., Oldfield, S., Rider, M., & Clark, C. (1971). Stages of group development: An empirical test of Tuckman's hypothesis. *Journal of Applied Behavioral Science, 7,* 180–193.

Scheerhorn, D., & Geist, P. (1997). Social dynamics in groups. In L. R. Frey & J. K. Barge (Eds.), *Managing group life: Communicating in decision-making groups* (pp. 81–103). Boston: Houghton Mifflin.

Sinclair-James, L., & Stohl, C. (1997). Group endings and new beginnings. In L. R. Frey & J. K. Barge (Eds.), *Managing group life: Communicating in decision-making groups* (pp. 308–334). Boston: Houghton Mifflin.

Socha, T. J. (1997). Group communication across the life span. In L. R. Frey & J. K. Barge (Eds.), *Managing group life: Communicating in decision-making groups* (pp. 3–28). Boston: Houghton Mifflin.

Street, M. D., & Anthony, W. P. (1997). A conceptual framework establishing the relationship between groupthink and escalating commitment behavior. *Small Group Research, 28,* 267–293.

Tuckman, B. W. (1965). Developmental sequence in small groups. *Psychological Bulletin, 63,* 384–399.

Tuckman, B. W., & Jensen, M. A. C. (1977). Stages of small-group development revisited. *Group & Organization Studies, 2,* 419–427.

Wheelan, S., Davidson, B., & Tilin, F. (2003). Group development across time: Reality or illusion? *Small Group Research, 34,* 223–245.

Wheelan, S. A., & Hochberger, J. M. (1996). Validation studies of the group development question-naire. *Small Group Research, 27,* 143–170.

Worchel, S. (1994). You can go home again: Returning group research to the group context with an eye on developmental issues. *Small Group Research, 25,* 205–223.

Characteristics of Small Group Tasks | 6

After reading this chapter, you should be able to:

1. identify and define the seven characteristics of a task,

2. distinguish between a decision-making and a problem-solving task,

3. identify and explain the five steps of the functional perspective of small group communication,

4. list the obstacles associated with task accomplishment, and

5. define groupthink and explain how to prevent it.

Case Study
Every Sunday, the Talagaviloni family gets together for dinner. The family comprises Stella; her adult children Stefano, Michaela, and Suzanna; Michaela's husband Ricardo; Michaela and Ricardo's daughters Maria and Nicolla; and Suzanna's friend Louisa. The family has just sat down to eat when Michaela mentions the idea of a family vacation.

Photo 6.1   Coordinating a family dinner is a common primary group task.

Source: ©iStockphoto.com/sjlocke.

Michaela:	Ricardo and I were thinking about taking the girls to Disney World for a weeklong vacation. What do you think about that idea, Ma?
Stella:	I think it's a wonderful idea. I remember when your father—may he and your brother Marco rest in peace—and I took the four of you to Disney World when you were little. Oh, the fun we had!
Stefano:	Oh yeah, a lot of fun. Michaela threw up all over me on the teacup ride, and Suzanna cried the entire time because she was afraid of Mickey Mouse. Oh yeah, a lot of fun.
Maria:	Why did Mommy throw up?
Stefano:	Because your Mommy is "delicate."
Michaela:	At least I didn't complain the whole time, Stefano. "It's hot." "My feet hurt." "I want to go home."
Stella:	Oh kids, knock it off. It wasn't that bad. Michaela, when are you going on this trip?
Michaela:	We were thinking October. Ricardo and I are taking a week off from work and making it a real vacation.

Suzanna:	If you're going in October, maybe I could go too. I have some vacation time I need to take before I lose it. Ma, what about you?
Stella:	Oh, I don't know. I really need to work. Besides, this is Michaela and Ricardo's vacation, not ours. And who would take care of the dogs? I can't leave Sage, Basil, and Paprika by themselves.
Suzanna:	Stefano could watch the dogs. This way he'll have something to do on Saturday night, right, Stefano? (laughs)
Stefano:	(glares) That's exactly what I was hoping to do on a Saturday night.
Michaela:	Think about it, Ma! This could be fun! We could rent a van, drive together, and stay at a nice hotel. We haven't done anything as a family in a long time. Plus, you could use a vacation. You haven't been anywhere in years.
Ricardo:	A family vacation could be fun. But if we're all going to go, maybe we should fly. I have a friend who works at a travel agency who could get us a good deal.
Suzanna:	But flying is so expensive. I would rather drive to keep costs low. I don't have a whole lot of money to spend on a vacation.
Stefano:	Then I guess you'll be the one who's watching the dogs on Saturday night.
Suzanna:	What about if we went in June? I bet travel is cheaper in the summer.
Stefano:	It doesn't matter when we go. Disney World is expensive, especially if you're there for a week. My neighbor went last year and said a 4-day pass to the parks cost $200 a person!
Suzanna:	What if we looked on the Internet for some discounts? I think my credit union has some way to purchase cheaper tickets.
Stefano:	What about the hotel? You think the hotels at Disney World are cheap?
Suzanna:	We could stay at a hotel on the edge of Orlando.
Louisa:	What about staying at a youth hostel or even the YMCA? I hear those places are really cheap.
Ricardo:	Hold on, ladies. If we're going to do this, we're going to do it right—meaning we'll fly and stay at a hotel close to the parks. I don't want to spend my vacation driving across the country only to have to spend more time driving around Orlando and then driving all the way back home.

Michaela:	And I'm not staying at a youth hostel. Sorry, Louisa, but I want to stay at a nice hotel with a pool and a fitness center. If we start looking now, I'm sure we can find someplace we all can afford.
Maria:	I want to stay somewhere with a pool.
Nicolla:	Me, too.
Stella:	We will, girls. I'll ask around at work about where to stay. Several of the girls in my department have been to Disney World the last few years, and I know they don't have a lot of money.
Michaela:	Just remember, Ma, check on hotels as close as possible to the park. No youth hostels, no YMCAs. And it has to have a pool.
Ricardo:	I'll call my friend at the travel agency and check on some cheap flights.
Suzanna:	This sounds like fun. I love planning a trip. Ricardo, I'll check the Internet also for plane fares, and I'll check with my credit union tomorrow about buying tickets for Disney World.
Michaela:	This sounds like a plan. If we all pitch in, this could be a lot of fun!
Stefano:	Oh yeah, a lot of fun. Just don't sit next to me when we ride the teacups.

U p to this point, we have focused on the components that comprise the small group communication process. Woven across these components is the reason small groups exist: a task. But as the preceding case study demonstrates, accomplishing the group task can be time-consuming, challenging, and intimidating.

This chapter purports to provide you with information about the group task. To do so, we first will identify and define the seven characteristics of a task and distinguish between a decision-making and a problem-solving task. We then will examine the functional perspective of small group communication, with a specific focus on the assumptions, steps, contexts, and obstacles associated with the perspective. Finally, we will explore groupthink and its implications for task accomplishment.

Characteristics of a Task

If you recall from Chapter 1, a task describes an activity in which no externally correct decision exists and whose completion depends on member acceptance (Fisher, 1971). To most efficiently assess a task, a group should consider the seven characteristics of a task as detailed below (Keyton, 1999; Shaw, 1981). Whether a group considers these characteristics affects not only how the group accomplishes its task but also whether the group decides to complete its task in an additive or a conjunctive manner. Truthfully addressing each characteristic allows a group not only to alleviate any obstacles that might arise but also to maximize its effectiveness when working toward task accomplishment.

The first characteristic, task difficulty, refers to the ease of task accomplishment. Although a task does not have to be overly difficult or extremely complex, an easy-to-accomplish task may not require full member participation or interest. In addition, the skills, abilities, and knowledge base of group members can enhance or alleviate task difficulty.

The second characteristic, solution multiplicity, refers to the number of alternatives that exist for accomplishing the task. The case study addresses solution multiplicity when the Talagaviloni family discusses its best option for lodging. The more alternatives a group identifies, the greater the effectiveness of the group's decision. Additionally, group members should strive to identify both positive and negative consequences of each alternative (Hirokawa, 1985). Doing so allows a group to consider more thoroughly the ways to complete a task.

The third characteristic, intrinsic interest, centers on what each group member finds interesting or fascinating about the task. For instance, in the case study, Suzanna finds the task of researching the trip costs appealing, in part because of her limited funds for the trip. Although group members' level of interest or fascination with a task should not affect the quality of the task, it stands to reason that when a group task genuinely interests or fascinates group members, they will be more involved in the task. When group members view a task as unimportant, meaningless, or boring, they will participate less in the group process (Latham, 1987). As such, it is no surprise that Stefano, uninterested in a trip to Disney World, does not offer to help the family.

The fourth characteristic, population familiarity, refers to the degree of group members' familiarity with the task. Being unfamiliar with a task can affect how quickly a group completes it, as can being overly familiar with a task. When a group knows a task too well, it may overlook some aspects of the task or not pay as much attention to the task as they probably should.

The fifth characteristic, acceptance level, describes the degree to which group members find the task outcome acceptable. In the case study, Michaela demonstrates acceptance level when she reminds her mother to find a hotel close to the park. Even if the outcome of a group's decision-making or problem-solving process does not directly impact each group member, group members, considered somewhat responsible for the outcome, still should consider whether the outcome is acceptable.

The sixth characteristic, **area of freedom**, centers on the amount of authority or responsibility the group possesses when it comes to implementing the task. Group members should consider that not all groups will have the authority to implement the task.

The seventh characteristic, **social complexity**, refers to the degree of ego involvement present among group members in accomplishing the task. As a rule of thumb, avoid ego involvement. Although group members should exhibit an interest in the task, they never should let their personal interest in the task (or the outcome) override their ability to objectively complete it.

Now that we have identified and defined the seven characteristics of tasks, we need to distinguish between a decision-making and a problem-solving task.

Engaging in Decision-Making and Problem-Solving Tasks

Decision making and problem solving present two approaches a group can take when faced with a task. When a group engages in **decision making**, it chooses one option from a set of already selected options in which no externally correct option exists (Frey, 1997). In this sense, view decision making as a judgment (Engleberg & Wynn, 2003). When a group engages in **problem solving**, it defines the problem, identifies the solutions, and chooses one solution from the set of identified solutions (Adams & Galanes, 2006). In this sense, view problem solving as a process (Engleberg & Wynn, 2003).

A group makes a decision in one of four ways: consensus, compromise, majority rule, and authority rule. In a group that makes a decision by **consensus,** all group members agree with and commit to the decision (DeStephen & Hirokawa, 1988). In a group that makes a decision by **compromise**, some group members may not agree with the decision (e.g., "I don't like arguing, so I'll give in"), but the group as a whole stands by the decision. Compromise presents one problem, however; some group members may feel their input is either ignored or not welcome. Over time, this can create resentment within the group if it consistently ignores a particular member's input. In a group that makes a decision by **majority rule**, the majority of the group members support the decision (e.g., "Three members win against two members").

To arrive at the decision, the group members usually take a vote, and the alternative that receives the majority of the votes becomes the group's decision. In a group that makes a decision by **authority rule**, someone in a position of power makes a decision on behalf of the group. In some cases, a group—unable for whatever reason to make a decision—may select an outside expert to make the decision (Rothwell, 2004).

> **?** Of these four decision-making techniques, which technique does your work group use most frequently? Why? How could you use the other three techniques in its place?

Ideally, a group will make a decision through consensus, or an open discussion that involves all group members and requires a commitment to behaving cooperatively (Renz, 2006). By engaging in consensus, member involvement is high, members feel satisfied with the group's decision, and members consider the decision-making process fair (Keyton, 1999; Sager & Gastil, 2006). To use consensus effectively, consult the tips listed in Table 6.1 (Gero, 1985; Hare, 1980). Making a decision by consensus can prove difficult, however, because (a) some group members may agree with the decision at the time it was made but change their mind later, and (b) this process is fairly time and skill intensive (Renz, 2006; Sager & Gastil, 2006).

For another way to work toward consensus, follow the functional perspective of small group communication (Gouran & Hirokawa, 1986). Use this perspective in addition to enhance the problem-solving abilities of any group.

Table 6.1 Tips on Using Consensus

1. Establish a climate that promotes cooperation.
2. Behave in a friendly yet sincere manner.
3. Own your viewpoint.
4. Approach the discussion in a logical manner.
5. Encourage all group members to own their viewpoints.
6. Encourage all group members to present their viewpoints.
7. Respond to each group member's viewpoint.
8. Avoid engaging in criticism or verbal aggressiveness.
9. Do not change your mind only to avoid conflict or disagreement.

Sources: Based on Gero, A. (1985). Conflict avoidance in consensual decision processes. *Small Group Behavior, 16,* 487–499, and Hare, A. P. (1980). Consensus versus majority: A laboratory experiment. *Small Group Behavior, 11,* 131–143.

Functional Perspective of Small Group Communication

The functional perspective of small group communication initially was conceptualized by Dennis Gouran and Randy Hirokawa (1983), professors of communication studies at Pennsylvania State University and the University of Hawaii, respectively. The **functional perspective of small group communication**, also known as functional theory, states that a group's performance directly relates to the communicative functions performed by a group (Hirokawa & Salazar, 1997). These functions emerge in the form of a five-step process in which group members should engage (Gouran & Hirokawa, 1996; Hirokawa, 1983b). Completing all five steps (i.e., satisfying all five functions) allows a group to arrive at a high-quality decision (Hirokawa, 1985).

To thoroughly understand the functional perspective, you must know the assumptions of the perspective, the five steps of the perspective, the two contexts that influence the perspective, and the obstacles associated with the perspective.

Assumptions of the Functional Perspective

Dennis Gouran and his colleagues (1993) identified seven assumptions that underlie the functional perspective:

1. The members of the group are motivated to participate.

2. The choice to be made is nonobvious.

3. The collective resources of the group exceed the resources of the individual members.

4. The guidelines for task accomplishment are provided to the group.

5. The information needed to complete the task is available or can be obtained easily.

6. The members possess the cognitive skills and abilities needed to complete the task successfully.

7. Communication is instrumental. (p. 579)

Note that not meeting these assumptions will lower the quality of the group's decision or solution (Gouran & Hirokawa, 2003).

Five Steps of the Functional Perspective

Central to the functional perspective is the notion that group members influence the quality of a group's decision through communication (Poole & Baldwin, 1996). By engaging in communication, group members can distribute and pool informational resources, identify and remedy errors in individual judgment, provide an opportunity for intragroup persuasion, and steer members away from poor alternatives (Gouran et al., 1993).

To fully understand this perspective, one must examine the five steps (see Table 6.2). The first step, developing a correct understanding of the issue (i.e., the decision to be made, the problem to be solved), includes the nature of the issue, the extent and seriousness of the issue, and/or the cause(s) behind the issue (Hirokawa, 1985). Many groups find this step difficult because they simply do not know enough about the issue, they do not possess the skills necessary to conduct research, or information about the issue is limited or unavailable. At other times, groups may feel unsure about the usefulness or importance of information they've gathered, which can impact the quality of their decision detrimentally (Mayer, Sonoda, & Gudykunst, 1997). To make a high-quality decision, the group must overcome any shortcomings it faces when gathering information to develop a correct understanding of the issue, which likely will enhance group performance (Hirokawa & Rost, 1992).

A group can enhance its understanding of the issue by determining the **charge**, or the direction given to the group about how to proceed with the task. Is the group charged with determining the facts about an issue? Is the group charged with identifying whether a plan has merit? Is the group charged with developing

Table 6.2   Five Steps of the Functional Perspective

---

1. Develop a correct understanding of the issue (i.e., the decision to be made, the problem to be solved).

2. Determine the minimal characteristics required of the alternative needed to resolve the issue.

3. Identify a relevant and realistic set of alternatives.

4. Examine the alternatives (step 3) in relation to the minimal characteristics of the alternative established in the second step (step 2).

5. Select the best alternative in light of the previous four steps.

Source: Based on Gouran, D. S., & Hirokawa, R. Y. (1996). Functional theory and communication in decision-making and problem-solving groups: An expanded view. In R. Y. Hirokawa & M. S. Poole (Eds.), *Communication and group decision making* (2nd ed., pp. 55–80). Thousand Oaks, CA: Sage.

Photo 6.2   Developing a correct understanding of an issue is the first step a group should take when making a decision or solving a problem.

Source: ©iStockphoto.com/Yuri_Arcurs.

a plan of action? A **question of fact** addresses whether something holds true. A **question of value** addresses whether something is viewed favorably or unfavorably (Infante, 1988). A **question of conjecture** addresses the possibility of whether something might occur (Gouran, 1997). A **question of policy** addresses whether a plan of action should be adopted.

In the case study, the members of the Talagaviloni family use each of these four questions as they discuss taking a family vacation. Suzanna and Stefano raise a question of fact when they discuss whether they can afford a trip to Disney World given their financial status. Michaela, Suzanna, and Louisa raise a question of value when they debate the merits of each lodging option based on their own needs and interests. Suzanna raises a question of conjecture when she asks whether the trip would be more financially feasible sometime earlier than October. The Talagaviloni family raises a question of policy when members discuss whether they should take a family vacation.

The second step involves determining the minimal characteristics required of the alternative needed to resolve the issue. Rather than jumping ahead to decide on an alternative, a group that makes a high-quality decision first identifies the minimal characteristics required of the alternative. Oftentimes, in their quest to make a decision or solve a problem, groups either progress through this stage too quickly or ignore this stage altogether. In fact, research shows that effective groups are more likely to establish evaluation criteria (i.e., identify the qualities a "good" decision or solution would possess) than less effective groups (Graham, Papa, & McPherson, 1997). Identifying the minimal characteristics helps a group focus on the alternative and determine whether the alternative ultimately presents a viable option.

The third step requires group members to identify an appropriate, adequate, and unambiguous (Gouran et al., 1993)—not to mention relevant and realistic— set of alternatives. Although no determined number of alternatives exists, the group should identify as many as possible (Hirokawa, 1983b). This enables a group to consider all feasible alternatives, of which one will emerge as the most feasible.

The fourth step involves examining the alternatives (step 3) in relation to the minimal characteristics of the alternative established in the second step. When a group carefully and thoroughly examines each alternative to determine whether it meets the criteria for a "good" decision, the group increases its chance of detecting any flaws or problems with the alternative (Hirokawa & Pace, 1983). Additionally, groups should examine both the positive and the negative consequences associated with each alternative (Graham et al., 1997; Hirokawa, 1985). Doing so makes it possible to determine which choice offers the most-desirable consequences and which choice offers the least-desirable consequences.

The fifth step is to select the best alternative in light of the previous four steps. Ideally, this alternative will allow group members to readily make a decision or easily solve a problem.

One note of caution: After reading the description of these five steps, it may appear that to make a high-quality decision, groups should follow the five steps in order. Surprisingly, this is not the case. Researchers have found that as long as a group goes through each step at some point (i.e., fulfills each function) in the decision-making or problem-solving process, the order of the steps emerges less important than the fact that the group

 Ethically Speaking: When faced with a task—particularly a task whose outcome affects people other than the group members—how essential is it for a group to complete the five steps of the functional perspective of small group communication? How acceptable (or unacceptable) is it for a group to ignore one (or more) of the five steps, knowing that the functional perspective works best when a group moves through all five steps?

has gone through each step (Hirokawa, 1983a, 1988). Fluctuating back and forth among the five steps creates a spiral effect, which reflects the fluid nature of group discussion (Scheidel & Crowell, 1964).

Additionally, not all five steps are equally important for every task. Small group communication researchers John Cragan and David Wright (1993) reported that the functions may depend on the task in that one step may pertain to a particular task more than the other four steps. In a meta-analysis of research published on groups that used the five steps, scholars Marc Orlitzky and Randy Hirokawa (2001) defined the top three steps with regard to importance: group members' assessment of the negative consequences of an alternative (step four), problem analysis (step one), and establishing the minimal characteristics required of the alternative (step two).

Contexts

In addition to these five steps, communication researchers Cynthia Stohl and Michael Holmes (1993) recommended groups consider the historical context and the institutional context in which they make a decision or solve a problem. By doing so, group members may grasp better the parameters surrounding their task. The **historical context** refers to the group's history of working together and whether the group qualifies as a zero history group. This context considers how the group has worked together in the past, how well the group is working together currently, and whether the group will have to work together in the future. The **institutional context** refers to the group's position within a larger group membership. For example, any classroom group you belong to this semester complements the many learning groups you will belong to during your college career.

Now that you understand the five steps of the functional perspective, as well as the historical and institutional contexts surrounding the group task, let's turn our attention to the obstacles that can impede decision making and problem solving.

Obstacles

Group members can encounter two sets of obstacles at any point in the decision-making or problem-solving process: task-related obstacles and relational obstacles (Gouran, 1997). **Task-related obstacles** refer specifically to the informational, analytical, and procedural problems that impede a group's ability to effectively accomplish its task. Informational problems include having too little or too much information, not having the proper information-gathering skills, and/or not having access to information. Analytical problems include being unable to interpret and evaluate the information at hand. This can range from lacking a fundamental understanding of reasoning skills to not being able to navigate the Internet and utilize search engines. Procedural problems center on a group's inability to establish and follow an agenda. An **agenda** comprises an outline of the specific objectives the group hopes to accomplish during a meeting. Although a group need not necessarily write a formal agenda each time it meets, it helps if a group has at least an idea of the specific objectives it hopes to accomplish at each meeting.

Relational obstacles refer specifically to the differences in attitudes, values, and goals that arise among members that impede a group's ability to effectively accomplish its task. An **attitude** reflects how favorable a person judges a person, a thing, or an event; a **value** reflects a belief or feeling about a person, a thing, or an event; and a **goal** reflects the end state of group activity (Gouran, 1997). Other obstacles include a member's communication and personality traits, such as verbal aggressiveness, Machiavellianism, and self-esteem (Frey, 1997; Keyton & Frey, 2002). If you refer back to the case study, obstacles associated with the Talagaviloni family include Stefano's lack of interest and use of sarcasm, Michaela's unwillingness to compromise on lodging, and Suzanna's preoccupation with the trip costs.

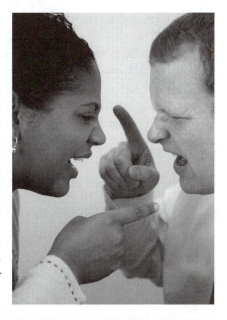

Photo 6.3   A group member's ineffective communication behaviors act as a relational obstacle to task accomplishment.

Source: ©iStockphoto.com/killerb10.

Whether faced with making a decision or solving a problem, a group may encounter any number of hurdles and barriers. To eliminate these hurdles and barriers, be aware of groupthink and its consequences. According to Irving Janis (1982), **groupthink** describes "a mode of thinking that [members] engage in when they are deeply involved in a cohesive group . . . which override[s] their motivation to realistically appraise

? What types of task-related obstacles and relational obstacles have arisen in your work group? How has your work group dealt with these obstacles?

alternative courses of action" (p. 9). Because groupthink can affect a group devastatingly, we will examine groupthink more thoroughly.

Groupthink

Think back to such historical events as the Bay of Pigs, the Cuban Missile Crisis, Watergate, and the explosion of the *Challenger* space shuttle. Or refer to such recent events as Enron, Tyco, and Qwest. What do these events have in common? According to researchers, groupthink, somehow, precipitated them all (Ginnett, 2005; Hirokawa, Gouran, & Martz, 1988; Park, 1990).

Groupthink presents a phenomenon of interest to small group communication researchers because of the argument that highly cohesive groups' ability to make an effective decision will be impeded by an implicit pressure to maintain cohesion. Recall that **cohesion** occurs when a group member reaches an acceptable level of desire to stay in the group. To learn more about groupthink, we need to examine its antecedent conditions, its symptoms, and ways to prevent it from occurring.

Antecedent Conditions of Groupthink

Although Janis (1982) stated that moderate to high amounts of cohesion must be present in order for groupthink to occur, the presence of cohesion is not enough. Rather, three sets of antecedent conditions, all of which are important to learning groups, must accompany cohesion (Aldag & Fuller, 1993; Janis, 1982; Janis & Mann, 1977).

The first set of conditions, called **decision characteristics** (Aldag & Fuller, 1993), refers to the parameters surrounding task assignment as experienced directly by the group. These parameters include the importance of the task, the time pressure faced by the group members, the procedural requirements of the task, and the seven task characteristics identified earlier in the chapter. For example, suppose Ricardo's friend at the travel agency finds the Talagaviloni family discounted airline tickets to Disney World but requires the family to purchase the tickets immediately. In its haste to purchase these inexpensive tickets, the family might not fully consider the ramifications of this decision, such as being able to make hotel reservations around the travel dates, finding the optimal hotel, or finding someone to watch Stella's dogs. Taking advantage of the opportunity to purchase the inexpensive tickets may steer the Talagaviloni family toward groupthink, particularly because the family hasn't taken the time to think about the impact of this decision, especially when coupled with its strong desire to visit Disney World.

The second set of conditions refers to the **group structure**, or the behaviors and characteristics unique to the group, and consists of six components (Janis, 1982). The first component, insulation of the group, occurs when a group—intentionally or unintentionally—insulates itself from other groups and individuals and thus lacks the opportunity to obtain expert information and seek critical evaluation. A group must maintain communicative ties with people outside the group.

The second component is a lack of impartial leadership. Rather than encouraging member participation as suggested by Zenglo Chen and Robert Lawson (1996), impartial leadership suggests that group members lead the group based on a hidden agenda or a personal motivation. As you will read in Chapter 9, groups function more effectively when they engage in shared leadership, meaning all group members take turns engaging in effective and appropriate communicative behaviors.

The third component comprises a lack of norms using methodical procedures surrounding how groups engage in task accomplishment. Groups that fail to follow a set procedure for making a decision or solving a problem or that rely on compromise or majority rule rather than consensus are headed toward groupthink. To prevent groupthink from occurring, a group should follow the five steps of the functional perspective discussed earlier in this chapter. This will put a group on the right track toward making a sound decision or solving a problem.

When a group possesses low group self-esteem, the fourth component, the members generally feel unworthy to complete the task. In most cases, low self-esteem is a temporary condition precipitated by one of several events, including a recent failure or being assigned a task that raises moral or ethical concerns or whose accomplishment requires abilities beyond those of the group members (Aldag & Fuller, 1993).

The fifth and sixth components are group member homogeneity (recall that a **homogeneous group** comprises members similar in demographic, cognitive, and cultural backgrounds) and a high amount of stress accompanying the small group task, respectively. Interestingly, political scientists Mark Schafer and Scott Crichlow (1996) examined 19 historical cases of groupthink and found group homogeneity and stress among the most frequent predictors of information-processing errors. This means that when group members share extremely similar viewpoints and opinions or experience high levels of stress, the group likely will encounter task-related obstacles as it proceeds through the decision-making and problem-solving process.

The third set of conditions, the **decision-making context** (Aldag & Fuller, 1993), similar to the historical and institutional contexts identified in the functional perspective of small group communication, refers to the organizational parameters surrounding task assignment that are independent of the group. These parameters include the political, social, and cultural norms of the group's parent organization; any prior discussion of the task initiated by the organization; and whether the organization has discussed the issues with its members (Aldag & Fuller, 1993; Whyman, 2005).

Symptoms of Groupthink

If these three conditions are met, the group may suffer from groupthink. Janis (1982) identified three symptoms of groupthink. The first occurs when a group overestimates its own mortality, creating an illusion of its own invulnerability. When a group considers itself invulnerable, it becomes overly optimistic and likely takes extreme risks. At the same time, such a group tends to ignore the moral or ethical consequences associated with a decision. Feeling overly confident about the group's decision also allows for groupthink to occur (Callaway & Esser, 1984).

The second symptom, **closed mindedness**, means a group relies solely on its members to gather and evaluate information. Closed-minded groups limit, if not terminate, communication with other groups; perceive these other groups as enemies; and may stereotype other group leaders as weak, ineffectual, or stupid. Eventually, the group discounts all other groups as ineffective.

When the third symptom, pressure toward uniformity, happens, group members engage in **self-censorship**. They monitor their reactions and contributions to the group discussion, making sure never to reveal their doubts and questions. If a group member does choose to express any doubts or raise any questions, the other group members apply direct pressure so the group member learns this behavior is not welcome. At the same time, members may engage in **mindguarding**, which Janis (1972) defined as a group member's attempt to keep adverse information from the other group members and provides another way group members facilitate groupthink.

Prevention of Groupthink

When groupthink occurs, the group makes a faulty decision. To prevent groupthink from occurring, experts recommend that groups follow four tips:

1. Allow sufficient time for discussion (Verderber, 1982). Sometimes groups make faulty decisions because they either receive a limited amount of work time or want to "hurry" the group process by spending as little time as possible working collectively on the task. Many students in classroom groups experience impatience with group work (Schullery & Gibson, 2001), but it is important to take the time necessary to complete the task.

2. Actively think about how group members' communication influences your group's decision-making and problem-solving processes (Hirokawa, Erbert, & Hurst, 1996). Several communicative behaviors, such as a lack of disagreement or a high ratio of agreement-to-disagreement statements (Callaway & Esser, 1984; Cline, 1994; Courtright, 1978), indicate groupthink may be occurring. Other dysfunctional communicative behaviors, such as not listening, interrupting each other, getting sidetracked by comments tangential to the group task, and behaving passively (DiSalvo, Nikkel, & Monroe, 1989), can lead to groupthink.

3. Probe each idea or statement offered by group members. "No idea [or statement] should be accepted at face value without some discussion" (Verderber, 1982, p. 129). One way to accomplish this involves the use of **verbal information probes**, or statements made by group members—"Explain that," "I'm not sure what that means," and "Now that we know this, perhaps we should rethink our position," for example (Propp & Julian, 1994)—intended to probe the accuracy of the information under examination by the group. Members also can probe ideas

or statements by asking questions, but surprisingly, this accounts for only 16% of a group's total time spent communicating, with the probing question emerging as the most frequently used question type (Hawkins & Power, 1999). By asking open-ended probing questions (e.g., "Why are probing questions vital to preventing groupthink?") rather than closed (e.g., "Are probing questions vital to preventing groupthink?"), members can provide more thoughtful and constructive answers to the questions that address the task.

4. Discourage promotional leadership, which refers to the behaviors a group leader uses early in the decision-making process to promote one idea rather than encourage the generation

> **?** Identify five ways in which you and the members of your work group could work actively toward preventing groupthink.

of multiple ideas (Flippen, 1999). By discouraging promotional leadership, group members will feel more inclined to offer their own ideas.

A Final Note About Small Group Tasks

It is important to remember that any time a group faces a task, the decision to be made or the solution to be generated ultimately results from several interrelated variables. To make satisfactory progress on a task, work groups require motivated members, adequate time and informational resources, competent leadership, and direct organizational assistance (Hirokawa & Keyton, 1995). Other influential variables include the cognitive abilities of group members, the communication and personality traits of group members, the relationships established among group members, and the communication that occurs during the decision-making or problem-solving process (Hirokawa & Johnston, 1989). The presence of these variables only serves as a reminder that task accomplishment may prove more difficult than groups sometimes believe. Following the functional perspective of small group communication discussed in this chapter allows for alleviating the problems that arise due to these interrelated variables.

Conclusion

This chapter provided you with information about the group task. We identified and defined the seven characteristics of a task and distinguished between a decision-making and a problem-solving task. We examined the functional perspective of small group communication, with a specific focus on the assumptions, steps, contexts, and obstacles associated with the perspective. Finally, we explored groupthink and its implications for task accomplishment. As you read the next chapter, consider how the decision-making and problem-solving process is enhanced through the use of decision-making procedures.

Discussion Questions

1. Identify a task recently accomplished by a group to which you belong. With this task in mind, indicate how each of the seven characteristics of tasks (i.e., task difficulty, solution multiplicity, intrinsic interest, population familiarity, acceptance level, area of freedom, and social complexity) influenced your group's ability to accomplish the task.

2. In examining the five steps of the functional perspective of group communication, which step would you argue is the most essential? Why? What practical experience do you have from working in groups to support your choice?

3. To what degree does the charge affect how group members approach a task? Why is it important to determine whether a group task is centered on a question of fact, value, conjecture, or policy?

4. What modifications or considerations, if any, would a virtual group need to make in order to use the functional perspective of small group communication? Can all types of group use this perspective in the same way?

5. What additional antecedent conditions of groupthink can you identify? To what extent do these conditions depend on the task assigned to the group? To what extent do these conditions depend on the relationships established among group members?

References

Adams, K., & Galanes, G. J. (2006). *Communicating in groups: Applications and skills* (6th ed.). Boston: McGraw-Hill.

Aldag, R. J., & Fuller, S. R. (1993). Beyond fiasco: A reappraisal of the groupthink phenomenon and a new model of group decision processes. *Psychological Bulletin, 113,* 533–552.

Callaway, M. R., & Esser, J. K. (1984). Groupthink: Effects of cohesiveness and problem-solving procedures on group decision making. *Social Behavior and Personality, 12,* 157–164.

Chen, Z., & Lawson, R. B. (1996). Groupthink: Deciding with the leader and the devil. *Psychological Record, 46,* 581–590.

Cline, R. J. W. (1994). Groupthink and the Watergate cover-up: The illusion of unanimity. In L. R. Frey (Ed.), *Group communication in context: Studies of natural groups* (pp. 199–223). Hillsdale, NJ: Erlbaum.

Courtright, J. A. (1978). A laboratory investigation of groupthink. *Communication Monographs, 45,* 229–246.

Cragan, J. F., & Wright, D. W. (1993). The functional theory of small group decision-making: A replication. *Journal of Social Behavior and Personality, 8,* 165–174.

DeStephen, R., & Hirokawa, R. (1988). Small group consensus: Stability of group support of the decision, task process, and group relationships. *Small Group Behavior, 19,* 227–239.

DiSalvo, V. S., Nikkel, E., & Monroe, C. (1989). Theory and practice: A field investigation and identification of group members' perceptions of problems facing natural work groups. *Small Group Behavior, 20,* 551–567.

Engleberg, I. N., & Wynn, D. R. (2003). *Working in groups: Communication principles and strategies* (3rd ed.). Boston: Houghton Mifflin.

Fisher, B. A. (1971). Communication research and the task-oriented group. *Journal of Communication, 21,* 136–149.

Flippen, A. R. (1999). Understanding groupthink from a self-regulatory perspective. *Small Group Research, 30,* 139–165.

Frey, L. R. (1997). Individuals in groups. In L. R. Frey & J. K. Barge (Eds.), *Managing group life: Communicating in decision-making groups* (pp. 52–79). Boston: Houghton Mifflin.

Gero, A. (1985). Conflict avoidance in consensual decision processes. *Small Group Behavior, 16,* 487–499.

Ginnett, R. (2005, May/June). What can leaders do to avoid groupthink? *Leadership in Action, 25*(2), 14.

Gouran, D. S. (1997). Effective versus ineffective group decision making. In L. R. Frey & J. K. Barge (Eds.), *Managing group life: Communicating in decision-making groups* (pp. 133–155). Boston: Houghton Mifflin.

Gouran, D. S., & Hirokawa, R. Y. (1983). The role of communication in decision-making groups: A functional perspective. In M. S. Mander (Ed.), *Communications in transition: Issues and debates in current research* (pp. 168–185). New York: Praeger.

Gouran, D. S., & Hirokawa, R. Y. (1986). Counteractive functions of communication in effective group decision-making. In R. Y. Hirokawa & M. S. Poole (Eds.), *Communication and group decision making* (pp. 81–90). Beverly Hills, CA: Sage.

Gouran, D. S., & Hirokawa, R. Y. (1996). Functional theory and communication in decision-making and problem-solving groups: An expanded view. In R. Y. Hirokawa & M. S. Poole (Eds.), *Communication and group decision making* (2nd ed., pp. 55–80). Thousand Oaks, CA: Sage.

Gouran D. S., & Hirokawa, R. Y. (2003). Effective decision making and problem solving in groups: A functional perspective. In R. Y. Hirokawa, R. S. Cathcart, L. A. Samovar, & L. D. Henman (Eds.), *Small group communication theory & practice: An anthology* (8th ed., pp. 27–38). Los Angeles: Roxbury.

Gouran, D. S., Hirokawa, R. Y., Julian, K. M., & Leatham, G. B. (1993). The evolution and current status of the functional perspective on communication in decision-making and problem-solving groups. In S. A. Deetz (Ed.), *Communication yearbook* (Vol. 16, pp. 573–600). Newbury Park, CA: Sage.

Graham, E. E., Papa, M. J., & McPherson, M. B. (1997). An applied test of the functional communication perspective of small group decision-making. *Southern Communication Journal, 62,* 269–279.

Hare, A. P. (1980). Consensus versus majority: A laboratory experiment. *Small Group Behavior, 11,* 131–143.

Hawkins, K., & Power, C. B. (1999). Gender differences in questions asked during small decision-making group discussions. *Small Group Research, 30,* 235–256.

Hirokawa, R. Y. (1983a). Group communication and problem-solving effectiveness: An investigation of group phases. *Human Communication Research, 9,* 291–305.

Hirokawa, R. Y. (1983b). Group communication and problem-solving effectiveness II: An exploratory investigation of procedural functions. *Western Journal of Speech Communication, 47,* 59–74.

Hirokawa, R. Y. (1985). Discussion procedures and decision-making performance: A test of a functional perspective. *Human Communication Research, 12,* 203–224.

Hirokawa, R. Y. (1988). Group communication and group decision-making performance: A continued test of the functional perspective. *Human Communication Research, 14,* 487–515.

Hirokawa, R. Y., Erbert, L., & Hurst, A. (1996). Communication and group decision-making effectiveness. In R. Y. Hirokawa & M. S. Poole (Eds.), *Communication and group decision making* (2nd ed., pp. 269–300). Thousand Oaks, CA: Sage.

Hirokawa, R. Y., Gouran, D. S., & Martz, A. E. (1988). Understanding the sources of faulty group decision making: A lesson from the Challenger disaster. *Small Group Behavior, 19,* 411–433.

Hirokawa, R. Y., & Johnston, D. D. (1989). Toward a general theory of group decision making: Development of an integrated model. *Small Group Behavior, 20,* 500–523.

Hirokawa, R. Y., & Keyton, J. (1995). Perceived facilitators and inhibitors of effectiveness in organizational work teams. *Management Communication Quarterly, 8,* 424–446.

Hirokawa, R. Y., & Pace, R. (1983). A descriptive investigation of the possible communication-based reasons for effective and ineffective group decision making. *Communication Monographs, 50,* 363–379.

Hirokawa, R. Y., & Rost, K. M. (1992). Effective group decision making in organizations: Field test of the vigilant interaction theory. *Management Communication Quarterly, 5,* 267–288.

Hirokawa, R. Y., & Salazar, A. J. (1997). An integrated approach to communication and group decision making. In L. R. Frey & J. K. Barge (Eds.), *Managing group life: Communicating in decision-making groups* (pp. 156–181). Boston: Houghton Mifflin.

Infante, D. A. (1988). *Arguing constructively.* Prospect Heights, IL: Waveland Press.

Janis, I. L. (1972). *Victims of groupthink.* Boston: Houghton Mifflin.

Janis, I. L. (1982). *Groupthink: Psychological studies of policy decisions and fiascoes* (2nd ed.). Boston: Houghton Mifflin.

Janis, I. L., & Mann, L. (1977). *Decision making: A psychological analysis of conflict, choice, and commitment.* New York: Free Press.

Keyton, J. (1999). *Group communication: Process and analysis.* Mountain View, CA: Mayfield.

Keyton, J., & Frey, L. R. (2002). The state of traits: Predispositions and group communication. In L. R. Frey (Ed.), *New directions in group communication* (pp. 99–120). Thousand Oaks, CA: Sage.

Latham, V. M. (1987). Task type and group motivation: Implications for a behavioral approach to leadership in small groups. *Small Group Behavior, 18,* 56–71.

Mayer, M. E., Sonoda, K. T., & Gudykunst, W. B. (1997). The effect of time pressure and type of information on decision quality. *Southern Communication Journal, 62,* 280–292.

Orlitzky, M., & Hirokawa, R. Y. (2001). To err is human, to correct for it divine: A meta-analysis of research testing the functional theory of group decision-making effectiveness. *Small Group Research, 32,* 313–341.

Park, W. (1990). A review of research on groupthink. *Journal of Behavioral Decision Making, 3,* 229–245.

Poole, M. S., & Baldwin, C. L. (1996). Developmental processes in group decision making. In R. Y. Hirokawa & M. S. Poole (Eds.), *Communication and group decision making* (2nd ed., pp. 215–241). Thousand Oaks, CA: Sage.

Propp, K. M., & Julian, K. M. (1994). Enhancing accurate information processing: An investigation of verbal information probes in decision making. *Communication Reports, 7,* 145–152.

Renz, M. A. (2006). Paving consensus: Enacting, challenging, and revising the consensus process in a cohousing community. *Journal of Applied Communication Research, 34,* 163–190.

Rothwell, J. D. (2004). *In mixed company: Small group communication* (5th ed.). Belmont, CA: Wadsworth.

Sager, K. L., & Gastil, J. (2006). The origins and consequences of consensus decision making: A test of the social consensus model. *Southern Communication Journal, 71,* 1–24.

Schafer, M., & Crichlow, S. (1996). Antecedents of groupthink: A quantitative study. *Journal of Conflict Resolution, 40,* 415–435.

Scheidel, T. M., & Crowell, L. (1964). Idea development in small discussion groups. *Quarterly Journal of Speech, 50,* 140–145.

Schullery, N. M., & Gibson, M. K. (2001). Working in groups: Identification and treatment of students' perceived weaknesses. *Business Communication Quarterly, 64*(2), 9–30.

Shaw, M. E. (1981). *Group dynamics: The psychology of small group behavior* (3rd ed.). New York: McGraw-Hill.

Stohl, C., & Holmes, M. E. (1993). A functional perspective for bona fide groups. In S. A. Deetz (Ed.), *Communication yearbook* (Vol. 16, pp. 601–614). Newbury Park, CA: Sage.

Verderber, R. F. (1982). *Working together: Fundamentals of group decision making.* Belmont, CA: Wadsworth.

Whyman, W. (2005, May/June). A question of leadership. *Leadership in Action, 25*(2), 13.

Small Group Decision-Making Procedures 7

After reading this chapter, you should be able to:

1. define decision-making procedures,
2. differentiate among the brainstorming, nominal group technique, ideawriting, and six thinking hats of decision-making procedures,
3. list the four rules members should follow when using the brainstorming decision-making procedure,
4. identify the six thinking hats and describe the concept represented by each hat, and
5. identify the advantages and disadvantages associated with use of the decision-making procedures.

Case Study | Jacob, Sarah, Joshua, Carolyn, and Tim work together in the public relations department of Andy's, a midsize fast-food chain. Three-year veterans of the same team, they pride themselves on getting along and occasionally meet for dinner with their partners or spouses. Although they

Photo 7.1   Similar to the process of serving a meal in a restaurant, a group should make a decision or solve a problem by coordinating the efforts of all group members.

Source: Chip Simons/Photographer's Choice/Getty Images.

disagree at times over work issues, they also take pride in reaching agreement on decisions surrounding tasks and solving problems without too much hassle or conflict. In fact, they laugh about how they could be clones of each other.

When the fourth-quarter results came out, Chris Bean, the new vice president, sent a memo to all department personnel reporting the continued slipping of sales since the first quarter of the year. To make matters worse, the company's closest competitors just announced a new public relations campaign promoting brand-name toys for kids and special deals for parents on repeat business. Since the competitor's campaign succeeded instantly, something had to be done to reverse the trend if Andy's was to regain its market share. Vice President Bean ordered each department to make recommendations by the end of the week on how to accomplish this trend reversal and move Andy's forward. As directed, the public relations team congregated to discuss its recommendations.

Jacob: Gosh, we're a solid company. I don't see what all the hype is about. We have lost market shares before and have always come back. Slipping sales for three quarters does not mean the end is coming tomorrow.

Carolyn: Well, we do have to respond to Bean's request. When the vice president sends a directive, we need to pay attention. What about if we brainstorm or use those other decision-making procedures we learned in college?

Joshua: We could examine our current promotional materials to see how we could make them more appealing. Perhaps we need more color in our print ads. Or maybe we should create a new jingle.

Sarah: As I remember, the last time we did that we had some success. How about going to dinner tomorrow night to discuss it?

Tim: Great idea! Why try to reinvent the wheel? We have enough to do around here. Besides, we are still the number-one fast-food company. I think it's too soon to be in a panic mode.

As demonstrated by this case study, in which the team must recommend how to move Andy's forward, group members can fall easily into the trap of not taking the decision-making process seriously. Group members should confront a complex task by generating several methods that lend themselves to choosing among alternative solutions (Laughlin, 1996). The norms and rules about how to generate ideas in response to problems maximize the quantity and quality of ideas and create the proper climate for groups to engage in the decision-making process (Jackson & Poole, 2003).

This chapter will introduce you to decision-making procedures. First, we will offer a definition of decision-making procedures. Then, we will examine four specific decision-making procedures: brainstorming, nominal group technique, ideawriting, and six thinking hats. Finally, we will identify the advantages and the disadvantages associated with using decision-making procedures.

Definition of Decision-Making Procedures

According to group communication scholars David Seibold and Dean Krikorian (1997), **decision-making procedures** describe structured methods of decision making that coordinate group members' communication, keep members focused on the issues at hand, and guide members through the process of problem diagnosis, solution selection, or solution implementation. Each decision-making procedure occurs within a controlled situation, in which one or two members facilitate the group's process. Because decision-making procedures impose structure on the group's discussion of an issue, groups can avoid haphazard or poor decision making or premature decisions that result in poor group performance. Furthermore, small group communication expert Randy Hirokawa (1980) found that members of effective groups use more procedural statements and spend more time discussing procedural matters than members of ineffective groups. To evaluate the quality of a group's decisions, examine the type of decision-making procedures it uses (Pavitt & Curtis, 1994).

> ? What are some decision-making procedures currently used by your work group? How effective are these procedures?

Types of Decision-Making Procedures

Although groups can choose among several types of decision-making procedures (Jarboe, 1999; Jones, 1998; Sunwolf, 2002; Sunwolf & Seibold, 1999), any group, including your classroom group, can use the following four procedures: brainstorming, nominal group technique, ideawriting, and six thinking hats.

Although the steps of each procedure vary, group scholars Michele Jackson and Marshall Scott Poole (2003) noted that most idea generation procedures share four common principles. First, these procedures encourage generation of many ideas. Second, the members focus on one single activity, the generation of ideas as a group. Third, groups that want to produce must make members follow a set of rules or steps in working through the decision-making process. Fourth, as a group activity, the members must commit to using the procedures in a cooperative group climate. As group experts Dennis Gouran and Randy Hirokawa (2003) noted, human nature causes group members to "follow the lines of least resistance and settle on only a few alternatives, rather than assess the merits of all [alternatives] that might be pertinent" (p. 31). By using these four decision-making procedures, a group can capitalize on their advantages.

Brainstorming

In 1953, advertising executive Alex F. Osborn introduced the first decision-making procedure, the concept of brainstorming, which group members can use to stimulate creativity in the idea generation process. Brainstorming allows groups to generate more ideas or solutions to problems than individuals might generate working alone, in part because innovation usually involves more than one person (Scheidel, 1986). Situations that warrant the appropriate use of brainstorming include facing a specific and fairly range-limited problem, facing a problem with many answers, needing to produce a range of options that will be evaluated at a later date, and needing to generate a large number of good ideas (Anderson, Foster-Kuehn, & McKinney, 1996; Price, 1985).

To use brainstorming effectively, a group needs to follow four rules (Osborn, 1953), as found in Table 7.1. Consider that although brainstorming centers on quantity of ideas rather than quality of ideas, offensive or derogatory ideas are unacceptable. Researcher William Cooper and his colleagues (1998) found one extremely offensive idea for every five ideas produced in their brainstorming sessions, so group members may require cautioning against being too wild and crazy.

In addition to these four rules, groups should follow three tips for making brainstorming more effective. First, before your group begins the brainstorming session, select one group member to write the ideas on a blackboard, a flip chart, or newsprint so all members can view them. Second, make sure all group members understand and agree to follow the four rules; otherwise, the brainstorming session will not be as effective as it could. Because not all members may be familiar with the four rules, one member may need to verbally state the rules before the brainstorming session begins. Third, remind group members to refrain from evaluating ideas during brainstorming. Brainstorming usually succeeds due to non-evaluation.

> **?** How helpful are these rules and these tips? When using brainstorming, does your work group follow these rules and consider these tips?

Table 7.1   Brainstorming Rules

Rule 1	No evaluation should occur during the session, no matter how outlandish or nonsensical the ideas may seem.
Rule 2	Members should generate as many ideas as possible without extended pauses.
Rule 3	Members should be encouraged to be creatively wild and crazy.
Rule 4	Piggybacking or hitchhiking on each other's ideas is important.

Source: Based on Osborn, A. F. (1953). *Applied imagination.* New York: Scribner.

Photo 7.2   Some decision-making procedures require a facilitator, whose purpose is to ensure that group members follow the procedures in the allotted time.

Source: ©iStockphoto.com/killerb10.

If you make sure your group members think creatively when generating ideas, you will realize the ease required to conduct a brainstorming session and the fun involved in unleashing creativity, although a brainstorming session should last no longer than 30 minutes (Gautschi, 1990a). Groups may want to use this procedure along with other decision-making procedures, such as the nominal group technique decision-making procedure.

Nominal Group Technique

The second decision-making procedure, a popular one, is nominal group technique or NGT (Delbecq, Van de Ven, & Gustafson, 1975). **Nominal group technique** allows members to independently and silently generate ideas, but not as a group. NGT permits members to work alone, combine ideas afterward, and later view the process as one in which they worked as a group (Green, 1975).

Although NGT compares to brainstorming in that it first requires members to engage in idea generation, the independence of idea generation and the silent recording of each member's ideas present NGT as a more democratic process. This procedure minimizes persuasive influences by group members, especially the influence of powerful and high-status members (Seibold & Krikorian, 1997). As such, NGT is an appropriate procedure to use when some group members dominate group discussion or when status differences in the group inhibit equal participation (Anderson et al., 1996).

An ideal decision-making procedure for use with 5 to 9 participants, NGT is guided by a facilitator, or an individual who purports to ensure that group members follow the decision-making procedure in the time allotted. Some behaviors used by the facilitator include engaging in active communication skills (e.g., listening, maintaining eye contact, paraphrasing members' statements), maintaining the group momentum, remaining neutral during the group discussion, and treating the information disclosed in the group as confidential (Anderson & Robertson, 1985; Zorn & Rosenfield, 1989). At no point does a facilitator evaluate an idea, become part of the discussion process, or interject an opinion (Offner, Kramer, & Winter, 1996).

To use NGT, a group must follow four steps. The first step involves the silent generation of ideas, with all members recording their responses to a stimulus question or problem. Members must use words or descriptive phrases and list as many opinions or ideas as possible. This step usually takes 3 to 5 minutes but should take no more than 15 to 20 minutes (Gautschi, 1990b). Once the time limit has expired, the facilitator instructs the members to stop writing. The case study's Sarah could exemplify NGT by writing, "Give free kids' DVDs with 10 meals" as one response to Bean's request of how to regain market share and counter the brand-named toys their company's competitors offer.

In the second step, the facilitator records the members' ideas. A critical component of this step is the recording, but not the discussion, of ideas. To execute this step, the facilitator writes members' responses on a blackboard, a flip chart, or newsprint so all members can view them. In a round-robin fashion, the facilitator asks each member to present one idea at a time until all ideas have been recorded. The facilitator helps members determine if their ideas duplicate or extend those ideas already stated. In these cases, the member can elect to piggyback or hitchhike on an existing idea rather than create a new idea. At any time, a member can pass when called upon if he has no more ideas on his list.

During the third step, the clarification of ideas, each member must understand what the recorded ideas mean. In response to Sarah's idea in the first step, for example, Joshua could ask if the 10 meals are kids' meals or parents' meals, and the facilitator then would ask Sarah to clarify for the team what she meant by her idea. This process continues until the facilitator feels confident all members understand each idea.

The fourth step requires members to vote on the best idea from among the list of ideas generated. This step forces members to take a stand by identifying the most important ideas and then rank-ordering the ideas, which means a member may favor another member's idea and choose not to vote for her own idea. For instance, the members in the case study might be asked to select and rank-order five ideas from the list they generated. Thus, each member not only chooses his or her top five ideas from the list but also must determine the order of these ideas using the ranking system provided by the facilitator. The facilitator then records each member's ranking in front of the group. At this stage, the facilitator could either dismiss the members and present the results to another group for discussion and eventual decision making or explain the voting patterns to the members who generated the ideas and they could begin to discuss the results.

> *Ethically Speaking:* Would it be wrong to vote for your own idea, even though the ideas presented by other group members are stronger, more relevant, or more appropriate?

The strength of this decision-making procedure lies in the short amount of time the group takes to generate, clarify, and vote on the best ideas. Furthermore, a diverse group of working members can participate (Ulschak, Nathanson, & Gillan, 1981). According to consultant and group scholar Carl Moore (1987), NGT is an enjoyable and successful decision-making procedure used in business, government, and community endeavors. On the downside, this procedure requires a facilitator (Ulschak et al., 1981), focuses on one problem only, and limits interaction among group members.

Some group members find ideawriting, the third decision-making procedure, enjoyable. This procedure also encourages participation from all members.

Ideawriting

According to Carl Moore (1987), **ideawriting** focuses on a single topic that produces a written product. Similar to the NGT procedure, ideawriting begins with a writing step. However, its strength lies in the inclusion of silent evaluation of ideas from each group member.

To use ideawriting, a group must follow four steps. First, members must react to a stimulus question or problem by listing three or four ideas and then supplying reason(s) why each has merit. Members should not worry about spelling or punctuation and should use phrases. When members finish, they place their list in a pile. Table 7.2 exemplifies a form used in ideawriting.

The second step requires members to select a list other than their own and respond to the list. They should read all the ideas and offer solutions, provide suggestions, and identify weaknesses. This process continues until each member has commented on all other members' ideas (i.e., has read all members' lists).

The third step requires members to read other members' comments on their list and respond, in writing, to the solutions, suggestions, and weaknesses

Table 7.2   Ideawriting Sample Form

Name: _____

Problem or Issue:

List of ideas: (use phrases)

1.

2.

3.

Responses:

1.

2.

3.

Source: Moore, C. M. (1987). *Group techniques for idea building.* Newbury Park, CA: Sage.

provided. In this manner, accomplishing criticism of ideas in writing helps neutralize conflict.

In the fourth step, members summarize, report, and evaluate their collective ideas and select those they think merit further discussion. They write this summary on a blackboard, a flip chart, or newsprint so all members can see the ideas. Recording the ideas helps the group develop each idea by prompting further discussion.

Ideawriting encourages full participation by members and utilizes simultaneous work by members to enhance productivity and efficiency. Additionally, several groups can work on the stimulus question or problem at the same time, and a facilitator quite feasibly can conduct a session with several groups in one room because ideawriting does not take long. Usually, in one hour or less, members generate ideas, have the ideas critiqued, and summarize the main ideas for future discussion.

Six Thinking Hats

The fourth decision-making procedure comprises six thinking hats. Unlike the aforementioned decision-making procedures, six thinking hats is a technique designed to simplify thinking by having a group focus solely on one aspect of a decision at a time. According to Edward de Bono (1999), often people focus on several aspects at once when thinking about making a decision or solving a problem. These aspects include emotion, logic, wishful thinking, procedures, and both positive and negative consequences. When using six thinking hats as a decision-making procedure, group members examine one aspect of a decision simultaneously from the same point of view based on the collective intelligence, experience, and knowledge of the group.

> ? In your work group, which hat is most appealing to you? Which hat is least appealing to you? To what degree is this appeal based on your communication and personality traits?

In other words, at any given point the group wears one of six color-coded hats, with the color representing one aspect. Table 7.3 identifies the aspect associated with each color. Once the group has examined the decision or problem from one hat, the group proceeds to examine the decision or problem from another hat.

Photo 7.3   Using the six thinking hats decision-making procedure requires group members to examine simultaneously one aspect of a decision from the same hat.

Source: Walter Lockwood Photography/Workbook Stock/Jupiterimages.

Table 7.3 Six Thinking Hats

Color	Aspect
White	Approaches the decision in a neutral and objective manner by providing facts and figures
Red	Approaches the decision in an emotional manner by legitimizing members' emotions and feelings about the decision
Black	Approaches the decision in a cautious manner by centering on the negative aspects (i.e., risks, differences) of the decision
Yellow	Approaches the decision in an optimistic manner by focusing on the positive aspects of the decision
Green	Approaches the decision in a creative manner by exploring alternatives of the decision
Blue	Approaches the decision in a procedural manner by monitoring the decision-making procedures used by the group

Source: Based on de Bono, E. L. (1999). *Six thinking hats.* New York: Little, Brown and Company.

Although there exists no predetermined sequence of hats, de Bono recommends that a group (a) begins with the blue hat, (b) uses at least two hats, and (c) spends no more than 1 minute per member per hat (e.g., a five-member group using three hats would spend approximately 5 minutes on each aspect, or hat, for a total of approximately 15 minutes). By doing so, a group not only maximizes its thinking on one aspect of a decision or problem; it also can switch between aspects with relative ease and clarity.

Why Use Decision-Making Procedures?

Using decision-making procedures offers four advantages. First, the rules a group follows in idea generation appear to create other benefits aside from the narrow focus on the quantity of ideas (Kramer, Kuo, & Dailey, 1997). For example, group members trained in decision-making procedures are less dominant and interact more positively with each other than group members not trained in decision-making procedures. Even after the idea generation process concludes, the rest of the group process usually becomes more democratic in nature.

The second advantage concerns the development of group and member creativity. If you recall from Chapter 1, **creativity** refers to the process by which members engage in idea generation. To enhance creativity, engage in **excursion** (Prince, 1970), or a three-stage process that requires group members to (a) put the problem or task out of mind, (b) focus on an irrelevant yet unrelated topic, and (c) force-fit the characteristics of the irrelevant topic to the original problem or task (Weaver & Prince, 1990). In this setting, creativity is considered a skill rather than a talent (Georgiou, 1994) and is based on the definition of creativity as purposeful imagination (Golen, Eure, Titkemeyer, Powers, & Boyer, 1982). Think about how you could enhance decision making in your classroom group if you and your group members subscribed to this consideration.

Third, decision-making procedures increase group efficiency (Moore, 1987) and enhance the quality of the decision (Hall & Watson, 1980). Regardless of whether a group uses face-to-face procedures or communicates through e-mail, using these procedures simultaneously forces a group to focus on the task and minimize non-task talk. As you now know, the steps in NGT and ideawriting do not permit task deviation. Furthermore, groups that do not use these procedures may not use their time effectively (Sunwolf & Seibold, 1999) and often think they must solve the problem quickly without taking the time to reach high-quality decisions (Poole, 1991).

The fourth advantage to decision-making procedures stems from the fact that facilitators (or leaders) can conduct sessions with a large number of groups. This means that an organization can amass larger data sets, engage a diverse number of employees in the decision-making process, and yet spend less time doing it (Moore, 1987). Groups larger than 7 to 9 members who must make decisions may find a buzz group decision-making procedure helpful (Phillips, 1948). In a **buzz group**, the larger group breaks into subgroups of 3 to 5 members (i.e., the buzz group). Each buzz group then generates ideas to take to the larger group for discussion and decision making. Using buzz groups facilitates member participation, efficiency, and diversity of opinion. Buzz groups "can also breathe life into a stagnant meeting" (Seibold & Krikorian, 1997, p. 301), in which organizational members feel invigorated, validated, and involved. Sessions also can be conducted via virtual groups, enabling members to utilize group decision-making procedures through e-mail, message boards, or chat rooms.

Decision-making procedures, however, also present three disadvantages. First, some group experts have argued that researchers have not consistently proven that groups outperform individuals, particularly in brainstorming sessions (Jablin & Seibold, 1978; Seibold & Krikorian, 1997). Second, some group members' communication and personality traits affect their participation in decision-making procedures. For example, in terms of brainstorming, group members who contribute a greater number of ideas tend to be low in communication apprehension, feel more attracted to the brainstorming task and more tolerant of ambiguity, and perceive all members as possessing the same group status (Comadena, 1984; Jablin, Seibold, & Sorenson, 1977; Jablin & Sussman, 1978). Similarly, groups composed of all low-communication-apprehensive members also produce more ideas than groups composed of all high-communication-apprehensive members (Jablin, 1981). Although not known, these findings likely may apply to the other three decision-making procedures as well.

Third, some group members may feel restrained by their lack of creativity. Because many people consider themselves better at routine thinking than creative thinking (Georgiou, 1994), they easily become self-conscious when placed in creativity-invoking situations (Gordon, 1961). As such, group members required to engage in creativity sometimes become frustrated or flustered. To combat this feeling, members should remember to value creativity for its own worth and not measure it against an objective standard (Golen et al., 1982).

A Final Note About Small Group Decision-Making Procedures

When we ask students if the groups to which they belong use these decision-making procedures, most students admit their groups do not use any of them, except some form of brainstorming. And even though some college textbooks mention decision-making procedures and professors may even train students to use them, many college students who work full-time state that their work and social groups fail to use them. Communication professor Marshall Scott Poole (1991) listed several reasons why group members resist using decision-making procedures. For example, some members feel awkward using these procedures, and some members feel these procedures impede the flow of discussion rather than enhance it. Other inhibiting effects on members from the use of decision-making procedures include frustration, boredom, grouphate, and destructive conflict (Sunwolf & Seibold, 1999). The next time you work in a group, we encourage you to (a) think about the advantages of decision-making procedures and (b) actively work toward implementing one of these procedures in your group. You might be surprised at not only the quality of the results your group attains but also the time, energy, and frustration that using these procedures alleviates.

Conclusion

This chapter introduced you to decision-making procedures, first by offering a definition of decision-making procedures. We then examined four specific decision-making procedures: brainstorming, nominal group technique, ideawriting, and six thinking hats. Finally, we identified the advantages and disadvantages associated with using these decision-making procedures. As you read the next chapter, consider whether your choice to use these decision-making procedures relates to the role you play in a small group.

Discussion Questions

1. Watch a reality television show (e.g., *Trading Spouses, Top Chef, Survivor*) that features a primary group or work group. How does this group utilize decision-making procedures? Would the outcome of a group decision be different had the group used one of the procedures discussed in this chapter?

2. What additional rules or tips would a virtual group need to effectively engage in brainstorming?

3. In your classroom group, use ideawriting to answer the following question: What can your university do to improve the quality of life for first-year students? (Use the sample form in Table 7.2 to complete this question.) How many ideas did your group generate?

4. Identify a primary group to which you belong. What are some advantages of using the decision-making procedures discussed in this chapter? What are some disadvantages of using the decision-making procedures discussed in this chapter?

5. Of the decision-making procedures discussed in this chapter, which procedures have been used in your classroom group to complete group activities and projects? How could these procedures help your group in completing any remaining group activities and projects?

References

Anderson, J., Foster-Kuehn, M., & McKinney, B. C. (1996). *Communication skills for surviving conflicts at work.* Creskill, NJ: Hampton Press.

Anderson, L. F., & Robertson, S. E. (1985). Group facilitation: Functions and skills. *Small Group Behavior, 16,* 139–156.

Comadena, M. E. (1984). Brainstorming groups: Ambiguity tolerance, communication apprehension, task attraction, and individual productivity. *Small Group Behavior, 15,* 251–264.

Cooper, W. H., Gallupe, R. B., Pollard, S., & Cadsby, J. (1998). Some liberating effects of anonymous electronic brainstorming. *Small Group Research, 29,* 147–178.

Delbecq, A., Van de Ven, A. H., & Gustafson, D. H. (1975). *Group techniques for program planning: A guide to nominal and Delphi processes.* Glenview, IL: Scott, Foresman.

de Bono, E. L. (1999). *Six thinking hats.* New York: Little, Brown, and Company.

Gautschi, T. F. (1990a). How to improve group decisions. *Design News, 46*(17), 188.

Gautschi, T. F. (1990b). Group decision-making—Part III. *Design News, 46*(19), 336.

Georgiou, S. N. (1994). Synectics: A problem-solving tool for educational leaders. *International Journal of Educational Management, 8,* 5–10.

Golen, S., Eure, J. D., Titkemeyer, M. A., Powers, C., & Boyer, N. (1982). How to teach students to improve their creativity in a basic business communication class. *Journal of Business Communication, 20,* 47–57.

Gordon, W. J. J. (1961). *Synectics: The development of creative capacity.* New York: Harper & Row.

Gouran, D. S., & Hirokawa, R. Y. (2003). Effective decision making and problem solving in groups: A functional perspective. In R. Y. Hirokawa, R. S. Cathcart, L. A. Samovar, & L. D. Henman (Eds.), *Small group communication theory and practice: An anthology* (8th ed., pp. 27–38). Los Angeles: Roxbury.

Green, T. B. (1975). An empirical analysis of nominal and interacting groups. *Academy of Management, 18,* 63–73.

Hall, J., & Watson, W. H. (1980). The effects of a normative intervention on group decision-making performance. *Human Relations, 23,* 299–317.

Hirokawa, R. Y. (1980). A comparative analysis of communication patterns within effective and ineffective decision-making groups. *Communication Monographs, 47,* 312–321.

Jablin, F. M. (1981). Cultivating imagination: Factors that enhance and inhibit creativity in brainstorming groups. *Human Communication Research, 7,* 245–258.

Jablin, F. M., & Seibold, D. R. (1978). Implications for problem-solving groups of empirical research on "brainstorming": A critical review of the literature. *Southern Speech Communication Journal, 43,* 327–356.

Jablin, F. M., Seibold, D. R., & Sorenson, R. (1977). Potential inhibitory effects of group participation on brainstorming performance. *Central States Speech Journal, 28,* 113–121.

Jablin, F. M., & Sussman, L. (1978). An exploration of communication and productivity in real brainstorming groups. *Human Communication Research, 4,* 329–337.

Jackson, M. H., & Poole, M. S. (2003). Idea-generation in naturally occurring contexts: Complex appropriation of a simple group procedure. *Human Communication Research, 29,* 560–591.

Jarboe, S. (1999). Group communication and creativity processes. In L. R. Frey (Ed.), D. S. Gouran, & M. S. Poole (Assoc. Eds.), *The handbook of group communication theory and research* (pp. 335–368). Thousand Oaks, CA: Sage.

Jones, M. D. (1998). *The thinker's toolkit: 14 powerful techniques for problem solving.* New York: Random House.

Kramer, M. W., Kuo, C. L., & Dailey, J. C. (1997). The impact of brainstorming techniques on subsequent group processes: Beyond generating ideas. *Small Group Research, 28,* 218–242.

Laughlin, P. R. (1996). Group decision making and collective induction. In E. H. Witte & J. H. Davis (Eds.), *Understanding group behavior: Consensual action by small groups* (pp. 61–80). Mahwah, NJ: Erlbaum.

Moore, C. M. (1987). *Group techniques for idea building.* Newbury Park, CA: Sage.

Offner, A. K., Kramer, T. J., & Winter, J. P. (1996). The effects of facilitation, recording, and pauses on group brainstorming. *Small Group Research, 27,* 283–298.

Osborn, A. F. (1953). *Applied imagination.* New York: Scribner.

Pavitt, C., & Curtis, E. (1994). *Small group discussion: A theoretical approach* (2nd ed.). Scottsdale, AZ: Gorsuch Scarisbrick.

Phillips, J. D. (1948). Report on discussion 66. *Adult Education Journal, 7,* 181–182.

Poole, M. S. (1991). Procedures for managing meetings: Social and technological innovation. In R. A. Swenson & B. O. Knapp (Eds.), *Innovative meeting management* (pp. 53–109). Austin, TX: 3M Meeting Management Institute.

Price, K. H. (1985). Problem-solving strategies: A comparison by problem-solving phases. *Group & Organization Studies, 10,* 278–299.

Prince, G. M. (1970). *The practice of creativity.* New York: Macmillan.

Scheidel, T. M. (1986). Divergent and convergent thinking in group decision-making. In R. Y. Hirokawa & M. S. Poole (Eds.), *Communication and group decision-making* (pp. 113–130). Beverly Hills, CA: Sage.

Seibold, D. R., & Krikorian, D. H. (1997). Planning and facilitating group meetings. In L. R. Frey & J. K. Barge (Eds.), *Managing group life: Communicating in decision-making groups* (pp. 270–305). Boston: Houghton Mifflin.

Sunwolf. (2002). Getting to "groupaha!": Provoking creative processes in task groups. In L. R. Frey (Ed.), *New directions in group communication* (pp. 203–217). Thousand Oaks, CA: Sage.

Sunwolf, & Seibold, D. R. (1999). The impact of formal procedures on group processes, members, and task outcomes. In L. R. Frey (Ed.), D. S. Gouran, & M. S. Poole (Assoc. Eds.), *The handbook of group communication theory and research* (pp. 395–431). Thousand Oaks, CA: Sage.

Ulschak, F. L., Nathanson, L., & Gillan, P. G. (1981). *Small group problem solving: An aid to organizational effectiveness.* Reading, MA: Addison-Wesley.

Weaver, W. T., & Prince, G. M. (1990). Synectics: Its potential for education. *Phi Delta Kappan, 71,* 378–388.

Zorn, T. A., & Rosenfeld, L. B. (1989). Between a rock and a hard place: Ethical dilemma in problem-solving group facilitation. *Management Communication Quarterly, 3,* 93–106.

Development of Small Group Roles 8

After reading this chapter, you should be able to:

1. explain the functional approach to roles,
2. identify the three general propositions of roles,
3. differentiate among formal, informal, and deviant roles,
4. identify and describe the five informal roles, and
5. identify and describe several deviant role behaviors.

Case Study | After working as an administrator for the Taylor County Department of Human Services in a small town in the Midwest for 40 years, Chris Simpson decides to retire. Tom Harrison, agency director, forms a committee to plan a retirement party for Chris, and drawing from the diverse workforce, he selects Ted (Caucasian male, new hire) and other employees from each 5-year category of service. The members chosen include Yang (Asian male, 5 years), Alicia (African-American female, 10 years), Leo (Caucasian male, 15 years), and Lucille (Caucasian female, 20 years), whom Tom appoints as

Photo 8.1   A group activity, such as the members of a social group playing golf, can reveal how group members embrace roles and role behaviors.

Source: ©iStockphoto.com/robh.

chair because she worked with him for many years. The agency's budgeted monies and employee donations allow the committee a considerable amount of money to spend. The group meets for the first time two months before Chris's retirement date.

Lucille: I must admit I've never chaired a committee before, but I know Chris well, so that should be helpful. Does anyone have any ideas?

Yang: Well, I have lots of experience chairing committees, although I don't know Chris as well as the rest of you. But I do know that someone should be taking the minutes of the meetings so we can record our work. Who wants to do that? How about you, Leo?

Leo: Isn't that a woman's role? Being a secretary?

Alicia: Excuse me, Leo, but is that intended to be a sexist remark?

Lucille: Hold on, you two. I don't want to see you putting on boxing gloves!

Alicia: (humorously) I'm a terrible boxer! Why don't we rotate taking the minutes? I'll take them today, and then Leo will have a good idea of what is expected. He can take them the next meeting. In fact, I bet he'll love taking the minutes once he tries it.

Yang: That's a great idea, Alicia. Now, let's brainstorm ideas for the party.

Ted: Before we do that, Yang, let's talk about Chris. I haven't had much of an opportunity to interact with our honoree. I would like to know more about Chris as a person and an employee.

Leo: Chris is a stellar employee and loves golf. What more do we need to know? I have access to a country club; we could play golf and follow it with dinner and dancing.

Ted: That sounds good, Leo, but that idea may not work for all employees who want to attend. I don't play golf. How many of our employees do? And does Chris's family play golf?

Yang: Those are good points, Ted. Perhaps we should find out more about Chris so we have a better idea of the type of party to plan.

Ted: Then why don't we just ask Chris to plan the party? Why do we need a committee? This is a waste of time. My desk is overflowing with work.

Lucille: Come on, Ted. I see this committee as having a fun assignment. Once we know more about Chris, we can put our great minds together and plan the best retirement party this agency has ever seen. Chris deserves it.

Yang: Let's each talk to the people we work with about Chris and find out all we can and meet again tomorrow.

An important function in small groups is establishing group members' roles. Think of roles as different hats members wear during the life span of group life. How many different hats do you wear in a current group? How many roles are you willing to play in a group? The answers depend on the fact that role performance varies with each unique group experience. For example, in the case study Lucille behaves as the appointed leader, and Alicia attempts to relieve group tensions, exercising behaviors crucial to a group's communication as members work on the task and attend to member relations. Thus, making sure group members understand which roles and role behaviors are needed and how members competently can perform these roles factor in significantly to group success.

This chapter endeavors to examine roles in the small group setting. To do so, we will explain the functional approach to roles and identify the three general propositions of roles. Then, we will differentiate among formal, informal, and deviant roles, with a specific focus on identifying and describing the five informal roles needed in any group. Finally, we will address deviant role behaviors, which serve as barriers to group success because deviant role behaviors create tension in the group and may even prevent the group from moving forward on tasks and maintaining relationships.

Functional Approach to Roles

Before learning about formal, informal, and deviant roles, we first must explain why a functional approach provides a useful foundation for understanding roles and role behaviors. Group scholars Dennis Gouran and Randy Hirokawa (1983) described groups as social systems with particular goals of making a decision or solving a problem. In other words, group members must perform certain functions to reach goals. Thus, a **functional approach to small groups** focuses on the communicative behaviors used by group members during group meetings. When group members communicate with each other, their communicative behaviors emerge in the form of statements (Yang: "Perhaps we should find out more about Chris so we have a better idea of the type of party to plan") that become the necessary functions that enable the group to reach its goals. Positive statements direct the group's discussion toward goal attainment; negative statements prevent the group from attaining their goals.

Consider two things when defining the word *role*. In keeping with the functional approach described above, group scholars Kenneth Benne and Paul Sheats (1948) suggested the communicative statements group members make during the group's discussion send messages to the other group members about who they are and what function in the group they serve. Benne and Sheats considered roles functional, which means roles include the speaker (e.g., Lucille, the appointed leader, appearing to lead the group) and the speech (e.g., Lucille's statement, "I see this committee as having a fun assignment").

Another way to define roles is to look at them as assignments. Steven Beebe and John Masterson (2003) suggested as group members engage in communication to reduce uncertainty about group work, they simultaneously evaluate the communicative behaviors of the other members. Based on these assessments, group members develop expectations for behaviors that each member is supposed to perform and, in essence, group members assign roles to each other. Furthermore, you harbor expectations for your own behaviors that help determine how you will communicate and behave in the group. For example, in the case study, Yang has leadership experience and feels he could lead the group. An individual who wants to lead a group will view himself or herself in that role, engage in leader-like communicative behaviors, and actually perform as a leader (i.e., keep the group on task).

Think of a role as a repeatable pattern of communicative behaviors that group members come to expect from each other. Group members base these expectations on their perceptions of themselves and other members that emerge during the process of group discussion.

Now that we have arrived at a definition, let's examine the general propositions of roles.

General Propositions of Roles

Three general propositions of roles may affect whether and how group members play a particular role. First, roles are learned behaviors. Whether members embody assigned roles (e.g., organizational supervisor, data entry operator, or receptionist) or roles that emerge though the group process, they must learn appropriate role behaviors. Distinguished group scholar Ernest Bormann (1990) offered that when a member knows what part he or she will play and what is expected, the member "has assumed a role" (p. 161). Thus, roles are learned behaviors. Group members learn by observing what other group members say and do. When new members enter established groups, they learn about roles by communicating with established group members who know the task, as well as by observing members' behaviors. If the group very recently formed, members must draw upon their lessons from belonging to other groups about communication and role behaviors.

The second general proposition is that self-concept affects role behavior. Although each individual plays an important part in group work by assuming various roles, the group, in turn, also influences each member in important ways. As group scholar Joann Keyton (2002) noted, "You are who you are in groups" (p. 98). This means that the group helps each member establish an identity. Through interactions with others, you learn what interests and skills you possess. Suppose you join Public Relations Student Society of America (PRSSA), a pre-professional organization for college students interested in public relations as a career choice. When a classmate asks what activities you participate in, you may describe yourself as a student leader of PRSSA. In turn, the members of PRSSA confirm and support your behaviors as a leader.

Other facets of self-concept include an outgrowth of cultural background and gender. Perhaps your cultural background does not encourage women to argue or engage in decision-making activities. Through group members' communicative influences and encouragement, you may find yourself more willing to communicate and argue issues. You also may have expectations for your behavior in groups, which may contradict with your actual contributions to the group. Sometimes, you consider your ideas or skills the best when, in fact, the group may choose other members' ideas or other members' skills surpass yours. As such, you may have to learn to adjust your view of self.

The third general proposition is that we play multiple roles simultaneously. In Chapter 2, we described five phases of the socialization process that members move through while working on the task and building relationships. We can assume safely, then, that different phases of the socialization process and group communication in general need different roles. Thus, groups may need multiple roles as they develop. For example, in the encounter phase of socialization when members first come together, they get to know one another and may not need a member to manage conflict. Conversely, in the assimilation phase when members establish a group culture, they may need a member to manage conflicts that arise over differences of opinions.

Although scholars know that group success depends on certain roles being played in each small group setting, Kenneth Benne and Paul Sheats (1948) suggested group members should not limit themselves by assuming only one or two roles. This type of limiting behavior by members, referred to as **role rigidity**, occurs when members do not play a variety of roles. Groups are less likely to succeed when their group structure sanctions role rigidity. When members assume multiple role positions, they permit the effective utilization of each member's strengths and talents.

Role conflict occurs when two or more members vie for the same role. Suppose the group contains no appointed leader. You want to be the leader because you are a high Mach and motivated to communicate for control whereas another member wants to be the leader because of his prior leadership experience. Communication among group members can get quite heated as each member tries to "win" by persuading the other members to choose him. This type of role competition likely causes tension among the group members because they ultimately must make a choice.

> **?** In your work group, have you experienced either role conflict or role strain? What impact did this have on your group performance?

Role strain occurs when the group requires members to assume a new role and they feel reluctant, at least initially, to do so. For example, you may be asked to assume the leadership role if the present leader resigns. In these instances, members must anticipate playing new roles and learn how to behave in new ways (Moreland & Levine, 1984). Additionally, at times, members will exit a group and new members will enter. This change in group composition can create role strain because the members not only must socialize the new members; they must adapt and adjust to the new members as well.

Role Development

So how does a group member learn to play a particular role? According to researchers, a member can learn to play a role in two primary ways.

The first way is to engage in information seeking. Communication in groups comprises what members say, how they say it, and to whom they say it. By asking questions and observing their own group as well as other small groups, group members seek information as one way to learn about their roles (Lester, 1987). Learning how to perform group role behaviors often comes from direct information obtained from other group members, people outside the group, friends, and family. Additionally, we gain insight and learn about role development by taking classes in small group communication and reading books that provide informative tips about the roles members play in groups.

The second way is to solicit feedback. In one sense, feedback comprises the other half of information seeking. Feedback, the response a listener gives to a speaker about the speaker's behavior (Ogilvie & Haslett, 1985), provides information about individual role behaviors, provides support or encouragement from other members, and evaluates member and group performance (Ashford, 1986). Effective feedback also serves as a means of motivation or incentive to perform well (Quaglieri, 1980) and describes, rather than evaluates, a group member's behavior (Harris, 1988).

Feedback can be positive, negative, or ambiguous. Positive feedback helps group members distinguish between typical and optimal behavior concerning task

Photo 8.2   Feedback never should be delivered to group members in an inappropriate manner.

Source: ©iStockphoto.com/lisegagne.

performance and relationship building, reinforcing the idea that the behavior should continue. Over time, the behavior becomes patterned and continues to improve as the group process develops. In a review of literature on feedback, group scholar Beatrice Schultz (1999) reported positive feedback about task accomplishments improves group task performance. Group communication scholars Sean Limon and Franklin Boster (2003) found that when task groups receive positive feedback, the group members perceive their group as having greater task competencies and prestige than task groups whose group members receive negative feedback. Equally, positive feedback strengthens the relational aspects leading to group cohesion and member satisfaction, in part because positive feedback is considered more accurate, easier to provide, more credible, and more desirable than negative feedback (Martin & Jacobs, 1980). As demonstrated in the case study, Lucille supports the idea that group members should find out all about Chris and then attempts to build cohesion in the group by suggesting they "plan the best retirement party this agency has ever seen."

> **Ethically Speaking:** Should a group permit a member to continue engaging in behaviors the other members don't expect, appreciate, think are appropriate, or even like? What steps should the members take to combat these behaviors?

Negative feedback helps group members identify weaknesses and make improvements. Sometimes members give negative feedback concerning role behaviors because they want the member to stop the behavior. Suppose the group leader behaves in a bossy manner, and the members, considering that style group inappropriate, tell the leader they don't like it. One of two things will happen: The behavior will continue, or the behavior will stop.

According to Abran Salazar (1996), negative role behavior continues if the behavior provides "utility value to the group and [is] perceived as such" (p. 493). Perhaps the bossy leader has powerful upward influence with top management that helps the group attain valuable resources it needs to succeed. Conversely, if the negative behavior provides no utility value, the group members will continue to give negative feedback with the hope the behavior will change or stop eventually. On the downside, when task groups receive negative feedback, group members perceive each other as engaging in higher amounts of social loafing (Limon & Boster, 2003).

Ambiguous feedback, neither positive nor negative, offers little information to the group member. In fact, ambiguous feedback can dishearten any member attempting to learn a new role, perform a difficult role, or assume multiple roles because of its lack of direction. Because one goal of feedback is role clarity (Nadler, 1979), feedback that accomplishes no role clarity leaves a member in a bind with unanswered questions, such as "How should I act?" and "Where do I go for information?" For example, if someone quits your work group and no one knows exactly what that person did or how he completed his tasks, the new member assuming his role may receive a variety of messages from other members on how he should perform. When confronted with this type of uncertainty, members must seek additional information, suffer through trial and error efforts, and/or learn the "ropes" as best they can. Obstacles to role performance, such as lack of information, take time to overcome.

In sum, teachers and trainers of small groups cannot stress enough the value and importance of constructive positive or negative feedback that contributes to group performance. As Ernest Bormann (1990) stated, feedback as honest feelings expressed from one member to another or to the group as a whole contributes to relationship building and satisfaction among group members. Group success, then, depends on the competent communicative skills of giving and receiving feedback.

Types of Roles

In any group, roles can be classified into three types: formal roles, informal roles, and deviant roles.

Formal Roles

Formal roles describe specific role positions assigned to one group member through appointment or election as part of the group's structure. Fast-food restaurants, for example, contain layers of such appointed formal roles as manager, supervisor, and crew leader. Legitimate formal roles carry certain powers to act in performing the requirements established for each role position. Furthermore, group members should acknowledge and respect such formal role positions as manager. Note in the case study that although Lucille is the formal leader, Yang is willing to help her fulfill that role by engaging in leadership behaviors.

In general, group scholars agree all types of formal groups, including those charged with making decisions or solving problems, are better served with the establishment or assignment of three formal roles in the group (Cragan & Wright, 1999; Keyton, 1999; Pavitt & Curtis, 1994). These formal roles—leader, recorder, and critical advisor—center on keeping the group on the task and moving toward goal achievement.

In the first formal role, the leader must move the group toward its goals and convince external audiences the group is achieving or has achieved its goals. Experts often view the leader role as complex due to its association with the ideas

Photo 8.3   Group members should alternate playing the role of recorder so each member can develop the skills necessary to perform this formal role.

Source: ©iStockphoto.com/lijlexmom.

of legitimate power for acting as leader (e.g., "I'm the boss"). Group members are expected to respect the position and person. Sometimes we do not like the leader as a person but accept his or her ability to lead; sometimes we like the leader as a person but disagree with his or her ability to lead. In one sense, no other role position carries as much weight in terms of both external and internal influences and evaluations.

According to John Cragan and David Wright (1999), the second formal role, recorder, is the only role "in which one communication behavior completely defines the role" (p. 194). The recorder takes the minutes of meetings and records any other actions of the group that need to be stored as permanent records. The recorder position often carries with it such specific duties as typing the agenda, making arrangements for group meetings, making sure members receive copies of minutes of the meeting, and sending pertinent information to prepare for the next meeting. Unless a definite term (e.g., 1 year) exists for this position, group members should rotate the role. Especially in classroom groups, this allows each member to develop the skills necessary to perform this needed function.

The third formal role, critical advisor, sometimes is referred to as the devil's advocate. The critical advisor challenges group members' ideas in a constructive manner. Ted plays this role in the case study by challenging Leo's idea. A critical advisor forces group members to think through the steps to decision making and weigh the positive and negative consequences of each option or solution under consideration. Because the critical advisor role can carry a negative connotation if always enacted by the same individual, group members also should rotate this role. By practicing being a critic, each group member learns to develop the skill of analyzing the benefits and consequences of group action before making decisions.

Keep in mind not all members who play the roles of leader, recorder, or critical advisor perform these roles competently. Equally, some members holding these role positions leave the group, become ill, or simply lose interest and perform the least amount of work possible, forcing the remaining group members to remove the obstacles confronting them by assuming these formal roles and working around the nonperformers.

In addition to these formal roles, informal group roles contribute to group success.

Informal Roles

In an historic study, Kenneth Benne and Paul Sheats (1948) observed and labeled a multitude of informal roles found to exist in small groups. Benne and Sheats also discovered that more than one member performed each informal role. An informal role emerges through group member interaction. In essence, any group member with the appropriate communicative and group skills often communicates in such a manner to fulfill the role function. Although most scholars agree not all small groups need a multitude of informal roles in order to succeed, several important informal roles must be played. In this section, we share with you these opinions about informal roles and how these informal roles contribute to group success. You and your group members can decide their relevance for your group's needs.

According to group communication scholars John Cragan and David Wright (1999), small groups need a minimum of five critical roles: task leader, social-emotional leader, information provider, central negative, and tension releaser. Notice when discussing informal roles, the role of leader divides into the two dimensions of small group work: task and relationships.

The task leader (who may or may not be the formal leader) typifies a *take-charge* group member with excellent technical skills and problem-solving abilities. The task leader must communicate competently in that she puts the rest of the group members at ease when confronting the processes of working on the group's task. Also, importantly, the task leader assumes the responsibility of making sure the group's discussion moves along on the task. In the case study, Yang performs this role by keeping the group on the task track. Because a group is expected to produce and complete its task in a timely manner, the task leader devotes her energies toward the group's goal attainment.

The social-emotional leader helps other group members maintain mutual respect for each other, promotes empathic listening, offers support for all members' ideas, and ensures that the self-worth of each member remains intact. Lucille performs this role in the case study. Consider the social-emotional leader role as the role concerned with the building and maintenance of group member relationships. When group members emerge from a satisfying group experience, they usually trace their satisfaction to the competent interpersonal care of the social-emotional leader. As such, and not surprisingly, group members like the social-emotional leader immensely, if not more than any other member in the group.

The information provider exercises the ability to synthesize information. In this role, the member contributes information in the form of facts, statistics, examples, and quotations. Additionally, in the technological world of today, the information provider may demonstrate competency in seeking relevant information on the Internet. Although the information provider is generally adept at finding information for, and providing information to, the group, the information provider may resist playing this role if he feels the group does not appreciate his efforts.

The central negative group member challenges the group's decisions. According to John Cragan and David Wright (1999), the member who plays this role feels unhappy with the group processes or group work and often tries to challenge the leader. The central negative—for example, the case study's Ted—may have similar characteristics as the task leader and therefore voice the loudest and strongest criticisms against the group's path. In one respect, the central negative often forces the group to think in different ways; in another respect, this role can result in blocking the group's progress toward goals as members strive to defend their stance on an issue.

The tension releaser, using light humor strategically, eases tensions in the group that may arise over role conflicts, personality clashes, or problems with the decision-making process associated with the task. Though thought of as friendly and funny, the member playing the tension releaser role need not be a comedian. Stories and jokes may be appropriate for the context surrounding the tension, but sometimes they may not. In small groups, humor serves to bring smiles or laughter to the members as a way of getting them to reexamine the communicative events surrounding the cause of the tension. In the case study, Alicia plays this role when she jokes about her lacking boxing skills.

> **?** In your work group, which informal role do you play? How does this role help your group? How does this role hinder your group?

Deviant Roles

Another category of informal roles falls under the negative and disruptive individual roles identified by Benne and Sheats (1948). These negative roles, referred to as deviant roles, destroy the group's productivity and success because the communicative focus centers on an individual member rather than on the best thing for the group. Group communication, thus, does not help the group make

Table 8.1   Deviant Roles

Role	*Description*
Airhead	Purposely acts stupid so other members will complete task
Aggressor	Attacks other members or the task
Blocker	Interferes with the group process by disagreeing frequently
Clown	Makes a fool of herself by acting dumb or saying stupid things
Dominator	Monopolizes group time and tries to show superiority
Egghead	Acts as if he is smarter than other members
Recognition seeker	Seeks attention by boasting
Self-confessor	Expresses personal feelings unrelated to group's goal
Special pleader	Introduces irrelevant information and supports it
Whiner	Complains about having to participate in group task

Source: Based on Benne, K., & Sheats, P. (1948). Functional roles of group members. *Journal of Social Issues, 4,* 41–49.

progress on its task or meet the relational needs of its members. Examine the list of deviant role behaviors identified by Benne and Sheats (1948) in Table 8.1. How many of these roles have you played at some point in your work groups?

When a member consistently engages in a deviant behavior or several deviant behaviors (e.g., whiner ["I don't want to do that"] or aggressor ["That was my idea. You stole it, you creep"]), the other members must decide what to do about the difficult member. They can delay doing anything, which includes ignoring the deviant behaviors in the hope that the member will stop them and learn what is or is not appropriate communication. If the person does not

> **?** In your work group, have you had to fire a member due to the member playing a deviant role? What tactics did your group members try to use to get that member to assimilate into the group? How was the tension handled?

"get it," the group members may resort to persuasive tactics, criticism, or verbal aggressiveness. As a last resort, the group may need to "fire" the member. Often, less competent communicators lack the appropriate group skills for effective communication in groups, resulting in their being fired as members.

A Final Note About Small Group Roles

To play the appropriate role for your group, remain flexible. **Role flexibility** refers to possessing the skills and abilities needed to engage in a variety of group member roles (Benne & Sheats, 1948). To maximize your role flexibility, it is essential that you (a) resist role rigidity, (b) place group goals above your own goals, and (c) identify how you can contribute to playing **group task roles** (i.e., roles that facilitate group movement toward task accomplishment) and **group building and maintenance roles** (i.e., roles that strengthen the group's collective bond). Refer to the list of these task roles and building and maintenance roles identified by Benne and Sheats (1948) in Table 8.2. The next time your learning or work groups meet,

Table 8.2 Task Roles [T] and Building and Maintenance Roles [BM]

Role	*Description*
Compromiser	Offers or accepts compromises [BM]
Elaborator	Supports suggestions through examples or evidence [T]
Encourager	Speaks positively to members and accepts their ideas [BM]
Energizer	Motivates the members to act [T]
Follower	Accepts members' ideas and goes along with group [BM]
Harmonizer	Reduces tension associated with conflict [BM]
Information giver	Offers relevant facts or draws upon personal experiences [T]
Information seeker	Requests facts and clarification [T]
Initiator	Defines the problem, proposes solutions, and offers ideas [T]
Interpreter	Paraphrases what members have said [BM]
Opinion giver	Offers feelings about suggestions and options [T]
Opinion seeker	Asks for members' feelings about task [T]
Orientor	Keeps group on task [T]

Source: Based on Benne, K., & Sheats, P. (1948). Functional roles of group members. *Journal of Social Issues, 4,* 41–49.

think about how the group's performance could be enhanced if members engaged in these roles in addition to both the formal and the informal roles already in place.

Conclusion

This chapter examined roles in the small group. To do so, we explained the functional approach to roles and identified the three general propositions of roles. We then differentiated among formal, informal, and deviant roles, with a specific focus on the identification and description of the five informal roles needed in any group. Finally, we addressed deviant role behaviors. With knowledge of how groups work and the importance of training in small groups, members most likely will perform the necessary formal and informal roles needed for group success. This notion also applies to the next chapter, which explores the role of leadership in small groups.

Discussion Questions

1. Which role definition—functional approach or assigned roles—best describes the behaviors in your prior group experiences? Why?

2. Refer to Chapter 3 on traits. Which communication and personality traits do you think are necessary for a group member to assume any of the three formal roles? Which communication and personality traits do you think are necessary for a group member to assume any of the five informal roles?

3. Refer to the descriptions of the five informal roles. In light of a group's dependence on technology, how might these descriptions change?

4. In this chapter, we listed several deviant roles that disrupt the group's progress. What rules would you establish for handling group members who engage in these roles?

5. Choose a work group in which you have played (or still play) a formal role. How did you learn this role? How has this role affected your beliefs about yourself?

References

Ashford, S. J. (1986). Feedback-seeking in individual adaptation: A resource perspective. *Academy of Management Journal, 29,* 465–487.

Beebe, S. A., & Masterson, J. T. (2003). *Communicating in small groups: Principles and practices* (7th ed.). Boston: Allyn & Bacon.

Benne, K., & Sheats, P. (1948). Functional roles of group members. *Journal of Social Issues, 4,* 41–49.

Bormann, E. G. (1990). *Communicating in small groups: Theory and practice* (5th ed.). New York: Harper & Row.

Cragan, J. F., & Wright, D. W. (1999). *Communication in small groups: Theory, process, skills* (5th ed.). Belmont, CA: Wadsworth.

Gouran, D. S., & Hirokawa, R. Y. (1983). The role of communication in decision-making groups: A functional perspective. In M. S. Mander (Ed.), *Communications in transition: Issues and debates in current research* (pp. 168–185). New York: Praeger.

Harris, T. E. (1988). Mastering the art of talking back. *Management World, 17*(3), 9–11.

Keyton, J. (1999). *Group communication: Process and analysis.* Mountain View, CA: Mayfield.

Keyton, J. (2002). *Communicating in groups: Building relationships for effective decision making* (2nd ed.). Boston: McGraw-Hill.

Lester, R. E. (1987). Organizational culture, uncertainty reduction, and the socialization of new organizational members. In S. Thomas (Ed.), *Culture and communication: Methodology, behavior, artifacts, and institutions: Selected proceedings from the Fifth International Conference on Culture and Communication* (pp. 105–113). Norwood, NJ: Ablex.

Limon, M. S., & Boster, F. J. (2003). The effects of performance feedback on group members' perceptions of prestige, task competencies, group belonging, and loafing. *Communication Research Reports, 20,* 13–23.

Martin, L., & Jacobs, M. (1980). Structured feedback delivered in small groups. *Small Group Behavior, 11,* 88–107.

Moreland, R. L., & Levine, J. M. (1984). Role transition in small groups. In V. L. Allen & E. Van de Vliert (Eds.), *Role transitions: Exploration and explanations* (pp. 181–195). New York: Plenum.

Nadler, D. A. (1979). The effects of feedback on task group behavior: A review of the experimental research. *Organizational Behavior and Human Performance, 23,* 309–338.

Ogilvie, J. R., & Haslett, B. (1985). Communicating peer feedback in a task group. *Human Communication Research, 12,* 79–98.

Pavitt, C., & Curtis, E. (1994). *Small group discussion: A theoretical approach* (2nd ed.). Scottsdale, AZ: Gorsuch Scarisbrick.

Quaglieri, P. L. (1980). Feedback on feedback. *Supervisory Management, 25*(1), 34–39.

Salazar, A. J. (1996). An analysis of the development and evolution of roles in the small group. *Small Group Research, 27,* 475–503.

Schultz, B. G. (1999). Improving group communication performance: An overview of diagnosis and intervention. In L. R. Frey (Ed.), D. S. Gouran, & M. S. Poole (Assoc. Eds.), *The handbook of group communication theory & practice* (pp. 371–394). Thousand Oaks, CA: Sage.

Approaches to Small Group Leadership | 9

After reading this chapter, you should be able to:

1. define leadership from a communication perspective,
2. distinguish between being a leader and sharing leadership,
3. identify and explain the classic approaches to leadership,
4. identify and explain the popular communication approaches to leadership, and
5. identify several guidelines for enhancing leadership competence.

Case Study

Professor Pat Howley was just appointed chair of the Department of Communication Studies at a midsize college in the Midwest. Dr. Howley, the senior member of the department, taught communication theory classes and has conducted research for over 20 years. The students and staff generally describe Dr. Howley as highly intelligent and somewhat friendly. Of the seven faculty members, including Dr. Howley, four have been hired

Photo 9.1   A group member who engages in shared leadership uses verbal and nonverbal behaviors that are appropriate given the task, the situation, and the group members.

Source: ©iStockphoto.com/diane39.

within the last three years due to retirements and college expansions. Dr. Kim Soo, a recent PhD graduate, specializes in intercultural communication. Dr. Pierre Rogert teaches the mass media courses and continues to gain scholarly recognition as an expert in radio and print media. Dr. Carolyn Andrews is a nontraditional PhD graduate with a history of business and leadership experiences as well as specialties in group and organizational communication. Dr. Harvey Rue left his previous public relations teaching position to join the staff. Drs. Faith Hall and Christopher Mofit are rhetorical communication scholars who have been ranked as distinguished faculty members for 20 and 19 years, respectively. Dr. Howley calls a faculty meeting to order on Friday the first week of classes.

Dr. Howley: Good afternoon, everyone. I welcome Dr. Harvey Rue to our department. The first order of business on the agenda is to discuss our financial needs for the coming academic term. We lost $25,000 of our state funding and must cut our operating budget.

Dr. Andrews:	Perhaps we could put our minds together and raise the monies from our alumni or business community partners. I would hate to see us take away from faculty development and growth by not funding such items as travel. The faculty needs to stay updated on teaching and research.
Dr. Rue:	I think that is a splendid idea. We did that at my last position, and it was successful for us. We need to be resourceful.
Dr. Hall:	Quite frankly, I think we need to consider the students first. After all, they pay the bills. Let's not cut from them by raising lab or computer fees. This budget cutting is so stressful.
Dr. Andrews:	I agree with you, Dr. Hall, but I wasn't suggesting we take from the students. The students are our top priority. I just think if we have the enthusiasm and self-confidence, we can raise the monies we need. I'm excited about the idea.
Dr. Howley:	I don't think the administration will go along. They like to contact possible donors. The administration handed down this directive to cut the budget, and we must comply.
Dr. Mofit:	In the years I've been here, I have never seen alumni donate anything. Personally, I don't like the idea of fundraising.
Dr. Rogert:	But we haven't tried it before. Perhaps we should entertain Dr. Andrews's idea.
Dr. Andrews:	Dr. Soo, what do you think?
Dr. Soo:	I am not a tenured faculty member yet, so I cannot afford to attend conventions and conduct research without financial support.
Dr. Howley:	Well, we can't please everyone here. I have made a list of possible cuts, and faculty needs are last.
Dr. Andrews:	Perhaps we could approach the administration and get their ideas about fundraising. I'd be happy to oversee this project.
Dr. Howley:	I don't see how it will work. Besides, it has never been done before.
Dr. Rue:	Perhaps we should give it a shot.
Dr. Rogert:	I think if anyone can convince the administration, Dr. Andrews can. She is assertive, persuasive, and knowledgeable and seems popular with the administration and students; plus, she has a business background.

Dr. Soo: I don't care where the money comes from. I just need support from the college to conduct my research.

Dr. Andrews: I agree. The faculty members should be supported in their research and teaching. Like I said before, I'm willing to tackle the problem.

Dr. Howley: And, as I said before, I don't like the idea. As chair, I have pre- pared a list of budget-cut items, and faculty travel is one of them. Please study the list and e-mail me your comments.

Dr. Rue: I would like to see Dr. Andrews make a few telephone calls con- cerning the fundraising idea. Would that be possible?

Dr. Howley: It's an unrealistic idea.

Dr. Andrews: That may be true, but I think we should give it a shot.

As discussed in the previous chapter, one necessary group role is leader. This chapter purports to dis- cuss what we know about leaders and leadership behaviors. Remember, though, that in a small group, the leader is also a group member, and this dual role requires communication competence in both areas.

This chapter aims to identify leadership behaviors that any group member can learn and display as part of his or her competent commu- nication. To do so, we will define leadership from a communication perspective, distinguish between being a leader and sharing leadership, trace classic approaches to leadership, and present popular communication approaches to leadership. Finally, we will offer several guidelines for enhancing leadership competence.

Being a Leader Versus Sharing Leadership

It is essential to understand who leaders are, what they think, how they talk, how they act, and what they feel. Northouse (2007) defined leadership as "a process whereby an individual influences a group of individuals to achieve a common goal" (p. 3). From another perspective, leadership and communication experts Michael Hackman and Craig Johnson (2004) pointed to leadership as a unique form of communicative behavior. In this respect, they identified three themes that run through most definitions of leadership. The first theme surrounds the idea of persuasive influence. In the case study, Dr. Andrews persuades the group members to agree to the idea of raising funds from alumni and the business community. In this instance, she is not the appointed leader, but she enacts a leadership behavior. The second theme anchors leadership in the group context, suggesting the group leader helps the group set goals, build and maintain relationships, and complete tasks. The third theme concerns the relationship between the leader and individual group members. In this sense, the leader and the group members collaborate by working together to meet the needs of the group. A leader cannot lead if he or she does not have followers with similar goals.

Yet, there exists a difference between being a leader and sharing leadership. A characteristic of the leader role depends on whether the leader is appointed or shares leadership with group members. An **appointed leader** assumes the role responsibility of controlling and directing the group. Researchers have found appointed leaders tend to be more leader-centered than group-centered. In the case study, Dr. Howley well exemplifies a leader-centered leader by expecting the group to follow the course of action put before them. The role position of an appointed leader can be appropriate for some groups. For example, a large group will need more structure than a small group. Another reason to appoint a leader stems from time constraints, with the appointed leader having more control of the group's activities (Cragan & Wright, 1999). Although appointed leaders have been perceived as more efficient and effective than group-centered leaders, group members tend to feel happier with group-centered leaders (Wischmeier, 1955). An **elected leader** enters a negotiated position. After careful discussion, the group elects one member as its leader. This type of leader is more likely to be group-centered because the members negotiated for the position and voted on the person of their choice (Wischmeier, 1955).

Examine shared leadership from two views. One view suggests the member with competence in the task or relational area assumes the leader role, with leadership becoming a shared function among members. Leaderless groups often function this way. This type of leadership applies to teams and work groups in organizations because it suggests one leader need not possess the skills required in both areas (i.e., task and relational). The flexibility of sharing leadership permits the most competent group member(s) to assume the role when needed. Shared leadership not unusually rotates among group members over the life span of a task (Kramer, 2006).

A second view suggests shared leadership emerges from any interested and talented group member (O'Hair & Wiemann, 2004). As demonstrated in the case study, Dr. Andrews offers a creative and original idea (i.e., raising funds) as well as communicates confirmation of Dr. Hall's position before presenting an opposite view—excellent examples of engaging in shared leadership behaviors, or the behaviors any group member can enact to demonstrate leadership. These behaviors include encouraging member participation, monitoring group progress toward the group task, promoting diversity of member opinion, building consensus, and engaging in effective communicative behaviors (Galanes, 2003). In the case study, Dr. Andrews demonstrates such other shared leadership behaviors as assertiveness, resourcefulness, and self-confidence. This acknowledgement reinforces the idea that some group members perceive Dr. Andrews as acting like a leader.

> **?** How does your work group engage in shared leadership behaviors? How are these behaviors linked to group success?

Thus, whether a leader is an appointed leader, an elected leader, or part of shared leadership, competent communication becomes a critical issue primarily with regard to group success. Researchers have noted leaders must attend to tasks and the building of group relations. Furthermore, any group member competent in communicating can enact leadership behaviors (Barge & Hirokawa, 1989).

We now turn our attention to discussing classic and popular communication approaches to leadership. These approaches have served as a foundation for the principles surrounding the phenomenon of leaders and leadership in small groups.

Classic Leadership Approaches

Though several classic approaches to leadership (Barge, 1997) exist, we will focus specifically on three approaches: the trait approach, the style approach, and the situational approach.

Trait Approach to Leadership

Historically, the trait approach to leadership research began in the 1920s when researchers sought to identify characteristics that set a certain individual or leader apart from another individual or nonleader. This approach, sometimes called the "Great Man Theory of Leadership," refers to those unique individuals considered born leaders (Kippenberger, 2002). Generally, the trait approach to leadership centers on the idea that people inherently possess characteristics that distinguish them as either a leader or a follower (Geier, 1967).

Photo 9.2   The trait approach to leadership is based on the idea that certain characteristics, such as physical traits, distinguish a leader from a follower.

Source: ©iStockphoto.com/jhorrocks.

An initial attempt to determine which traits make good leaders identified physical traits, personality traits, communicative behaviors, and social skills. Physical traits comprise such characteristics as height (e.g., tall versus short), weight (e.g., heavy versus thin), and personal appearance (e.g., attractive versus unattractive). According to speculations based on the attempt, a short, stocky man with an ugly nose does not possess the physical traits of a leader. Group specialists Charles Pavitt and Ellen Curtis (1994) noted researchers have found attractive group members receive more attention from other group members and impact decision making to a greater extent than less attractive group members. According to the trait approach, the attractive group members would be viewed as more likely to have leadership potential.

Scholars also thought of personality traits as key factors. For example, if you recall the traits discussed in Chapter 3, group members who are high in Machiavellianism, are high self-monitors, and have self-esteem more likely will emerge as leaders. Suppose the same short, stocky man with an ugly nose was also low in Machiavellianism, was a low self-monitor, and had little self-esteem. Here again, trait researchers would speculate this individual would not make a good leader.

Some examples of communicative behaviors, also thought of as important, include communication apprehension (Hawkins & Stewart, 1991) and argumentativeness (Schultz, 1982); some examples of social skills, additionally important, include sociability (i.e., a person's degree of pleasantness and agreeableness) and social sensitivity (e.g., a person responds to the needs of others). Additionally, a group member with a strong command of her verbal and nonverbal communicative behaviors is thought to have greater leadership ability. In the case study, Dr. Howley does not demonstrate effective communicative behaviors or social skills, which could impact whether (and how) the faculty members consider their department chair to act as a leader.

Numerous studies have examined the trait approach to leadership. Social psychologist Ralph Stogdill (1948, 1974) conducted two reviews to determine the consistency of these studies' findings. His first review produced for the most part inconsistent findings. In his second review, he reported somewhat better findings in that a few traits emerged as predictors of leadership, such as intelligence and sociability. In the end, however, he offered that traits alone might not fully explain the makeup of a good leader, although recent research has found that intelligence and dominance positively relate to perceptions of leadership (Lord, De Vader, & Alliger, 1986). Thus, some researchers began to pay less attention to the trait approach and investigated other factors associated with leadership, such as the factors that might influence the "way" leaders lead.

> **?**
> Make a list of the traits that best describe the person you perceive as the leader of your work group. How similar are these traits to your traits or the traits of the other group members?

Style Approach to Leadership

The way leaders lead, sometimes referred to as the style approach to leadership, emerged from the idea that the method or style a leader uses to lead followers determines success or failure of the leader and the group. This approach provides a framework for assessing leadership behaviors from both a task and a relationship dimension. Generally, the **style approach to leadership** stems from the idea that leaders display different styles, which then differently impact group outcomes (White & Lippitt, 1960). The secret to successful leadership involves balancing these styles by employing appropriate communicative behaviors (Hackman & Johnson, 2004).

In a landmark study, social psychologists Kurt Lewin, Ronald Lippitt, and Ralph K. White (1939) tested three leadership styles: democratic, autocratic, and laissez faire. A leader who uses a **democratic style** believes group members should be involved in the decision-making or problem-solving process. This leader asks for member input, offers suggestions, helps the group set rules and regulations, displays a nonjudgmental stance, solicits interaction from nonparticipating members, and maintains relationships with all members (O'Hair & Wiemann, 2004). A leader with a democratic style possesses a "people orientation," meaning the leader treats group members as equals by sharing both the rewards achieved and the punishments received by the group (Rosenfeld & Plax, 1975).

A leader who uses an **autocratic style** believes group members need controlling. This leader is more likely to give orders, set policies for the group, criticize members' ideas, and control the decision-making or problem-solving process by not soliciting members' opinions or ideas (O'Hair & Wiemann, 2004). A leader with an autocratic style possesses an "object orientation," meaning the leader fails to consider the feelings of group members and does not treat group members as people (Rosenfeld & Plax, 1975). Additionally, a leader with an autocratic style may be characterized as aggressive, revengeful, and expressing a strong desire to be recognized as an authority figure (Rosenfeld & Fowler, 1976).

A leader who uses a **laissez faire style** believes group members should function independently, with little direction or personal involvement by the leader. This leader only participates in the group process if the group has arrived at a standstill or requested his assistance. Once the group resolves the issue, the laissez faire leader lets the group return to its independent status.

Not surprisingly, the style used by a leader affects the communication that occurs in a group. Examine Table 9.1, which lists five ways communication differs among the democratic, autocratic, and laissez faire styles of leadership (Hackman & Johnson, 2004).

At the same time, the three leadership styles differ in their perceived communicator style attributes as defined in Chapter 3. Democratic leaders perceivably use the relaxed, animated, attentive, and friendly communicator style attributes; autocratic leaders perceivably use the dominant communicator style attribute; and laissez faire leaders perceivably use the relaxed, attentive, and friendly communicator style attributes (Bradley & Baird, 1977).

It is important to note each style's merits depend on the situation, the group composition, and time constraints. For example, if group members must leave the group with feelings of satisfaction, the democratic style might be the best style to employ (Foels, Driskell, Mullen, & Salas, 2000). On the other hand, if a group desires efficiency, the autocratic style might be the better style to use. Complete the Leadership Questionnaire on page 169 to assess your style.

Situational Approach to Leadership

The **situational approach to leadership** rests on the idea that leadership behavior depends on situational variations. This approach first became popular in organizational

Table 9.1   Communication Differences Among Leadership Styles

Democratic	Autocratic	Laissez-faire
Engages in two-way, open communication	Engages primarily in one-way, downward communication	Engages in noncommitted, superficial talk
Focuses on interaction	Dominates interaction	Avoids interaction
Provides frequent positive feedback	Provides infrequent positive feedback	Provides infrequent feedback of any kind
Uses effective listening skills	Uses poor listening skills	May use either effective or poor listening skills
Mediates conflict for group gain	Uses conflict for personal gain	Avoids conflict

Source: Reprinted by permission of Waveland Press, Inc. from M. Z. Hackman & C. E. Johnson, *Leadership: A communication perspective* (4th ed.). (Long Grove, IL: Waveland Press, Inc., 2004). All rights reserved.

communication research of leaders and their relationships with workers (i.e., employees). A central idea of this approach holds that effective leading requires different strategies, depending on the type of worker or group. Scholar Fred Fiedler (1978) introduced the contingency model of leadership as an attempt to identify factors that affect what type of power and how much influence the leader has over other individuals. Fiedler claimed there exist three primary situational factors. The first factor, power, generally is contained within the leader position. Strong leaders can reward or punish workers (e.g., bonus or no bonus) and have the power to control work life and careers. Weak leaders have little say in granting rewards or punishments and thus have less influence over others. The second factor is task structure. A leader easily can evaluate highly structured tasks (e.g., accounting department reporting) whereas unstructured tasks (e.g., sales department reporting) offer several options or solutions for goal achievement. The latter type of task makes evaluation more difficult for leaders. The third factor comprises member relations, or how well the leader gets along with his followers. For example, a leader who communicates well with group members more likely receives their trust, loyalty, and respect. Conversely, if a leader does not interact well with members, the members may lack commitment and feel less motivated to do quality work. Together, these three factors influence the situation and the leadership that consequently emerges from it.

In sum, this chapter discusses the trait, style, and situational approaches to leadership because of their relevance to classic leadership research. However,

Assessment Tool 9.1   Leadership Questionnaire

Listed below are several pairs of statements. Read each pair and choose the statement you believe is more important.

In a group, it is more important . . .

 1. A. to give everyone a chance to express an opinion.
    B. to know what the group and its members are doing.

 2. A. to assign members to tasks so more can be accomplished.
    B. to let members reach a decision all by themselves.

 3. A. to know what the group and its members are doing.
    B. to help members see how the discussion is related to the group's purpose.

 4. A. to assist the group members in getting along well together.
    B. to help the group members get to what they think is their best answer.

 5. A. to get the job done.
    B. to let members reach a decision all by themselves.

 6. A. to know what the group and its members are doing.
    B. to let members reach a decision all by themselves.

 7. A. to get the job done.
    B. to assist the group members in getting along well together.

 8. A. to help members see how the discussion is related to the group's purpose.
    B. to assign members to tasks so more can be accomplished.

 9. A. to ask questions that will cause members to do more thinking.
    B. to get the job done.

10. A. to let members reach a decision all by themselves.
    B. to give new information when you feel the members are ready for it.

Scoring:

1. If you answered "A" to items 1, 4, 8, 9, and 10, give yourself one point for each "A."
2. If you answered "B" to items 2, 3, 5, 6, and 7, give yourself one point for each "B."
3. Add the summed scores from step 1 and step 2. This is your leadership style score. Scores closer to 0 indicate an autocratic style; scores closer to 10 indicate a democratic style.

Source: Reprinted by permission of Blackwell Publishing from Sargent, J. F., & Miller, G. R. (1971). Some differences in certain communication behaviors of autocratic and democratic group leaders. *Journal of Communication, 21,* 233–252.

group scholar Charles Pavitt (1999) suggested these particular approaches do not represent approaches whose foundations center on communication. One reason is they focus on "such factors as follower characteristics, situational constraints, and possible leadership styles" (p. 328). Furthermore, these approaches were designed not with the small group in mind but rather to measure what happens in other contexts, such as organizations and public arenas. Nonetheless, the trait, style, and situational approaches to leadership provide a relevant background from which to study leadership.

Popular Communication Leadership Approaches

From a communication perspective, the following three approaches—emergent, charismatic, and counteractive influence—address the interaction between the leader and the group members. These approaches focus on the communication among group members, as well as the leader's communication competence and skills.

Emergent Leader Approach to Leadership

The emergent leader approach to leadership centers on what happens in leaderless groups. Classroom groups well exemplify leaderless groups. Ad hoc work groups that meet for only one time provide another example. In ongoing groups, however, a leader emerges "as a result of consensual agreement in the perception of fellow group members" (Gershenoff & Foti, 2003, p. 170). The perception is based on the member's behavior and group outcomes directed by him thought to be leader-like. Prominent group scholar Ernest Bormann (1975) and his colleagues reported from their studies that the group tends not to select a leader at first but instead to eliminate members who are not good choices. Group members look for a member who displays excellent communication skills and appears natural at leadership and group work. Thus, with the **emergent leader approach to leadership**, a group member emerges as a leader based on communicative behaviors and persuasive influence. Experts believe emergent leadership also results from the leader's perceived intellectual competence (Rubin, Bartels, & Bommer, 2002).

Group leadership specialists Michael Hackman and Craig Johnson (2004) offered three communication strategies that can increase your chances of emerging as a leader. First, they recommend you participate from the moment the group forms because you want group members to recognize your will to lead and commitment to them and the task. Second, they suggest you engage frequently in quality communication. This means you must demonstrate you can guide the group's decision-making and problem-solving process, manage conflicts, and challenge poor decisions. Other emergent leadership behaviors include taking charge, being task-oriented, contributing and soliciting input, and working well with others (Kolb, 1997). Third, they believe you must demonstrate good character by respecting group members. Communication professors Scott Johnson and Curt Bechler (1998) offered a fourth strategy: Listen to group members. They reported that group members who engage in leadership behaviors utilize a variety of effective listening behaviors, such as staying focused, asking questions, demonstrating interest in what group members say, and not interrupting group members when they speak. However, emergent leadership lasts only as long as the group members grant emergent leadership status to the member (Kolb, 1998).

> **Ethically Speaking:** How ethical is it to purposely engage in communicative behaviors that would allow you to NOT emerge as a leader? In which of your work group situations would you use the guidelines to NOT emerge as a leader?

Suppose, however, you do not want to emerge as a leader. You likely won't emerge as a group leader if you use any of the six behaviors contained in Table 9.2. Take a minute to read this list. Additionally, if group members perceive you as having communication anxiety, you will not emerge as a leader (Hawkins & Stewart, 1990). Why would group members let you lead the group if you engage in any of these behaviors? If you use too many of these behaviors, group members may go a step further and not let you remain as a member of the group.

Table 9.2 How NOT to Emerge as a Leader

1. Don't attend group meetings.
2. If you attend group meetings, don't speak.
3. If you speak, do so in a dominant and contentious manner.
4. At group meetings, indicate you would rather be a follower than a leader.
5. At group meetings, volunteer to play the formal recorder role.
6. At group meetings, play the clown or egghead deviant roles.

Source: Based on Fisher, B. A. (1980). *Small group decision making: Communication and the group process* (2nd ed.). New York: McGraw-Hill.

Charismatic Approach to Leadership

The charismatic approach to leadership has been attributed to such notable public leaders as John F. Kennedy, Jr., former president of the United States, and Lee Iacocca, former president of Chrysler Corporation. Recently, however, scholars suggest that charismatic leadership is appropriate at any level of leadership, including small groups. According to Michael Hackman and Craig Johnson (2004), "charisma is the product of communication" (p. 116). Generally, the **charismatic approach to leadership** states that a leader possesses the ability to accomplish extraordinary things (Kouzes & Posner, 1987) while simultaneously exerting a powerful influence on members (Holladay & Coombs, 1994).

Group members perceive charismatic leaders as visionaries who energize others and risk takers who challenge conventional norms. Considered extremely knowledgeable, self-confident, and hard working, as well as skillful at building relationships, from a communication perspective these leaders communicate vision masterfully by employing the rhetorical techniques of emotional appeals, picturesque language, and appropriate gesturing (Pavitt, 1999). They possess competent skills in communication, persuasion, and relationship building. As Malcolm Parks (1994) suggested, charismatic leaders know what to say, how to say it, and when to say it to reach goals. If they do not reach their goals, charismatic leaders analyze the situation and fix it by learning the appropriate behaviors and abandoning the behaviors that do not work.

In one respect, we could consider the charismatic approach to leadership closely aligned with the emergent approach to leadership because both approaches depend on the perceptions of group members. Yet this dependency places charismatic leaders more at risk if visions fail or task goals are not met. Because group members' impressions can and do change, group members sometimes view charismatic leaders as dictatorial, poor at detail work, inflexible, and demanding (Conger, 1989). Thus the downside to charismatic leadership comes from the fact that it can boomerang, causing group members to become dissatisfied with the group and the leader.

Counteractive Influence Approach to Leadership

Dennis Gouran (1982) introduced the idea of viewing leadership in decision-making and problem-solving groups as counteractive influence. When group members' communication behaviors move them along on their tasks or problems without encountering any obstacles, neither a leader nor leadership behaviors need emerge. When the group faces a task-related or a relational obstacle, however, the leader (i.e., appointed, elected, emergent) must draw upon persuasive skills to counter the force presented by the group member pulling rank, displaying

Photo 9.3   Group members perceive a charismatic leader as possessing the communication, persuasion, and relationship-building skills needed to energize and motivate the group.

Source: Allison Michael Orenstein/Photonica/Getty Images.

disruptive behaviors, or pressuring other group members to conform. Simply put, the counteractive influence approach to leadership centers on the notion that when the group encounters an obstacle, the leader needs to draw upon a repertoire of communicative skills that (a) counters what other group members have said or done and (b) influences members to resolve or remove whatever caused the obstacle.

Along a similar line of thinking, leadership scholar J. Kevin Barge (1994) introduced a communication-based skill model of leadership, the premise of which is that leaders must know how to communicate in the form of mediation or intervention when conditions in the group process interfere with the group's ability to meet task requirements. The conditions could be associated with either the task or group member relationships. For example, the group may lack the information it needs to make high-quality decisions surrounding the task, the group may not understand the information it has, the members may lack problem-solving skills, or the members may have relational problems. Barge stated a leader needs to utilize her communicative skills to get information, make sense of information, help the members learn problem-solving methods, and manage conflict. Although Barge does not refer to his communication skill model of leadership as counteractive influence, the model fundamentally fits with the counteractive influence approach to leadership primarily because a leader, or a group member acting as the leader, must counter the communicative behaviors (influence) in the group setting that block the group's progress toward goal achievement.

Guidelines to Enhance Leadership Competence

Now that we have explored the classic and the popular communication approaches to leadership, let's examine some ways to enhance your leadership competence. As group expert B. Aubrey Fisher (1986) stated, leadership is a "property of any successful group" (p. 200). In this section, we offer several guidelines you can follow to enhance your leadership potential and effectiveness. Though not exhaustive, these guidelines simply provide a template for individuals who want to succeed as leaders of small groups.

1. Strive toward engaging in competent group member communicative behaviors. Consider that a competent communicator engages in simultaneously effective and appropriate behavior (Spitzberg & Cupach, 1984). In a small group, competent communicative behaviors that suggest leadership include, among others, being self-assured, tolerating uncertainty, listening, providing autonomy, formulating goals, giving directions, and being able to convert negative or angry comments into more positive and constructive comments (Bechler & Johnson, 1995; Gouran, 2003; Kolb, 1995, 1996; Schultz, 1974). Group members perceived as task attractive also are more likely to be targeted as leaders (Lashbrook, 1975).

2. Set realistic and manageable goals for the group. Scholars Carl Larson and Frank LaFasto (1989) found leadership occurs when members exhibit personal commitment to the group goal—for example, by understanding what such constraints as time, money, personnel, and goals allow the group to possibly achieve.

3. Foster a supportive communication climate. Consultant Jack Gibb (1961) posited most groups communicate through an underlying tone of defensiveness, meaning that group members may devote considerable amounts of time to defending themselves, their ideas, and their actions. Rather, group members should strive to be open, approachable, and flexible (Galanes, 2003) to allow for the establishment of a supportive communication climate. We will explore the importance of establishing a supportive communication climate further in Chapter 12.

4. Watch the use of humor. Although group members will evaluate a leader's use of humor differently, they will consider the leader who uses self-disparaging humor a better tension releaser than the leader who targets humor at group members or fails to use humor at all (Smith & Powell, 1988). Moreover, a

member who demonstrates "good" leadership is perceived to use humor that puts group members at ease and maintains group morale (Priest & Swain, 2002).

5. Encourage group members to engage in orientation behaviors, which refer to a group's tendency to examine the procedures it uses while engaging in the decision-making or problem-solving process and to include the use of verbal behaviors that direct members to handle conflict, make helpful suggestions, lessen tension, and facilitate agreement (Knutson & Holdridge, 1975).

6. Set high standards for group members' behaviors, such as by developing a code of conduct and a charter that specifies acceptable and unacceptable group member behavior. A code of conduct lists behaviors by which group members agree to abide; a charter lists goals the group hopes to achieve. By doing this, group members may be accountable for not only their behaviors but their contributions toward task accomplishment as well. At the same time, expectations for group membership are clarified, and norms for group behavior are established.

7. Foster creativity. If you recall from Chapter 1, creativity refers to idea generation and allows members to consider a decision or a problem from a different point of view without thinking about how to implement a decision, solve a problem, or evaluate the effectiveness of the decision. Doing so motivates group members and encourages them to "think outside the box." As such, creativity emerges through the messages exchanged among group members rather than through the mind-sets of group members (Sunwolf, 2002).

> Referencing your work group, what other guidelines could you add to this list? Should these guidelines be discussed with group members when they first meet? Why?

8. Celebrate successes. Enjoy the rewards of group work and member relationships! Recognize and reward the efforts put forth by group members (Kolb, 1995). Group members respect and like good leaders (Rees & Segal, 1984), so don't take the leader role so seriously you jeopardize the positive affect created among group members.

A Final Note About Small Group Leadership

Through leadership, group members make sense of their group (Meindl, Ehrlich, & Dukerich, 1985). To enhance this sense making process, it is essential that a group retain a group-centered focus. To do so, leadership expert Gary Yukl (2002) recommended that group members share responsibility for all facets of task accomplishment. This means all group members should participate in the decision-making or problem-solving process, embrace the discussion techniques used by the group, and refrain from playing deviant roles. Moreover, group-centered leadership requires group members to use effective interpersonal communication behaviors, demonstrate maturity, and develop trust in each other (Bradford, 1976), as well as to encourage both participation and the statement of divergent opinions (Neck & Moorhead, 1995). Retaining a group-centered focus allows all group members to engage in shared leadership.

Conclusion

This chapter purported to identify leadership behaviors that any group member can learn and execute as part of communicating competently. To do so, we defined leadership from a communication perspective, distinguished between being a leader and sharing leadership, traced classic approaches to leadership, and presented popular communication approaches to leadership. Finally, we offered several guidelines for enhancing leadership competence. As you read the next chapter, consider how your use of relational communication (i.e., verbal communication skills, nonverbal communication skills, and listening skills) contributes to whether group members perceive you as exhibiting leadership.

Discussion Questions

1. In your classroom group, define leadership. Should classroom groups appoint a leader, or should group members share the leadership role? Why?

2. In the case study, Dr. Pat Howley can be a gender-neutral name. Would the group members in the case study respond differently if Dr. Pat Howley was a woman? Why? Would the group members in the case study respond differently if Dr. Pat Howley was a man? Why?

3. Refer to the Communicator Style Measure you completed in Chapter 3. Does your communicator style cluster identify you as using a democratic style, an autocratic style, or a laissez faire style of leadership? Does this identification make sense?

4. Of the three popular communication approaches to leadership, which approach has surfaced in one of your social groups? What were the outcomes of this approach?

5. What additional guidelines to enhance leadership competence would you suggest to members of a virtual group? How can virtual group members engage in shared leadership?

References

Barge, J. K. (1994). *Leadership: Communication skills for organizations and groups*. New York: St. Martin's Press.

Barge, J. K. (1997). Leadership as communication. In L. R. Frey & J. K Barge (Eds.), *Managing group life: Communicating in decision-making groups* (pp. 202–233). New York: Houghton Mifflin.

Barge, J. K., & Hirokawa, R. Y. (1989). Toward a communication competency model of group leadership. *Small Group Behavior, 20*, 167–189.

Bechler, C., & Johnson, S. D. (1995). Leadership and listening: A study of member perceptions. *Small Group Research, 26*, 77–85.

Bormann, E. G. (1975). *Discussion and group methods* (2nd ed.). New York: Harper & Row.

Bradford, L. P. (1976). *Making meetings work: A guide for leaders and group members*. La Jolla, CA: University Associates.

Bradley, P. H., & Baird, J. E., Jr. (1977). Management and communicator style: A correlational analysis. *Central States Speech Journal, 28*, 194–203.

Conger, J. A. (1989). Leadership: The art of empowering others. *The Academy of Management Executive, 3*, 17–24.

Cragan, J. F., & Wright, D. W. (1999). *Communication in small groups: Theory, process, skills* (5th ed.). Belmont, CA: Wadsworth.

Fiedler, F. (1978). The contingency model and the dynamics of the leadership process. In L. Berkowitz (Ed.), *Advances in experimental social psychology* (Vol. 11, pp. 59–112). New York: Academic Press.

Fisher, B. A. (1980). *Small group decision making: Communication and the group process* (2nd ed.). New York: McGraw-Hill.

Fisher, B. A. (1986). Leadership: When does the difference make a difference? In R. Y. Hirokawa & M. S. Poole (Eds.), *Communication and group decision-making* (pp. 197–215). Beverly Hills, CA: Sage.

Foels, R., Driskell, J. E., Mullen, B., & Salas, E. (2000). The effects of democratic leadership on group member satisfaction: An integration. *Small Group Research, 31*, 676–701.

Galanes, G. A. (2003). In their own words: An exploratory study of bona fide group leaders. *Small Group Research, 34*, 741–770.

Geier, J. G. (1967). A trait approach to the study of leadership in small groups. *Journal of Communication, 17*, 316–323.

Gershenoff, A. B., & Foti, R. J. (2003). Leader emergence and gender roles in all-female groups: A contextual examination. *Small Group Research, 3*, 170–196.

Gibb, J. R. (1961). Defensive communication. *Journal of Communication, 11*, 141–148.

Gouran, D. S. (1982). *Making decisions in groups: Choices and consequences*. Glenview, IL: Scott, Foresman.

Gouran, D. S. (2003). Leadership as the art of counteractive influence in decision-making and problem-solving groups. In R. Y. Hirokawa, R. S. Cathcart, L. A. Samovar, & L. D. Henman (Eds.), *Small group communication theory & practice: An anthology* (8th ed., pp. 172–183). Los Angeles: Roxbury.

Hackman, M. Z., & Johnson, C. E. (2004). *Leadership: A communication perspective* (4th ed.). Long Grove, IL: Waveland Press.

Hawkins, K., & Stewart, R. A. (1990). Temporal effects of leadership style on state communication anxiety in small task-oriented groups. *Communication Research Reports, 7*, 3–8.

Hawkins, K., & Stewart, R. A. (1991). Effects of communication apprehension on perceptions of leadership and intragroup attraction in small task-oriented groups. *Southern Communication Journal, 57*, 1–10.

Holladay, S. J., & Coombs, W. T. (1994). Speaking of visions and visions being spoken: An exploration of the effects of content and delivery on perceptions of leader charisma. *Management Communication Quarterly, 8*, 165–189.

Johnson, S. D., & Bechler, C. (1998). Examining the relationship between listening effectiveness and leadership emergence: Perceptions, behaviors, and recall. *Small Group Research, 29*, 452–471.

Kippenberger, T. (2002). *Leadership styles.* Oxford, UK: Capstone.

Knutson, T. J., & Holdridge, W. E. (1975). Orientation behavior, leadership and consensus: A possible functional relationship. *Speech Monographs, 42,* 107–114.

Kolb, J. A. (1995). Leader behaviors affecting team performance: Similarities and differences between leader/member assessments. *Journal of Business Communication, 32,* 233–248.

Kolb, J. A. (1996). A comparison of leadership behaviors and competencies in high- and average-performance teams. *Communication Reports, 9,* 173–183.

Kolb, J. A. (1997). Are we still stereotyping leadership? A look at gender and other predictors of leader emergence. *Small Group Research, 28,* 370–393.

Kolb, J. A. (1998). The relationship between self-monitoring and leadership in student project groups. *Journal of Business Communication, 35,* 264–282.

Kouzes, J. M., & Posner, B. Z. (1987). *The leadership challenge: How to get extraordinary things done in organizations.* San Francisco: Jossey-Bass.

Kramer, M. W. (2006). Shared leadership in a community theater group: Filling the leadership role. *Journal of Applied Communication Research, 34,* 141–162.

Larson, C. E., & LaFasto, F. M. (1989). *Teamwork: What must go right, what can go wrong.* Newbury Park, CA: Sage.

Lashbrook, V. J. (1975). Leadership emergence and source valence: Concepts in support of interaction theory and measurement. *Human Communication Research, 1,* 308–315.

Lewin, K., Lippitt, R., & White, R. K. (1939). Patterns of aggressive behavior in experimentally created "social climates." *Journal of Social Psychology, 10,* 271–299.

Lord, R. G., De Vader, C. L., & Alliger, G. M. (1986). A meta-analysis of the relation between personality traits and leadership perceptions: An application of validity generalization procedures. *Journal of Applied Psychology, 71,* 402–410.

Meindl, J. R., Ehrlich, S. B., & Dukerich, J. M. (1985). The romance of leadership. *Administrative Science Quarterly, 30,* 78–102.

Neck, C. P., & Moorhead, G. (1995). Groupthink remodeled: The importance of leadership, time pressure, and methodical decision-making procedures. *Human Relations, 48,* 537–557.

Northouse, P. A. (2007). *Leadership: Theory and practice* (3rd ed.). Thousand Oaks, CA: Sage.

O'Hair, D., & Wiemann, M. O. (2004). *The essential guide to group communication.* Boston: Bedford/St. Martin's.

Parks, M. (1994). Communication competence and interpersonal control. In M. L. Knapp & G. R. Miller (Eds.), *Handbook of interpersonal communication* (2nd ed., pp. 589–620). Thousand Oaks, CA: Sage.

Pavitt, C. (1999). Theorizing about the group communication-leadership relationship: Input-process-output and functional models. In L. R. Frey (Ed.), D. S. Gouran, & M. S. Poole (Assoc. Eds.), *The handbook of group communication theory and research* (pp. 313–334). Thousand Oaks, CA: Sage.

Pavitt, C., & Curtis, E. (1994). *Small group discussion: A theoretical approach* (2nd ed.). Scottsdale, AZ: Gorsuch Scarisbrick.

Priest, R. F., & Swain, J. E. (2002). Humor and its implications for leadership effectiveness. *Humor, 15,* 169–189.

Rees, C. R., & Segal, M. W. (1984). Role differentiation in groups: The relationship between instrumental and expressive leadership. *Small Group Behavior, 15,* 109–123.

Rosenfeld, L. R., & Fowler, G. D. (1976). Personality, sex, and leadership style. *Communication Monographs, 43,* 320–324.

Rosenfeld, L. R., & Plax, T. G. (1975). Personality determinants of autocratic and democratic leadership. *Speech Monographs, 42,* 203–208.

Rubin, R. S., Bartels, L. K., & Bommer, W. H. (2002). Are leaders smarter or do they just seem that way? Exploring perceived intellectual competence and leadership emergence. *Social Behavior and Personality, 30,* 105–118.

Schultz, B. (1974). Characteristics of emergent leaders of continuing problem-solving groups. *Journal of Psychology, 88,* 167–173.

Schultz, B. (1982). Argumentativeness: Its effect in group decision-making and its role in leadership perception. *Communication Quarterly, 30,* 368–375.

Smith, C. M., & Powell, L. (1988). The use of disparaging humor by group leaders. *Southern Speech Communication Journal, 53,* 279–292.

Spitzberg, B. H., & Cupach, W. R. (1984). *Interpersonal communication competence.* Beverly Hills, CA: Sage.

Stogdill, R. M. (1948). Personal factors associated with leadership: A survey of the literature. *Journal of Psychology, 25,* 35–71.

Stogdill, R. M. (1974). *Handbook of leadership.* New York: Free Press.

Sunwolf. (2002). Getting to "groupaha!": Provoking creative processes in task groups. In L. R. Frey (Ed.), *New directions in group communication* (pp. 203–217). Thousand Oaks, CA: Sage.

White, R., & Lippitt, R. (1960). *Autocracy and democracy.* New York: Harper & Row.

Wischmeier, R. R. (1955). Group and leader-centered leadership: An experimental study. *Speech Monographs, 22,* 43–48.

Yukl, G. (2002). *Leadership in organizations* (5th ed.). Upper Saddle River, NJ: Prentice Hall.

Relational Communication Among Small Group Members

10

After reading this chapter, you should be able to:

1. define relational communication,
2. identify the three components of relational communication,
3. list and explain the characteristics of verbal communication,
4. list and define the codes of nonverbal communication, and
5. define listening and distinguish among the four listening styles.

Case Study | At 11 a.m. the members of Weight Loss for Healthy Living (WLHL) gather for their weekly meeting. New members Kathleen and Peggy walk into the room and look for an empty seat. Noticing the first two

Photo 10.1   For many group members, relational communication is key to task accomplishment.

Source: ©iStockphoto.com/Cimmerian.

rows are empty, they select seats in the front row. Dorcas, the group facilitator, walks in, glares at the women, and begins the meeting.

Dorcas: Good afternoon, folks, and welcome to another session of Weight Loss for Healthy Living, the weight maintenance program designed to help you lose weight and keep it off for life—or at least until you gain it all back again.

Kathleen: (nudges Peggy and speaks in a whisper) Did she just say until we gain it all back again? Was she serious?

Peggy: (whispers back) I don't know. She didn't smile when she said it, and she looks mean. What did we get ourselves into?

Dorcas: (looks sternly at Kathleen and Peggy) I hear talking. Ladies, do you have a question?

Kathleen: No, not at all. We weren't sure what you said.

Dorcas: Fine. Let's begin our meeting. My name is Dorcas, I've lost 65 pounds on the WLHL program, and I've kept it off for four years.

Kathleen:	(pokes Peggy and raises her eyebrows) Wow! Did you hear that? 65 pounds!
Peggy:	She doesn't look like she was once a tank.
Dorcas:	Chuckie, why don't you start by sharing with the group your numbers for the week?
Chuckie:	Sure, Dorcas. I had 26 frugans, hit the grand slam, did 1,250 AEA, and had 17 substance substitutes.
Dorcas:	And how much weight did you lose?
Chuckie:	So far, 27 pounds.
Dorcas:	Good job. Jeff, what are your numbers?
Jeff:	Just a triple, but 43 frugans, 2,700 AEA, and 27 subs.
Dorcas:	Weight loss?
Jeff:	(beams) Over 150 pounds!
Kathleen:	(nudges Peggy again) Check out his body! Did you hear that? 150 pounds!
Peggy:	(looking wistfully toward Jeff) He must have had some surgery. There is no way he could lose 150 pounds and look like that.
Lois:	(waves her arm) Excuse me, Dorcas, but I have a question. How many subs a week should we eat?
Dorcas:	It depends on your weight loss goal, but at least 14.
Kathleen:	(whispers to Peggy) A sub sounds good right about now.
Peggy:	Do you want to go to Panera after this meeting? They have a great turkey and avocado sandwich.
Kathleen:	Their avocado is a little too bitter for me. I'm in the mood for some spicy horseradish. How about Arby's? (looks up and notices Dorcas staring at her)
Dorcas:	Ladies, I know you're new to the group, but it's important you listen while we share our numbers. You can't learn if you don't listen. Would you like to introduce yourselves?
Kathleen:	Well, my name is Kathleen, and I'm new to the group. My friend Peggy and I would like to drop a few pounds.

Dorcas:	What do you mean by a few pounds?
Kathleen:	Maybe 10, 15.
A voice from the back of the room:	(laughing) Did you say 10 pounds? Somebody hold me back.
Dorcas:	Who said that? Suzanne, was that you?
Suzanne:	Yes. You know my voice, Dorcas. (rest of group starts laughing)
Dorcas:	Yes, I do. I'd recognize that voice anywhere. What's so funny about Kathleen's comment?
Suzanne:	Because for me, a few pounds are more like 60! (rest of group laughs again) Besides, you don't look like you need to lose any weight. (other group members nod in agreement)
Dorcas:	Now Suzanne, keep in mind weight loss will be different for each person. Peggy, why are you interested in joining this group?
Peggy:	I'd like to lose a few pounds, too.
Suzanne:	(rolls her eyes) Great, another one who wants to lose a "few pounds."
Dorcas:	(with an edge to her voice) Be nice, Suzanne. Why don't we move on to today's topic? We only have 45 minutes to cover the topic. Today I want to discuss . . .

After the meeting, Kathleen and Peggy stand in the hallway, trying to make sense of frugans, grand slams, and AEA. Suzanne walks over to the women.

Suzanne:	Welcome to the group. By the way, you may not want to sit in the front row next week. Dorcas always gets a little cranky when people are too close to her, and besides, she can hear you when you talk. If you sit toward the back, she can't hear you, and you can avoid being suffocated by her perfume. I have the most sensitive nose and those scents she wears . . . (shakes her head and walks away)
Kathleen:	What do you think, Peggy? Should we come back next week?
Peggy:	We better. I just bought a box of those substance substitutes. But next time, let's sit in the back row and keep our mouths shut.

Up to this point, we have focused on the idea that the primary purpose behind group work is task accomplishment. But as the preceding case study illustrates, the relational aspect of group work proves just as important. Author Joann Keyton (1999) argued that studying the relational aspect of group work is important for three reasons. First, many groups exist to satisfy group members' interpersonal needs. Think for a moment about why we join primary, social, and self-help groups. Membership in these groups makes many of us feel needed and important. Second, relational issues can't help but surround the group task. For instance, when group members engage in conflict, their interaction may be influenced more by how members state their positions than by the position taken. Third, as discussed in Chapter 1, group members' relationships are interdependent. When the relationship between two group members becomes strained, all group members experience this strain.

Aiming to introduce you to relational communication, this chapter will provide you with a definition of relational communication and its three components—verbal communication, nonverbal communication, and listening, which we will explore further. Once we explore these components, we will explain the four listening styles used by group members.

Definition of Relational Communication

Relational communication describes "the verbal and nonverbal messages that create the social fabric of a group by promoting relationships between and among members" (Keyton, 1999, p. 192). Because listening is regarded as a relational process that occurs before, during, and after an interaction (Halone & Pecchioni, 2001) and is considered the most important communication skill needed by group members (Hawkins & Fillion, 1999), we also consider it a vital part of the social fabric of any group

> **?** How is relational communication used in your work group? Of the three components—verbal communication, nonverbal communication, and listening—which component is the most vital to promote member relationships?

interaction. For our purposes, then, we define relational communication as the use of verbal communication, nonverbal communication, and listening to develop and maintain relationships between and among group members.

To explore the components of relational communication, we will start by examining verbal and nonverbal communication.

Verbal and Nonverbal Communication

Although researchers define verbal communication and nonverbal communication in several ways, at the heart of all definitions lies the distinction between the two concepts. In its simplest form, verbal communication comprises the words and phrases used by group members through which meaning is created whereas nonverbal communication comprises all communication other than words (Andersen, 1999) through which meaning is created. As such, verbal and nonverbal communication serve several functions in any small group interaction, such as relaying, structuring, and regulating interaction; forming and managing impressions; establishing and maintaining relationships; and conveying relational messages (Ketrow, 1999; Trenholm & Jensen, 2007).

Learning more about the distinction between verbal communication and nonverbal communication requires an understanding of the characteristics of each communication component. We'll start by examining the three characteristics of verbal communication.

Characteristics of Verbal Communication

The first characteristic of verbal communication is that it can have both a denotative meaning, referred to as the dictionary or literal meaning of a word, and a connotative meaning, referred to as the personal response to a word. To examine the difference between a denotative meaning and a connotative meaning, think of how your group members would respond to a word. For instance, if you tell your roommates you want to rescue a dog from the county animal control shelter, they know you want to get a "domesticated canid" (*American Heritage College Dictionary*, 2000), which is the denotative meaning of the word *dog*. Connotatively, however, their definition of a dog may differ. One roommate (who loved Bruiser the chihuahua in *Legally Blonde* and wants to get one when she graduates) may envision a small animal who will sit quietly in her lap and shower her with affection; another roommate (who reads the cartoon *Marmaduke* every morning in the school newspaper) may imagine a large animal who will eat its weight in food and roam the neighborhood looking for an open trashcan lid.

The second characteristic is that verbal communication can be either concrete or abstract. When verbal communication is concrete, the word or phrase has an identifiable referent and its meaning is clear. When verbal communication is abstract, the word or phrase has no identifiable referent and the meaning is less clear. Additionally, a concrete word refers to something in a specific sense whereas an abstract word refers to something in a general sense. Suppose you decide to paint your kitchen walls yellow. For most of us, the word *yellow* is concrete. When you think of yellow, the referent is clear—you can envision a school bus, Big Bird, or one of the primary colors you learned in elementary school. When you go to the local home improvement store to purchase yellow paint, you are surprised when you can't find it. Instead, you find yarrow, daylily, saffron, and gilded shore, all labels for a shade of yellow paint. Not surprisingly, when you tell your mom you've painted your kitchen walls the color gilded shore, she cannot picture the color. This characteristic also can affect group work in a number of ways. Suppose during class on Tuesday, your group decides to meet to work on your group project. Which message is concrete: agreeing to meet at 5 p.m. Wednesday in front of Burger King at the Student Center to finish the outline for your group symposium or suggesting the group meet later in the week to get some work done?

The third characteristic is that verbal communication can emerge in the form of either a restricted or an elaborated code. According to sociologist Basil Bernstein (1971), individuals who speak in a restricted code use short, simple, and conventional language. Individuals who speak in an elaborated code use more complex, extensive, and precise language. In many cases, using a restricted code reflects group membership because the code emphasizes shared assumptions and solidarity. Consider the members of the Weight Loss for Healthy Living learning group in the case study. Kathleen and Peggy, newcomers to the group, have no idea what frugans, grand slams, substance substitutes, and AEA are. When Chuckie and Jeff speak using this restricted code, they implicitly communicate their group membership in WLHL because they know frugans refers to fruits and vegetables; grand slam refers to eating the required amount of fruits and vegetables and engaging in the minimal amount of exercise; substance substitutes refers to the pre-prepared meals WLHL sells to its members; and AEA refers to exercise.

Now that you understand the characteristics of verbal communication, let's turn our attention to the codes of nonverbal communication. Nonverbal communication consists of several codes.

Codes of Nonverbal Communication

The seven primary nonverbal codes include personal appearance, kinesics, oculesics, facial expression, proxemics, haptics, and vocalics. Two secondary nonverbal codes are olfactics and chronemics (Hickson, Stacks, & Moore, 2004).

Photo 10.2 Personal appearance is the nonverbal code to which group members initially pay the most attention.

Source: Tony Metaxas/Asia Images/Jupiterimages.

Of the seven primary nonverbal codes, we pay the most attention to personal appearance, at least initially when we interact with our group members. **Personal appearance** refers to how a group member looks and can encompass many dimensions, including height, weight, skin color, hair and eye color, body shape, choice of clothing and jewelry, and hairstyle. Many people base their perceptions of an individual's likeability, competence, and attractiveness (Molloy, 1988) on personal appearance.

Kinesics refers to a group member's use of body movement (Birdwhistell, 1970). This movement includes a person's posture, use of gestures, and behaviors such as walking and sitting. Through kinesics, we display our emotional state, regulate our interactions with others, emphasize a key idea or point during discussion, adapt to the situation, or send a message without having to speak (Ekman & Friesen, 1969).

Oculesics refers to a group member's eye behavior (Andersen, 1999). Eye behavior can take many forms, including staring, gazing, winking, scanning, blinking, and glancing. Of these forms, eye contact (when two individuals look each other in the eye) is perhaps the most important type of eye behavior because it intensifies emotional expression (Kimble, Forte, & Yoshikawa, 1981). In many cases, eye contact signals assertiveness, confidence, intelligence, and self-esteem (Napieralski & Brooks, 1995) and leads to greater compliance and liking (Gueguen & Jacob, 2002).

Facial expression refers to how a group member conveys meaning through the face. In our culture, the seven facial expressions easily interpreted by others include sadness, anger, disgust, fear, interest, surprise, and happiness (Ekman, 1982). Because the face is considered the richest source of emotional information (Leathers, 1997), we often rely on facial expression to determine how a person feels about the group task or group members.

Proxemics refers to a group member's use of space and can be broken into two types: distance and territory. Distance refers to the amount of physical space that exists between two or more group members as they communicate. According to anthropologist Edward Hall (1966), distance can be broken into four zones: the intimate zone, which is 0–18 inches and used when communicating with close others, such as relatives and romantic partners; the personal zone, which is 18 inches–4 feet and used when communicating with friends; the social zone, which is 4–8 feet and used when communicating with colleagues; and the public zone, which is 8 feet and beyond. These zones are used as an indicator of our relationships with others. Territory refers to the ownership of space. Sociologist Erving Goffman (1971) identified several ways individuals "mark" their territory—for example, leaving your books on a table at the Student Center while you get a cup of coffee at the kiosk, putting your backpack on the seat next to you in your history class, and writing your initials on the inside cover of your small group communication textbook.

Haptics refers to a group member's use of touch. Of the primary nonverbal codes, haptics is the most open to interpretation due to the varieties of touch that exist. Michael Argyle (1975) identified 16 types of touch, which include, among others, slapping, punching, shaking, kissing, holding, pinching, patting, and embracing. Additionally, these 16 types of touch can occur on any part of the body, including the head, the face, the chest, the arms, the hands, the waist, and the legs. For many people, touch is the primary way relational partners reveal liking, loving, and affection (Nguyen, Heslin, & Nguyen, 1975).

Vocalics, sometimes called paralanguage, refers to qualities of a group member's voice, including rate, pitch, volume, tempo, articulation, pronunciation, inflection, pauses, and silence. Vocalics complements verbal communication by emphasizing how something is said. For instance, the phrase "I love working in small groups" can be interpreted in several ways based on the emphasis of each word. As this interpretation can range from enthusiasm to sarcasm, vocalics is central to understanding the meaning of any verbal message.

The two secondary codes are olfactics and chronemics. Olfactics refers to scent and smell; chronemics refers to the use of time and structure of time. Although these two codes are present in interactions, they cannot be seen or heard and thus are considered covert (Hickson et al., 2004). Olfactics and chronemics play a secondary role in some people's interactions with others until their awareness of the code is heightened. For instance, smell may not become a consideration unless it is extremely pleasant or unpleasant, and time may not be an issue until group members realize they have either too little or too much of it.

> **?** When a new member joins your work group, to which primary nonverbal codes do you pay the most attention? How do you use these nonverbal codes to form an initial impression of this member?

Now that we have reviewed the characteristics of verbal communication and the codes of nonverbal communication, let's examine the relationship that exists between these two concepts. Although a message usually contains both a verbal component and a nonverbal component, most adults rely more on the nonverbal component to determine its meaning. This reliance on the nonverbal component results from the belief that a message contains more elements of the nonverbal component than the verbal component; the nonverbal component represents a more accurate display of an individual's emotional state than the verbal component; and the nonverbal component is used to illustrate, clarify, or reinforce the verbal component of a message (Afifi, 2007; Guerrero & Floyd, 2006). For example, in the case study when Suzanne welcomes Kathleen and Peggy to the WLHL group, she warns them about Dorcas's behavior, and then she shakes her head and walks away from the ladies without finishing her sentence. These nonverbal behaviors make Kathleen and Peggy question whether they should join the group, although Suzanne verbally welcomes the women. Moreover, when the verbal and nonverbal components of a message contradict each other, adults usually believe the nonverbal component over the verbal component (Afifi, 2007). In interpreting Suzanne's behaviors, Kathleen and Peggy may pay more attention to Suzanne's disconfirming behaviors (e.g., shaking her head, walking away) than her welcoming (i.e., verbal) comments.

As you may surmise, verbal communication and nonverbal communication exert a powerful influence on listening, the third component of relational communication.

Listening

Listening describes "the process of receiving, constructing meaning from, and responding to spoken and/or nonverbal messages" (International Listening Association, 2005). Listening allows individuals to organize information; learn, integrate, and evaluate information; and build relationships (Imhof & Janusik, 2006). And although business students identify listening as one of the most important communication skills to learn (McPherson, 1999), most individuals do not perform this behavior very well (Robertson, 1994). Reporter Don Oldenburg (2001) of the

> **" Ethically Speaking:** According to researchers, many people need to be provided with an incentive to listen (Smeltzer & Watson, 1984). In a work group, do members have an ethical obligation to listen to each other without incentive? **"**

Table 10.1   Types of Listening

Type	Definition
Discriminative	The ability to differentiate among various stimuli
Appreciative	The desire to listen for reasons of enjoyment
Empathic	The willingness to listen to understand how someone feels
Comprehensive	The need to comprehend information in order to learn
Evaluative	The need to evaluate information in light of some criteria

Washington Post has compiled some interesting statistics about listening. According to Oldenburg, 85% of what we know is learned by listening, 45% of our day is spent listening, and 75% of our time spent listening is plagued by distractions, preoccupations, and forgetfulness. Given these statistics, no wonder listening is one communicative behavior group members need to improve.

In the small group, five types of listening—discriminative, appreciative, empathic, comprehensive, and evaluative—are essential to task accomplishment and relational development (see Table 10.1). Although we engage in all five types of listening, most people have a preference for what they listen to, how they listen, and why they listen. These preferences have been conceptualized as the Listening Styles Profile and consist of four listening styles: the people-oriented listener, the content-oriented listener, the action-oriented listener, and the time-oriented listener (Watson, Barker, & Weaver, 1995). Complete the Listening Styles Profile to determine your listening style.

People-oriented listeners listen primarily out of concern for other people's feelings and emotions. These responsive listeners strive to find areas of interest between themselves and the speaker. People-oriented listeners also tend to be sympathetic, nonjudgmental, caring, and understanding (Bodie & Villaume, 2003; Weaver & Kirtley, 1995).

Action-oriented listeners prefer concise, efficient, and error-free messages. Action-oriented listeners are interested in listening to well-organized presentations (Imhof, 2004) and dislike ambiguity (Worthington, 2005a). At times, action-oriented listeners may get impatient or frustrated when communicating with a disorganized speaker and may interrupt the speaker or finish the speaker's statements (Bodie & Villaume, 2003; Keyton & Rhodes, 1994). Unlike the people-oriented listener, an action-oriented listener is less likely to pay attention to the relational communication dimension of a message (Worthington, 2005b).

Assessment Tool 10.1 Listening Styles Profile

Indicate how true each statement is for you by using the following scale.

If the statement is **always true**, write a **5** in the blank.

If the statement is **frequently true**, write a **4** in the blank.

If the statement is **sometimes true**, write a **3** in the blank.

If the statement is **infrequently true**, write a **2** in the blank.

If the statement is **never true**, write a **1** in the blank.

_____ 1. I focus my attention on the other person's feelings when listening.

_____ 2. When listening to others, I quickly notice if they are pleased or disappointed.

_____ 3. I become involved when listening to the problems of others.

_____ 4. I nod my head and/or use eye contact to show interest in what others are saying.

_____ 5. I am frustrated when others don't present their ideas in an orderly, efficient way.

_____ 6. When listening to others, I focus on any inconsistencies and/or errors in what is being said.

_____ 7. I jump ahead and/or finish thoughts of speakers.

_____ 8. I am impatient with people who ramble on during conversations.

_____ 9. I prefer to listen to technical information.

_____10. I prefer to hear facts and evidence so I can personally evaluate them.

_____11. I like the challenge of listening to complex information.

_____12. I ask questions to probe for additional information.

_____13. When hurried, I let the other person know I have a limited amount of time to listen.

_____14. I begin a discussion by telling others how long I have to meet.

_____15. I interrupt others when I feel time pressure.

_____16. I look at my watch or clocks in the room when I have limited time to listen to others.

Scoring:

1. Add your scores for items 1, 2, 3, and 4. This is your **people-oriented** listening style score.

2. Add your scores for items 5, 6, 7, and 8. This is your **action-oriented** listening style score.

3. Add your scores for items 9, 10, 11, and 12. This is your **content-oriented** listening style score.

4. Add your scores for items 13, 14, 15, and 16. This is your **time-oriented** listening style score.

Source: Watson, K. W., Barker, L. L., & Weaver, J. B., III. (1995). The listening styles profile (LSP-16): Development and validation of an instrument to assess four listening styles. *International Journal of Listening, 9,* 1–13. Copyright © 1995 by International Listening Association. Reproduced with permission of International Listening Association.

Photo 10.3 Group members who are people-oriented listeners generally are responsive.

Source: ©iStockphoto.com/lisafx.

Content-oriented listeners enjoy receiving complex or challenging information. These listeners carefully evaluate information before forming an opinion about the information by asking questions, listening to both sides of an issue, and withholding judgment (Bodie & Villaume, 2003; Imhof, 2004), thereby eliminating any bias they may have toward the speaker or the topic.

Time-oriented listeners measure interactions by informing their relational partners how much time they have available to listen (Worthington, 2005b). These listeners prefer brief interactions and are more likely to interrupt or express displeasure with their conversational partner (Bodie & Villaume, 2003).

> **?** What is your listening style? How does this style help your work group? How does this style hinder your work group?

Research conducted to date on the four listening styles has discovered five general findings. First, people-oriented and content-oriented listeners are low in interpersonal, small group, and meeting communication apprehension (Sargent, Weaver, & Kiewitz, 1997). People-oriented listeners also are low in receiver apprehension (Bodie & Villaume, 2003). Second, people-oriented and content-oriented listeners are low in verbal aggressiveness (Worthington, 2005b). If you recall the characteristics associated with the communication apprehensive and the verbally aggressive group member discussed in Chapter 3, it makes sense these two listener types not only would have less fear about communicating with group members but also would refrain from being hurtful in their communication. Third, people-oriented listeners are higher in extroversion than action-oriented and content-oriented listeners (Weaver, Watson, & Barker, 1996).

Fourth, people-oriented and content-oriented listeners engage in conversational sensitivity (Chesebro, 1999). Conversational sensitivity refers to a person's ability to pay attention to and make inferences about the meaning generated in a conversation (Daly, Vangelisti, & Daughton, 1987). Fifth, content-oriented and action-oriented listeners are more likely to engage in second-guessing (Kirtley & Honeycutt, 1996). Second-guessing refers to when a listener questions the literal meaning of a message to determine the truthfulness of the message. If the listener doubts the message's truthfulness, she engages in second-guessing in an attempt to attach an alternative meaning to the message.

A Final Note About Relational Communication

Groups sometimes fail due specifically to the group members' use of relational communication. Small group communication researchers Vincent DiSalvo and his colleagues (1989) reported group members' communication skills as the most frequently noted dysfunctional group problem. Specifically, they found that the use of jargon, ineffective use of vocalics, and poor listening skills exemplify how group members do not pay attention to the potential impact of their relational communication. The best way to maximize relational communication in the small group is by monitoring your use of relational communication during group meetings. To maximize verbal and nonverbal communication when working in groups, simply think before communicating. To maximize listening when working in groups, reflect on the barriers (see Table 10.2) that might impede your listening (Golen, 1990; Watson & Smeltzer, 1986). Doing so will allow you to choose the most effective words and phrases, use the appropriate nonverbal codes to complement these words and phrases, and engage in listening behaviors that focus on the message rather than the speaker or yourself. To remain an effective and productive group member across all groups, always reflect on your use of relational communication and make the appropriate modifications.

Table 10.2   Barriers to Listening

1. Viewing a topic as boring or uninteresting
2. Refusing to consider an alternative viewpoint or perspective on a topic
3. Thinking emotionally rather than logically
4. Disagreeing outwardly with a speaker
5. Becoming impatient with a speaker
6. Focusing on the speaker (e.g., appearance, nonverbal behavior) rather than the topic
7. Daydreaming or thinking about another topic
8. Being distracted by physical noise

Source: From Golen, S. (1990). A factor analysis of barriers to effective listening. *Journal of Business Communication, 27,* 25–36. Reprinted with permission of Sage.

Conclusion

This chapter introduced you to relational communication by providing you with a definition of relational communication and its three components: verbal communication, nonverbal communication, and listening. We then explored these three components further and explained the four listening styles used by group members. As you read the next chapter, consider how group members' use of relational communication contributes to their choice and use of a conflict-handling style.

Discussion Questions

1. Review the case study at the beginning of the chapter. Identify an example for each of the three characteristics of verbal communication and the nine codes of nonverbal communication. Identify the listening style employed by Dorcas.

2. Consider a campus group to which you belong. What are some examples of how your group uses a restricted code?

3. Identify a group to which you belong. Provide an example of how group members use personal appearance, kinesics, oculesics, facial expression, proxemics, haptics, and vocalics.

4. In your work group, what barriers to listening exist? What could you do to become a more effective listener?

5. What recommendations would you make to your primary group as to how the group could improve its relational communication?

References

Afifi, W. A. (2007). Nonverbal communication. In B. B. Whaley & W. Samter (Eds.), *Explaining communication: Contemporary theories and exemplars* (pp. 39–60). Mahwah, NJ: Erlbaum.

American Heritage College Dictionary (3rd ed.). (2000). Boston: Houghton Mifflin.

Andersen, P. A. (1999). *Nonverbal communication: Forms and function.* Mountain View, CA: Mayfield.

Argyle, M. (1975). *Bodily communication.* New York: International Universities Press.

Bernstein, B. (Ed.). (1971). *Class, codes, and control (Vol. 1, Theoretical studies towards a sociology of language).* London: Routledge & Kegan Paul.

Birdwhistell, R. L. (1970). *Kinesics and context.* Philadelphia: University of Pennsylvania Press.

Bodie, G. D., & Villaume, W. A. (2003). Aspects of receiving information: The relationship between listening preferences, communication apprehension, receiver apprehension, and communicator style. *International Journal of Listening, 17,* 47–67.

Chesebro, J. L. (1999). The relationship between listening styles and conversational sensitivity. *Communication Research Reports, 16,* 233–238.

Daly, J. A., Vangelisti, A. L., & Daughton, S. M. (1987). The nature and correlates of conversational sensitivity. *Human Communication Research, 14,* 167–202.

DiSalvo, V. S., Nikkel, E., & Monroe, C. (1989). Theory and practice: A field investigation and identification of group members' perceptions of problems facing natural work groups. *Small Group Behavior, 20,* 551–567.

Ekman, P. (1982). *Emotion in the human face.* Cambridge, UK: Cambridge University Press.

Ekman, P., & Friesen, W. V. (1969). The repertoire of nonverbal behavior: Categories, origins, usage, and coding. *Semiotica, 1,* 49–98.

Goffman, E. (1971). *Relations in public: Microstudies of the public order.* New York: Harper Colophon.

Golen, S. (1990). A factor analysis of barriers to effective listening. *Journal of Business Communication, 27,* 25–36.

Gueguen, N., & Jacob, C. (2002). Direct look versus evasive glance and compliance with a request. *Journal of Social Psychology, 142,* 393–396.

Guerrero, L. K., & Floyd, K. (2006). *Nonverbal communication in close relationships.* Mahwah, NJ: Erlbaum.

Hall, E. T. (1966). *The hidden dimension.* Garden City, NY: Anchor Books.

Halone, K. K., & Pecchioni, L. L. (2001). Relational listening: A grounded theoretical model. *Communication Reports, 14,* 59–71.

Hawkins, K., W., & Fillion, B. P. (1999). Perceived communication skill needs for work groups. *Communication Research Reports, 16,* 167–174.

Hickson, M., III, Stacks, D. W., & Moore, N-J. (2004). *Nonverbal communication: Studies and applications* (4th ed.). Los Angeles: Roxbury.

Imhof, M. (2004). Who are we as we listen?: Individual listening profiles in varying contexts. *International Journal of Listening, 18,* 36–45.

Imhof, M., & Janusik, L. A. (2006). Development and validation of the Imhof-Janusik Listening Concepts Inventory to measure listening conceptualization differences between cultures. *Journal of Intercultural Communication Research, 35,* 79–98.

International Listening Association. (2005). *Definition of listening.* Retrieved May 10, 2007, from http://www.listen.org

Ketrow, S. M. (1999). Nonverbal aspects of group communication. In L. R. Frey (Ed.), D. S. Gouran, & M. S. Poole (Assoc. Eds.), *The handbook of group communication theory & research* (pp. 251–287). Thousand Oaks, CA: Sage.

Keyton, J. (1999). Relational communication in groups. In L. R. Frey (Ed.), D. S. Gouran, & M. S. Poole (Assoc. Eds.), *The handbook of group communication theory & research* (pp. 192–222). Thousand Oaks, CA: Sage.

Keyton, J., & Rhodes, S. (1994). The effects of listener preference styles on identifying sexual harassment. *Journal of the International Listening Association, 8,* 50–79.

Kimble, C. E., Forte, R. A., & Yoshikawa, J. C. (1981). Nonverbal concomitants of enacted emotional intensity and positivity: Visual and vocal behavior. *Journal of Personality, 49,* 271–283.

Kirtley, M. D., & Honeycutt, J. M. (1996). Listening styles and their correspondence with second guessing. *Communication Research Reports, 13,* 174–182.

Leathers, D. G. (1997). *Successful nonverbal communication: Principles and applications* (3rd ed.). Boston: Allyn & Bacon.

McPherson, B. (1999). Correlating students' personality types with their rating of topics covered in business communication classes. *Business Communication Quarterly, 62,* 46–53.

Molloy, J. T. (1988). *New dress for success.* New York: Warner.

Napieralski, L. P., & Brooks, C. I. (1995). The effect of duration of eye contact on American college students' attributions of state, trait, and test anxiety. *Journal of Social Psychology, 135,* 273–280.

Nguyen, T., Heslin, R., & Nguyen, M. L. (1975). The meanings of touch: Sex differences. *Journal of Communication, 25,* 92–103.

Oldenburg, D. (2001, February 27). Ear this: Listening is a must. *Omaha World Herald,* B30-31.

Robertson, A. K. (1994). *Listening for success: A guide to effective listening.* Burr Ridge, IL: Irwin Press.

Sargent, S. L., Weaver, J. B., III, & Kiewitz, C. (1997). Correlates between communication apprehension and listening styles preferences. *Communication Research Reports, 14,* 74–78.

Smeltzer, L. R., & Watson, K. W. (1984). Listening: An empirical comparison of discussion length and level of incentive. *Central States Speech Journal, 35,* 166–170.

Trenholm, S., & Jensen, A. (2007). *Interpersonal communication* (6th ed.). New York: Oxford University Press.

Watson, K. W., Barker, L. L., & Weaver, J. B., III. (1995). The listening styles profile (LSP-16): Development and validation of an instrument to assess four listening styles. *International Journal of Listening, 9,* 1–13.

Watson, K. W., & Smeltzer, L. R. (1986). Barriers to listening: Comparison between students and practitioners. *Communication Research Reports, 1,* 82–87.

Weaver, J. B., III, & Kirtley, M. D. (1995). Listening styles and empathy. *Southern Journal of Speech Communication, 60,* 131–140.

Weaver, J. B., III, Watson, K. W., & Barker, L. L. (1996). Personality and listening preferences: Do you hear what I hear? *Personality and Individual Differences, 20,* 381–387.

Worthington, D. L. (2005a). Exploring the relationship between listening style preference and personality. *International Journal of Listening, 19,* 68–87.

Worthington, D. L. (2005b). Exploring the relationship between listening style preference and verbal aggressiveness. *International Journal of Listening, 19,* 3–11.

Conflict in the Small Group | 11

After reading this chapter, you should be able to:

1. define conflict and identify its three dimensions,
2. differentiate among the four types of group conflict,
3. list and explain the five conflict-handling styles,
4. list five guidelines for handling conflict, and
5. pose five questions to answer when a group experiences conflict.

Case Study

At 5:45 p.m., the members of Water Exercise Techniques (WET) are finishing their workout in the pool at the local community center. The members of WET include Sadie, the instructor who has led WET groups for 20 years; college professors Schlomo, Tandy, Jonetta, and Hector; Micah, who works as a systems analyst for a computer systems corporation; and Patsy, a nurse at County General. The group meets three times a week and has been swimming together for two years.

Sadie: (blows whistle) Okey-dokey, everyone, swim to the deep end. Tread water. Now, we need to start planning our end-of-the-semester party. Any ideas on where we should eat?

Photo 11.1   Even members of a social group, such as a swimming club, need to be reminded that conflict can surface in the most unexpected places.

Source: ©iStockphoto.com/elkor.

Tandy:	I think we should try Maxim's. We've never been there.
Schlomo:	I've been there, and it's like eating dinner in your grandmother's basement.
Hector:	So have I, although I wouldn't compare it to my grandmother's basement. I used to love exploring my grandmother's basement! She had the most interesting items she gathered from her travels all over the world. That reminds me, Sadie, aren't you and your husband heading off on another trip to Greece?
Sadie:	Yes, Bert and I are going to Greece in July. Remember that means there's no class for two weeks.
Tandy:	I won't be here, either. My husband and I are going to Alaska on a cruise.
Hector:	I thought you already went to Alaska.
Tandy:	We did—nine years ago. Really, Hector. You need to keep up.
Schlomo:	Speaking of keeping up, Tandy, we're talking about our dinner plans, not your travel plans. And we're treading water, not flutter kicking.
Tandy:	So should we try Maxim's then?

Sadie:	Switch to body pendulum. Are there any other ideas?
Patsy:	What about Pippi's? I liked the portabella mushroom sandwich I had there last year.
Hector:	Pippi's is too dark and too cold.
Tandy:	As I recall, Patsy, you ordered the mushroom sandwich because you thought it was a hamburger.
Patsy:	I still liked it. What about La Hacienda? I ate there a few years ago, and it was quite tasty.
Tandy:	La Hacienda closed last year. Don't you ever go downtown, Patsy?
Patsy:	What about Gilligan's? My daughter Libby works there, and she can reserve us a table.
Tandy:	We had our holiday party there, remember? Of course you don't— you didn't show up!
Patsy:	I didn't show up because it was snowing heavily. How many times do I have to tell you that? And it was Schlomo's idea to go to Gilligan's, not mine.
Schlomo:	Yes, it was.
Tandy:	It was hardly snowing. Besides, my salad was wilted.
Patsy:	What about the French Bistro?
Tandy:	That place is too casual. My husband refuses to go there.
Patsy:	Well, I'm not here to cause any trouble. Hector, Schlomo, Jonetta, feel free to make a suggestion.
Sadie:	Switch to body rotation. Micah, what do you think?
Micah:	Why get worked up over dinner? I'll go wherever the group wants to go.
Schlomo:	I will too. Since I chose Gilligan's last time, it's only fair that someone else gets to choose the restaurant this time.
Jonetta:	We're running out of choices, folks. Let's try to choose a restaurant that doesn't resemble a basement; isn't too dark, cold, or loud; doesn't have a relative working there; and is open. Considering these issues, everyone e-mail me a choice of two places. I'll compile a list and bring it to class next week, and we can go from there. Why ruin our friendships over a restaurant?
Tandy:	I still think we should go to Maxim's.
Sadie:	Switch to body vertical. We know, Tandy. You've made that very clear. But I think we'll follow Jonetta's suggestion, take a vote, and let the best restaurant win! Now, take a deep bite of air and go into a tuck float.

As illustrated in the case study, conflict can surface in the most unexpected places and involve the most mundane topics. Who among us hasn't engaged in conflict over where to eat dinner? Regardless of the place and topic, however, conflict, if left unresolved, can affect a small group's performance devastatingly. As researchers have discovered, unresolved or an excessive amount of conflict causes a decrease in commitment to the group, group member satisfaction and interest, and overall group performance (Bishop & Scott, 1997; O'Connor, Gruenfeld, & McGrath, 1993; Wall & Nolan, 1986).

This chapter endeavors to examine conflict in the small group. To do so, we first will define conflict and identify the three dimensions of conflict. We then will explore the four types of conflict small group members experience and the five conflict-handling styles they use. Finally, we will offer five guidelines for handling conflict as it arises in the small group.

Definition of Conflict

People often think of conflict in negative terms. Conflict experts William Wilmot and Joyce Hocker (2001) compiled a list of common images individuals liken to conflict. These images include conflict as a war, an explosion, a struggle, a mess, a trial, a heroic adventure, a balancing act, and a tide. Although these images vary in intensity and personal involvement, they are similar in that group members must communicate with each other for conflict to occur (Folger, Poole, & Stutman, 2005).

> In your work group, what image would you liken to conflict? How does this image affect how you feel about work group conflict?

As such, most experts not surprisingly believe conflict is an expressed (i.e., verbally communicated) struggle among group members (Filley, 1975). Experts disagree, however, about what causes the struggle. Small group experts Victor Wall and Linda Nolan (1987) reported conflict routinely arises in groups due to the interdependence of group members. Communication scholars Janice Anderson, Myrna Foster-Kuehn, and Bruce McKinney (1996) posited conflict centers on the perception of incompatible goals, which influences group member interaction. In addition to incompatible goals, scarce resources and interference from group members affect group member interaction (Wilmot & Hocker, 2001).

Small group experts Victor Wall, Gloria Galanes, and Sue Love (1987) believed conflict arises when group members attempt to reach consensus. Author Daniel Dana (2001) stated conflict occurs when group members assign fault to specific group members. Combining these various viewpoints, we define conflict as the process that occurs when group members, due to their interdependence, their real and perceived differences, and their emotions, engage in an expressed struggle that impedes task accomplishment.

Regardless of its definition, conflict comprises three dimensions—affective, behavioral, and cognitive (Barki & Hartwick, 2001, 2004)—to which group members respond. The affective dimension refers to the negative emotions group members associate with conflict. These emotions usually center on the anger and frustration that group members sometimes experience when engaged in a conflict with each other. Other negative emotions include jealousy, anxiety, and fear. The behavioral dimension refers to the behaviors group members use during conflict. Although these behaviors may vary, group members usually engage in some form of inappropriate behavior (e.g., yelling, shaking a fist, pounding a table) that interferes with conflict resolution. The cognitive dimension refers to the differences in opinion among group members. Most group members view conflict as some form of a disagreement, with a focus on the discrepancy among members' values, opinions, goals, or objectives.

Now that we have defined conflict and identified its three dimensions, let's examine the types of conflict often experienced in the small group.

Types of Small Group Conflict

Conflict is almost always either constructive or destructive. Group members gain something as a result of a constructive conflict (Deutsch, 1973); these gains include, among others, pride, satisfaction, public acknowledgment of the group's task, and friendships established among group members. On the other hand, a destructive conflict causes group members to feel as if they lost something (Deutsch, 1973); these losses include, among others, embarrassment, dissatisfaction, public acknowledgement of the group's failures, and a lack of friendships established among group members.

Considering conflict constructive or destructive may depend on its type. Generally, four types of conflict emerge in the small group: substantive, affective, procedural, and inequity (see Table 11.1). At any point, a group can engage in more than one type of conflict (Nicotera, 1997).

The first type of conflict in the small group, substantive conflict, centers on group members' critical evaluation of ideas and can occur over a fact, an interpretation of a fact, a definition, or a choice (Verderber, 1982). Substantive

Table 11.1 Types of Conflict

Type	Definition
Substantive	Conflict centers on group members' critical evaluationof ideas.
Affective	Conflict centers on individual group members' communication and personality traits.
Procedural	Conflict centers on the procedures group members use to critically evaluate ideas or confront member behavior.
Inequity	Conflict centers on a group member's perceived imbalance between his contribution to the group and the contributions made by the group members.

conflict, also known as productive conflict (Witteman, 1991), is considered constructive and beneficial because how the conflict is handled ultimately affects the quality of the group's decision making or problem solving (Falk, 1982; Guetzkow & Cyr, 1954). When group members critically evaluate ideas, engage in idea generation, discuss group goals, are flexible in their behaviors and attitudes, and work toward a win-win outcome, the conflict becomes more productive (Witteman, 1991).

The second type of conflict in the small group, affective conflict, centers on individual group members' communication and personality traits. In many cases, affective conflict is disruptive, creates frustration, and reduces task quality (Falk, 1982; Guetzkow & Cyr, 1954) because the focus on a group member's communication or personality traits overshadows the group task. When decision making rests in the hands of one group member, or if group members consistently disagree, affective conflict likely will occur (Witteman, 1991). In the case study, the disagreement over where to hold their end-of-the-semester dinner party causes the WET members to focus on member traits or behaviors. For example, Tandy engages in affective conflict when she attacks Hector for his faulty memory and Patsy for her absence at the holiday dinner.

The third type of conflict in the small group, procedural conflict, often stems from substantive or affective conflict (Putnam, 1986). Procedural conflict centers on the procedures group members use to critically evaluate ideas or confront member behavior. For some groups, procedural conflict is tied to a disagreement about how to work on a task (Nicotera, 1997). In the case study, Jonetta attempts to resolve the group's procedural conflict by suggesting the group members e-mail her their choice of restaurants, and Sadie attempts to resolve it by announcing a vote will be taken at the next group meeting.

The fourth type of conflict in the small group, inequity conflict, centers on a group member's perceived imbalance between his contribution to the group and

Photo 11.2   Substantive, affective, procedural, or inequity conflict easily can make a group member feel frustrated or annoyed.

Source: ©iStockphoto.com/Cimmerian.

the contributions made by the group members. A group member who experiences inequity often feels less satisfied and perceives a greater amount of conflict occurring in the group (Wall & Nolan, 1987). Greater inequity also is associated with conflict centered on a group member rather than on the task (Wall & Nolan, 1986). In the case study, Patsy experiences inequity conflict when she finally asks Hector, Schlomo, and Jonetta to suggest a restaurant.

Now that we have examined the types of conflict experienced in the small group, let's examine the five conflict-handling styles used by group members.

Conflict-Handling Styles

Adapted from the work of Robert Blake and Jane Mouton (1964) and influenced by the work of Kenneth Thomas and Ralph Kilmann (1974), conflict expert M. Aflzalur Rahim (1983, 2002; Rahim & Bonoma, 1979) developed a taxonomy of five conflict-handling styles. Central to understanding this taxonomy is the notion that when group members handle conflict, they consider two factors: their concern for themselves (i.e., their own needs) and their concern for others (i.e., the needs of their group members). Based on the levels (i.e., high, moderate, low) of these two concerns, five categories of conflict-handling styles emerge (see Figure 11.1): avoiding, dominating, compromising, obliging, and integrating (Rahim, 1983).

Figure 11.1   Model of Conflict-Handling Styles

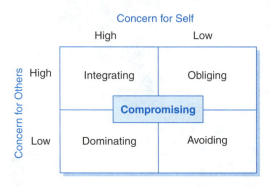

Source: From Rahim, M. A. (1983). A measure of styles of handling interpersonal conflict. *Academy of Management Journal, 26,* 368–376. Copyright © Academy of Management. Reprinted with permission.

Avoiding Conflict-Handling Style

A group member who uses an **avoiding conflict-handling style** has a low concern for both the self and the group members (Rahim, 2002). This means a group member may appear uninterested in the conflict, in part because he views conflict as hopeless, useless, or punishing (Filley, 1975), or in part because he views the issues surrounding the conflict as trivial (Rahim & Bonoma, 1979). Consequently, an avoider psychologically—and, if possible, physically—will leave the conflict situation. An avoider will not openly take sides in group conflict (Filley, 1975) and often does not disclose his feelings or thoughts about the conflict issue (Folger et al., 2005). In some instances, an avoider may appear apathetic, which may or may not be an accurate perception made by group members. In the case study, Micah illustrates the avoiding style when he informs the group he will abide by whatever decision the group makes about the restaurant. In fact, if Sadie hadn't asked Micah a question, he wouldn't have participated in the discussion at all! Luckily, group members infrequently use this conflict-handling style (Farmer & Roth, 1998).

Dominating Conflict-Handling Style

A group member who uses a **dominating conflict-handling style** places a priority on satisfying her own concerns instead of satisfying the concerns of group members (Rahim, 1983). This style represents a "win-lose" mentality in that the group member views winning as the ultimate goal (Rahim, Buntzman, & White, 1999) and often ignores the expectations or needs of her group members (Rahim, 2002). Because winning gives a dominator a sense of exhilaration and excitement (Filley, 1975), she may hide her true motives and withhold information that would weaken her position (Folger et al., 2005). In the case study, Tandy uses the dominating style by

> ❝ *Ethically Speaking:* In a work group, under what circumstances is using an avoiding or a dominating conflict-handling style an appropriate behavior? Why? ❞

finding fault with each restaurant suggestion Patsy makes. At the end of the interaction, Tandy reiterates the group should eat at Maxim's, which further demonstrates her assertiveness and lack of cooperativeness.

Compromising Conflict-Handling Style

A group member who uses a compromising conflict-handling style agrees to be agreeable (Blake & Mouton, 1970) and strives to find a middle ground between satisfying his own needs and satisfying his group members' needs (Rahim et al., 1999). A group member using the compromising style, therefore, will alternate between satisfying his own needs and satisfying the needs of group members. Although this member may make other group members aware of his will to compromise, he may not explain his reasons for the compromise (Folger et al., 2005). In the case study, Schlomo compromises when he tells the group he will go to whatever restaurant the group chooses since the group went to Gilligan's (his choice) the previous semester. Use this conflict-handling style as a last resort, however, because its use forces one group member—as evidenced by Schlomo— to give up something (Nicotera, 1997).

Obliging Conflict-Handling Style

A group member who uses an obliging conflict-handling style concerns herself highly with the needs of her group members (Rahim, 1983) and emphasizes finding commonalities among members (Rahim, 2002). A member who uses the obliging style tends to be highly flexible (Folger et al., 2005), in part because she overvalues the maintenance of group member relationships (Filley, 1975), in part because she may consider herself to have lower status than the other members (Rahim, 1983), and in part to maximize group harmony (Blake & Mouton, 1970). At the same time, a member who uses the obliging style desires the other members' acceptance and does not like to be confrontational because she fears hurting another member's feelings (Filley, 1975). In the case study, Patsy exemplifies the obliging style when she suggests a variety of restaurants from which the group could choose. Her use of this style becomes even more apparent when she continues to offer suggestions, even though Tandy responds in a disconfirming manner.

Integrating Conflict-Handling Style

A group member who uses an integrating conflict-handling style works toward developing a solution that satisfies the needs of all members (Ruble & Thomas, 1976). This group member does not view satisfying group members' needs and satisfying his own needs as mutually exclusive; rather, this member attempts to simultaneously satisfy his own needs and the needs of his group members. Considering conflict natural and helpful and refusing to sacrifice the needs of other members for the good of the group (Filley, 1975), this member engages in behaviors that stress openness, examination of differences, and a candid exchange of logic and emotion (Blake & Mouton, 1970; Rahim, 2002). In the case study, Jonetta illustrates the integrating style when she combines the concerns raised by the group and suggests how the group could arrive at a mutually desirable solution.

Not surprisingly, the integrating style is the preferred conflict-handling style among group members because using this style produces higher-quality outcomes (Wall et al., 1987), members regard it as the most effective style when it comes to decision making or problem solving (Kuhn & Poole, 2000), and it relates positively to group member satisfaction (Wall & Galanes, 1986). In addition, small group members frequently use this conflict-handling style (Farmer & Roth, 1998), which is considered the most appropriate and effective conflict-handling style (Gross & Guerrero, 2000).

Complete the ROCI-II instrument (Rahim, 1983). This instrument gives you a good indication of the conflict-handling style you are most likely to use in a group. Consider, however, that although the choice of a conflict-handling style usually is habitual (Folger et al., 2005), it can be situational (Nicotera, 1997), particularly if the group member considers the issue of conflict important or if the circumstance dictates the use of a particular style (Callahan, Benzing, & Perri, 2006). Rahim (2002) identified several situations in which each conflict-handling style is considered appropriate to use (see Table 11.2). As you read these situations, consider whether you would use the identified style to handle the conflict or if you would use a combination of styles. Researchers have found the use of a combination of conflict-handling styles (i.e., using the integrating, obliging, and compromising styles or the integrating and compromising styles simultaneously) can be more effective than relying on the use of a single style (Munduate, Ganaza, Peiro, & Euwema, 1999; Weider-Hatfield & Hatfield, 1995). As such, it might prove prudent to assess the conflict situation and consider using another style or a combination of styles when appropriate.

> **?** What is your conflict-handling style? How does this style help your work group? How does this style hinder your work group?

Now that we have examined the five conflict-handling styles used by small group members, let's explore some guidelines for handling conflict in small groups.

Assessment Tool 11.1   Rahim Organizational Conflict Inventory-II

This questionnaire contains statements about your communicative behaviors in a conflict situation with your group members. Indicate how often each statement is true for you personally according to the following scale.

If the statement is **almost always true**, write **5** in the blank.

If the statement is **often true**, write **4** in the blank.

If the statement is **occasionally true**, write **3** in the blank.

If the statement is **rarely true**, write **2** in the blank.

If the statement is **almost never true**, write **1** in the blank.

_____   1.   I try to investigate an issue with my group members to find a solution acceptable to us.

_____   2.   I attempt to avoid being "put on the spot" and try to keep my conflict with my group members to myself.

_____   3.   I use my influence to get my ideas accepted.

_____   4.   I generally try to satisfy the needs of my group members.

_____   5.   I try to find a middle course to resolve an impasse my group has reached.

_____   6.   I try to integrate my ideas with those of my group members to come up with a decision jointly.

_____   7.   I usually avoid open discussion of my differences with my group members.

_____   8.   I use my authority to get my ideas accepted.

_____   9.   I usually accommodate the wishes of my group members.

_____ 10.   I usually propose a middle ground for breaking deadlocks.

_____ 11.   I try to work with my group members to find solutions to a problem that satisfy all our expectations.

_____ 12.   I try to stay away from disagreeing with my group members.

_____ 13.   I use my expertise to help my group members make a decision in my favor.

_____ 14.   I give in to the wishes of my group members.

_____ 15.   I negotiate with my group members so we can reach a compromise.

_____ 16.   I exchange accurate information with my group members so we can solve a problem together.

_____ 17.   I avoid any unpleasant exchanges with my group members.

_____ 18.   I am usually firm in pursuing my side of an issue.

_____ 19.   I usually concede to my group members.

(Continued)

(Continued)

_____ 20. I "give and take" so a compromise can be made.

_____ 21. I try to bring all our concerns out in the open so that the issues can be resolved in the best possible way.

_____ 22. I try to keep any disagreement with my group members to myself in order to avoid hard feelings.

_____ 23. I sometimes use my power to win a competitive situation.

_____ 24. I often go along with the suggestions of my group members.

_____ 25. I collaborate with my group members to come up with decisions acceptable to us.

_____ 26. I try to satisfy the expectations of my group members.

_____ 27. I try to work with my group members to develop a proper understanding of the task.

Scoring:

1. Add your scores for items 1, 6, 11, 16, 21, 25, and 27. Divide by 7. This is your **collaborating** conflict-handling score.

2. Add your scores for items 2, 7, 12, 17, and 22. Divide by 5. This is your **avoiding** conflict-handling score.

3. Add your scores for items 3, 8, 13, 18, and 23. Divide by 5. This is your **competing** conflict-handling score.

4. Add your scores for items 4, 9, 14, 19, 24, and 26. Divide by 6. This is your **accommodating** conflict-handling score.

5. Add your scores for items 5, 10, 15, and 20. Divide by 4. This is your **compromising** conflict-handling score.

Source: From Rahim, M. A. (1983). A measure of styles of handling interpersonal conflict. *Academy of Management Journal, 26,* 368–376. Copyright © Academy of Management. Reprinted with permission.

Guidelines for Handling Conflict

Victor Wall and Linda Nolan (1986) found that in a survey of 375 groups, 75% reported the presence of conflict. Based on this statistic, group members should expect to handle conflict at some point during the group's history. Any time a conflict arises, group members should consider the following five guidelines.

1. Group conflict sometimes causes decreased affect for the group. When groups experience little conflict, members report more positive feelings about

Table 11.2   Appropriate Situations for Conflict-Handling Styles

Style	*Appropriate Situation*
Avoiding	1. The issue is trivial. 2. Group members need to take a break. 3. Confronting group members is unnecessary.
Dominating	1. The issue is trivial. 2. A timely decision is needed. 3. The group members lack expertise.
Compromising	1. The group members can't reach consensus. 2. The dominating style has no effect. 3. A temporary solution is needed.
Obliging	1. The issue is more important to group members than you. 2. The relationship among group members is worth preserving. 3. You lack expertise.
Integrating	1. The issue is complex. 2. The group has the necessary resources. 3. The issue requires group member collaboration.

Source: Reprinted by permission of Emerald Group Publishing Ltd. from Rahim, M. A. (2002). Toward a theory of managing organizational conflict. *International Journal of Conflict Management, 13*(3), 206–235.

each other than groups that report moderate or high amounts of conflict (O'Connor et al., 1993). According to Susan Jarboe and Hal Witteman (1996), the presence of substantive, affective, and procedural conflict can result in the development of negative feelings for the group. Individuals are less likely to quit a group when affective conflict is low (Bayazit & Mannix, 2003).

2. Group conflict may have nothing to do with the task. In fact, conflict can occur over such issues as struggles for leadership, perceived unequal workloads, group member personality differences, procedural issues, differences in group goals, and differences in ideology (Sell, Lovaglia, Mannix, Samuelson, & Wilson, 2004; Wall & Nolan, 1986). Kenneth Thomas and Warren Schmidt (1976) reported that conflict most often stems from misunderstandings among group members, which they consider a communication failure. Communication professor Sue Pendell (1990) offered that at times conflict arises when group members engage in

?

Identify the last time you engaged in a deviant behavior in your work group. Did conflict occur as a result of your behavior? If so, how was the conflict handled?

deviant behaviors. Similar to the notion of deviant role behaviors discussed in Chapter 8, deviant behaviors enacted by group members violate group norms (Putnam, 1986). Examples of deviant behaviors include not participating in group discussion, missing group meetings, fighting for leadership, "testing" members' opinions, and forming coalitions (Pendell, 1990). Group members who engage in these deviant behaviors unwittingly may cause conflict to occur.

3. Group conflict may prove irresolvable. As much as members would like to resolve group conflict, sometimes they simply cannot. In some cases, breakdowns in communication between and among group members create a rift that cannot be repaired (Thomas, 1976). In other cases, we belong to groups in which no amount of interaction can change a difficult member's lack of willingness to resolve conflict. In still other cases, a group member's communication and personality traits may influence whether conflict can be resolved. Communication scholars Randall Rogan and Betty La France (2003) reported that verbally aggressive individuals are more likely to approach a conflict situation in a controlling manner and are less likely to approach a conflict situation in a nonconfrontational manner. Scholars Robert Jones and Charles White (1985) found that high Machs prefer to approach conflict in a forcing or confrontational manner rather than in an obliging manner. In these cases, rather than wasting time, energy, and group resources in trying to resolve conflict, group members should recognize that some conflict is irresolvable and focus their energy elsewhere.

4. Group conflict has both short- and long-term benefits (Thomas, 1990). In the short term, the benefits of conflict include coping with the immediate issue and arriving at a decision or solution that satisfies the group members; in the long term, the benefits of conflict include establishing norms and procedures for group members to consider in conflict situations and influencing the development of group culture and member identification.

5. Group conflict produces both short- and long-term consequences (Thomas, 1976). In addition to benefiting a group, the consequences of group conflict can affect how group members communicate with each other, how they feel about each other, and whether they feel motivated to handle conflict. These consequences subsequently may act as a moderator between group conflict and group performance, which can become detrimental over the life span of a group.

A Final Note About Small Group Conflict

As we conclude this chapter, we want to reiterate that conflict creates both constructive and destructive consequences. As stated by conflict expert Linda Putnam (1986), "conflict typically evokes high levels of interpersonal anxiety and yet it aids in making top quality decisions" (p. 194). After experiencing constructive conflict, group members feel a sense of energy and a greater connection to the group, develop a greater sense of self-worth, and learn how to act in a productive manner; after experiencing destructive conflict, group members avoid each other, engage in less direct interaction, and harbor resentment and disappointment (Hocker & Wilmot, 1991). To make conflict as constructive as possible, group members should reflect on not only how they define the conflict but how best to handle it as well. Doing so allows group members to reduce both the frequency and the intensity of any conflict situation.

Conclusion

This chapter examined conflict in the small group. To do so, we first defined conflict and identified its three dimensions. We then explored the types of conflict experienced by small group members and examined the five conflict-handling styles used by group members. Finally, we offered five guidelines for handling conflict as it arises in the small group. As you read the next chapter, consider how your group members' conflict-handling styles impact the establishment of your group's communication climate.

Discussion Questions

1. Refer to a recent conflict that occurred in one of the groups to which you belong. How did you respond affectively, behaviorally, and cognitively?

2. Using a primary group to which you belong, identify an example of a substantive, an affective, a procedural, and an inequity conflict experienced by the group. Of these four types of conflict, which type(s) would you consider constructive? Which type(s) would you consider destructive?

3. Identify the advantages and disadvantages of using each conflict-handling style in your work group. Which style has the most advantages? Which style has the most disadvantages? To what extent are the advantages and disadvantages you identified unique to your work group?

4. What are some deviant group member behaviors that could cause conflict in a virtual group? Would these behaviors be considered deviant if the group met face-to-face?

5. What are some additional short- and long-term benefits of group conflict?

References

Anderson, J. W., Foster-Kuehn, M., & McKinney, B. C. (1996). *Communication skills for surviving conflicts at work.* Cresskill, NJ: Hampton Press.

Barki, H., & Hartwick, J. (2001). Interpersonal conflict and its management in information system development. *MIS Quarterly, 25,* 195–228.

Barki, H., & Hartwick, J. (2004). Conceptualizing the construct of interpersonal conflict. *International Journal of Conflict Management, 15,* 216–224.

Bayazit, M., & Mannix, E. A. (2003). Should I stay or should I go? Predicting team members' intent to remain in the team. *Small Group Research, 34,* 290–321.

Bishop, J. W., & Scott, K. D. (1997, February). How commitment affects team performance. *HR Magazine, 42*(2), 107–111.

Blake, R. R., & Mouton, J. S. (1964). *The managerial grid.* Houston, TX: Gulf.

Blake, R. R., & Mouton, J. S. (1970). The fifth achievement. *Journal of Applied Behavioral Science, 6,* 413–426.

Callahan, G. A., Benzing, C. D., & Perri, D. F. (2006). Choice of conflict-handling strategy: A matter of context. *Journal of Psychology, 140,* 269–288.

Dana, D. (2001). *Conflict resolution: Mediation tools for everyday worklife.* New York: McGraw-Hill.

Deutsch, M. (1973). *The resolution of conflict: Constructive and destructive processes.* New Haven, CT: Yale University Press.

Falk, G. (1982). An empirical study measuring conflict in problem-solving groups which are assigned different decision rules. *Human Relations, 35,* 1123–1138.

Farmer, S. M., & Roth, J. (1998). Conflict-handling behavior in work groups: Effects of group structure, decision processes, and time. *Small Group Research, 29,* 669–713.

Filley, A. C. (1975). *Interpersonal conflict resolution.* Glenview, IL: Scott, Foresman & Co.

Folger, J. P., Poole, M. S., & Stutman, R. K. (2005). *Working through conflict: Strategies for relationships, groups, and organizations* (5th ed.). Boston: Allyn & Bacon.

Gross, M. A., & Guerrero, L. K. (2000). Managing conflict appropriately and effectively: An application of the competence model to Rahim's organizational conflict styles. *International Journal of Conflict Management, 11,* 200–226.

Guetzkow, H., & Cyr, J. (1954). An analysis of conflict in decision-making groups. *Human Relations, 7,* 367–382.

Hocker, J. L., & Wilmot, W. W. (1991). *Interpersonal conflict* (3rd ed.). Dubuque, IA: Wm. C. Brown.

Jarboe, S. C., & Witteman, H. R. (1996). Intragroup conflict management in task-oriented groups: The influence of problem sources and problem analyses. *Small Group Research, 27,* 316–338.

Jones, R. E., & White, C. S. (1985). Relationships among personality, conflict resolution styles, and task effectiveness. *Group & Organization Studies, 10,* 152–167.

Kuhn, T., & Poole, M. S. (2000). Do conflict management styles affect group decision-making? Evidence from a longitudinal field study. *Human Communication Research, 26,* 558–590.

Munduate, L., Ganaza, J., Peiro, J. M., & Euwema, M. (1999). Patterns of styles in conflict management and effectiveness. *International Journal of Conflict Management, 10,* 5–24.

Nicotera, A. M. (1997). Managing conflict communication in groups. In L. R. Frey & J. K. Barge (Eds.), *Managing group life: Communicating in decision-making groups* (pp. 104–130). Boston: Houghton Mifflin.

O'Connor, K. M., Gruenfeld, D. H., & McGrath, J. E. (1993). The experience and effects of conflict in continuing work groups. *Small Group Research, 24,* 363–382.

Pendell, S. D. (1990). Deviance and conflict in small group decision making: An exploratory study. *Small Group Research, 21,* 393–403.

Putnam, L. L. (1986). Conflict in group decision-making. In R. Y. Hirokawa & M. S. Poole (Eds.), *Communication and group decision-making* (pp. 175–196). Beverly Hills, CA: Sage.

Rahim, M. A. (1983). A measure of styles of handling interpersonal conflict. *Academy of Management Journal, 26,* 368–376.

Rahim, M. A. (2002). Toward a theory of managing organizational conflict. *International Journal of Conflict Management, 13,* 206–235.

Rahim, M. A., & Bonoma, T. V. (1979). Managing organizational conflict: A model for diagnosis and intervention. *Psychological Reports, 44,* 1323–1344.

Rahim, M. A., Buntzman, G. F., & White, D. (1999). An empirical study of the stages of moral development and conflict management styles. *International Journal of Conflict Management, 10,* 154–171.

Rogan, R. G., & La France, B. H. (2003). An examination of the relationship between verbal aggressiveness, conflict management strategies and conflict interaction goals. *Communication Quarterly, 51,* 458–469.

Ruble, T. L., & Thomas, K. W. (1976). Support for a two-dimensional model of conflict behavior. *Organizational Behavior and Human Performance, 16,* 143–155.

Sell, J., Lovaglia, M. J., Mannix, E. A., Samuelson, C. D., & Wilson, R. K. (2004). Investigating conflict, power, and status within and among groups. *Small Group Research, 35,* 44–72.

Thomas, K. W. (1976). Conflict and conflict management. In M. D. Dunnette (Ed.), *Handbook of industrial and organizational psychology* (pp. 889–935). Chicago: Rand McNally.

Thomas, K. W. (1990). Conflict and negotiation processes in organizations. In M. D. Dunnette & L. M. Hough (Eds.), *Handbook of industrial and organizational psychology* (Vol. 3, 2nd ed., pp. 651–717). Palo Alto, CA: Consulting Psychologists Press.

Thomas, K. W., & Kilmann, R. H. (1974). *The Thomas-Kilmann conflict MODE instrument.* Tuxedo Park, NY: Xicom.

Thomas, K. W., & Schmidt, W. H. (1976). A survey of managerial interests with respect to conflict. *Academy of Management Journal, 19,* 315–318.

Verderber, R. F. (1982). *Working together: Fundamentals of group decision making.* Belmont, CA: Wadsworth.

Wall, V. D., Jr., & Galanes, G. J. (1986). The SYMLOG dimensions and small group conflict. *Central States Speech Journal, 37,* 61–78.

Wall, V. D., Jr., Galanes, G. J., & Love, S. B. (1987). Small, task-oriented groups: Conflict, conflict management, satisfaction, and decision quality. *Small Group Behavior, 18,* 31–55.

Wall, V. D., Jr., & Nolan, L. L. (1986). Perceptions of inequity, satisfaction, and conflict in task-oriented groups. *Human Relations, 39,* 1033–1052.

Wall, V. D., Jr., & Nolan, L. L. (1987). Small group conflict: A look at equity, satisfaction, and styles of conflict management. *Small Group Behavior, 18,* 188–211.

Weider-Hatfield, D., & Hatfield, J. D. (1995). Relationships among conflict, management styles, levels of conflict, and reactions to work. *Journal of Social Psychology, 135,* 687–698.

Wilmot, W. W., & Hocker, J. L. (2001). *Interpersonal conflict* (6th ed.). Boston: McGraw-Hill.

Witteman, H. (1991). Group member satisfaction: A conflict-related account. *Small Group Research, 22,* 24–58.

Cohesion and Climate in the Small Group 12

After reading this chapter, you should be able to:

1. explain the importance of cohesion in a small group,
2. define communication climate,
3. identify and define the six dimensions of a supportive communication climate,
4. identify and define the six dimensions of a defensive communication climate, and
5. identify four ways to turn a defensive communication climate into a supportive communication climate.

Case Study | During the final week of COMM 112, the group we met in Chapter 1 is finalizing its group project. At 10 p.m. on the night before the project's due date, the group is working at the Student Center.

Photo 12.1   Maintaining a supportive communication climate is essential when working in any small group, including learning groups.

Source: ©iStockphoto.com/ericsphotography.

David: Whew! I'm glad this project is almost done. I can't believe I had to spend as much time on this class as I have. I had better get an A in this class!

Shanika: You make it sound like you did all the work. Don't forget I was the one who went and found the books we needed at the library after you said you couldn't find them.

Hassan: That's right, Dave. If it weren't for Shanika, we'd be in bad shape.

David: Oh, yeah, I keep "forgetting." (rolls his eyes) You're absolutely right, Hassan. If it weren't for Shanika, we wouldn't have made it through this class. And don't forget your contributions. After all, if it weren't for you, Shanika wouldn't have had to retype the bibliography you "lost" when your computer "crashed."

Hassan: At least I volunteered to help the group.

David: How? Unless volunteering the radio station as a place to meet counts, you really didn't do much. And it's not as if that went well. What was it your boss said when she kicked us out—something like "Hassan has no authority to use U-101.5 for his own personal use"?

Hassan: At least I tried to do something. That's more than I can say for you, Dave. You've spent this entire semester being nothing but a . . .

Julie: All right, guys, knock it off. This has been a difficult task to accomplish, and we don't need to spend our last work session arguing with each other. For the most part, we've done a great job, and we need to stay positive as we finish working on our presentation.

David: Oh, I'm positive all right. I'm positive we're not going to get this done.

Shanika: We could get this done if you would quit being so negative. You know, if you had just followed the directions I provided when this project was assigned, we wouldn't still be working on it. And it's not as if this is the only class I'm taking. Between school, my job at Payless, being on the dance team, and running for homecoming court, I haven't had time to breathe, let alone do all the work for this group. With you and Hassan fighting the entire semester, it's a wonder we got anything accomplished at all. Right, Joe?

Joseph: (looks up from his newspaper) Did you say something, Shanika?

Shanika: Thanks for paying attention, Joe.

Julie: Now, Shanika, it wasn't that bad.

Shanika: Maybe not to you, Mary Sunshine. You find something positive in everything. Where were you when I had to go to the library at 11 p.m. at night in a torrential downpour to get a book Dave insisted he couldn't find or when I had to retype the bibliography Hassan lost because he never thought of making a backup copy on his computer?

Julie: It's understandable why you're angry, Shanika. But we have to remember, because we're different people, we all work differently. Think about the special qualities each of us brought to this group. Dave is phenomenal at finding resources on the Internet, Hassan knows how to makes us laugh when we need to, Joe is really good at playing the devil's advocate, and Shanika, you've been great at keeping us on task all semester. Yes, perhaps Dave and Hassan could have been more thoughtful at times, but we need to put aside our differences and finish our work.

David: Shanika, have you thought about majoring in theater? Because you've been putting on a great performance for us this entire semester.

Hassan: (laughs) And it's not my fault the computer crashed. You make it sound like I did it on purpose.

Julie: I'm sure it wasn't on purpose, Hassan. Now listen, everyone. We've had such a great semester working together I would hate for our last night to be filled with such bitterness. Don't you all agree?

Shanika: Whatever, Julie. At this point, I really don't care. All I know is we have a presentation tomorrow for which we are not ready. Could we just get to work and skip the pep talk?

David: That's part of the problem. You never seem to care. As long as we all agree with what Shanika thinks, feels, and believes, Shanika cares. It's when the rest of us have an opinion that Shanika doesn't care. It's always Shanika, Shanika, Shanika.

Joseph: For a bunch of comm. majors, you guys are lousy at communication. Let's finish this presentation so I can go to BW 3's, eat a few wings, and put this semester behind me.

During any group meeting, communication among members can produce either a facilitating or a debilitating effect. In this case study, the communication occurring among David, Hassan, Julie, Shanika, and Joseph is generally debilitating. David and Hassan bicker, Shanika attacks, Joseph doesn't listen, and Julie defends. Together, the five members demonstrate a lack of cohesion and exemplify an undeniably defensive communication climate. Unfortunately, this scenario commonly occurs. Failing to consider the interdependent nature of group members' communicative behaviors can produce detrimental results.

This chapter purports to introduce you to the concepts of cohesion and climate. To do so, we first will reexamine cohesion and explain its importance to small group members. We then will define communication climate, focusing specifically on the six dimensions that comprise a supportive communication climate and the six dimensions that comprise a defensive climate. Finally, we will examine four ways a group can turn a defensive communication climate into a supportive communication climate.

The Importance of Cohesion

You may have noticed the mention of cohesion in several places in this textbook. To refresh your memory, recall from Chapter 2 that **cohesion**, a behavior that can change over the course of a group's existence (Carron & Brawley, 2000), occurs when a member reaches an acceptable level of desire to stay in the group. The most effective groups balance task and social cohesion (Craig & Kelly, 1999). **Task cohesion** refers to the degree to which group members work toward a common goal whereas **social cohesion** reflects the level of positive affect among group members (Kjormo & Halvari, 2002).

Although both task and social cohesion are important to group members, members may pay more attention to social cohesion because it reflects their feelings about the group process and their relationships with group members. Moreover, social cohesion helps group members feel successful, connected, valued, and supported (Fujishin, 2007). When a group member feels successful, she contributes to the group's task accomplishment. When a group member feels connected, he communicates with his group members and partici-

> **?** Reflect on your work group. Identify how you make each group member feel successful, connected, valued, or supported.

pates in group interaction. When a group member feels valued, she appreciates her group members. When a group member feels supported, he expresses caring, empathy, and concern about his group members. Together, these feelings contribute to the development of trust among members (Fujishin, 2007), which is vital to the development of a supportive communication climate.

Definition of Communication Climate

Cohesion sometimes surfaces through a group's communication climate, which, as suggested by Corwin King (1986), comprises a free and open exchange of ideas and information among group members. John Veiga (1991) suggested an indifferent communication climate exists when one group member perceives the other group members as unwilling to commit themselves to task accomplishment. Nancy Evans and Paul Jarvis (1986) considered communication climate to reflect group members' feelings toward the group. For our purpose, we define **communication climate** as the relative acceptance or rejection a group member feels based on the social and psychological tone of the relationships established among group members (Rosenfeld, 1983).

Regardless of its definition, communication climate is created by the relational communication of group members—that is, the verbal communication behaviors, the nonverbal communication behaviors, and the listening behaviors used by each group member collectively create a group's communication climate.

Photo 12.2 A supportive communication climate encourages group members to share their opinion, offer their feedback, and contribute to the group task.

Source: ©iStockphoto.com/Yuri_Arcurs.

From these behaviors, two types of climate can emerge: a supportive communication climate and a defensive communication climate.

In a **supportive communication climate**, group members feel their contributions are welcomed and valued. Authors Charles and Elizabeth Beck (1986) stated a supportive communication climate invites openness among group members. Additionally, establishing a supportive communication climate allows group members to remain highly involved in the group process, to use empathic listening, and to engage in constructive conflict management procedures (Larsen & Folgero, 1993). A supportive communication climate provides group members with the information they need to perform their tasks, build morale, and encourage creativity (King, 1986). According to consultant Jack Gibb (1961), group members with a supportive communication climate communicate through the dimensions of description, problem orientation, spontaneity, empathy, equality, and provisionalism.

> **?** In your work group, has there been a time when you felt your contributions were neither welcomed nor valued? How did this affect your communication with your members?

In a **defensive communication climate**, group members feel their contributions are neither welcomed nor valued. Ultimately, a defensive communication climate results in resentment or a lack of communication among group members (Beck & Beck, 1986). A defensive climate implicitly encourages group members to work by themselves and to monitor the comments made to one another (Larsen & Folgero, 1993). Doubt, confusion, and demotivation to complete the group task can emerge, leading perhaps to cynicism (King, 1986). A defensive communication climate is communicated through the dimensions of evaluation, control, strategy, neutrality, superiority, and certainty (Gibb, 1961).

How Communication Climate Is Established

For a group to establish a supportive communication climate, group members essentially must utilize all six dimensions of a supportive climate (Beck & Beck, 1986; Gibb, 1961). Unfortunately, at any given point, a group member can engage in behaviors that promote a defensive communication climate. Even an unintentional engagement (Beck & Beck, 1986) can produce horribly damaging ramifications. Communication professor Ronald Gordon (1988) found that when people feel defensive, they report feeling physically tense, physiologically overwhelmed, and mentally confused. As such, group members should maximize their use of the six dimensions that promote a supportive communication climate and minimize their use of the six dimensions that promote a defensive communication climate. Table 12.1 explains these dimensions (Gibb, 1961).

To understand the differences between a supportive communication climate and a defensive communication climate, it is important to examine each dimension.

Description Versus Evaluation

Description and evaluation focus on how group members take ownership of their verbal and nonverbal expressions. A group member who engages in **description** describes her feelings and presents her viewpoints as her own; a group member who engages in **evaluation** passes judgment, assigns blame, and interrogates group members (Beck & Beck, 1986). Group members who describe often use the pronoun *I* (which implies ownership of the feeling) whereas group members who evaluate often use the pronoun *you* (which implies criticism or judgment and relegates blame to the receiver rather than the sender). Consider several of the statements made by Shanika, David, and Hassan. Rather than describing how she feels

Table 12.1   Dimensions of Communication Climate

Supportive Climate	Defensive Climate
Description	Evaluation
Problem orientation	Control
Spontaneity	Strategy
Empathy	Neutrality
Equality	Superiority
Provisionalism	Certainty

Source: Reprinted by permission of Blackwell Publishing from Gibb, J. R. (1961). Defensive communication. *Journal of Communication, 11,* 141–148. Copyright © Blackwell Publishing, Inc. Reprinted with permission of the editor.

taken advantage of by David and Hassan, Shanika evaluates both men's group performance, causing them to react in a negative manner. To describe rather than evaluate, group members should monitor how they talk to each other.

Problem Orientation Versus Control

Problem orientation and control deal with how group members approach task accomplishment. A group member who stresses **problem orientation** focuses on collaborating with group members by seeking a mutually defined and acceptable solution (Gibb, 1961). A group member who exhibits **control** imposes his point of view on group members. When a group member uses problem orientation, he endeavors to make a decision or solve a problem without inhibiting the behaviors of group members; when a group member uses control, he attempts to influence or change the behaviors of group members (Beck & Beck, 1986). To become more adept at problem orientation, group members should consider that task accomplishment requires all members' input.

Spontaneity Versus Strategy

Spontaneity and strategy center on the degree of openness that exists among group members. A group member who uses **spontaneity** openly expresses her thoughts, feelings, or emotions upfront whereas a group member who uses **strategy** shares her thoughts, feelings, or emotions less than honestly. Although a group member need not self-disclose highly intimate information in order to stimulate relational development (Anderson, 1985), it is important not to view a group member as having a hidden agenda or as using the group as a way to satisfy her personal needs. Group members can express spontaneity by discussing a variety of group-related topics,

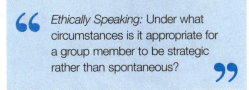

Ethically Speaking: Under what circumstances is it appropriate for a group member to be strategic rather than spontaneous?

such as individual expectations, prior group experiences, and expectations about the current group experience (Kavanaugh & Bollet, 1983), as well as by engaging in problem-solving, role, consciousness-raising, and encounter talk.

Empathy Versus Neutrality

Empathy and neutrality focus on how group members demonstrate concern or indifference toward one another. A group member displaying **empathy** identifies with the group members and attempts to understand their feelings, needs, and interests. A group member displaying **neutrality** indicates her indifference toward the other group members and their feelings, needs, and interests. The case study's Shanika exemplifies neutrality, which occurs in many groups, when she states "I really don't care" in response to Julie's request for everyone to get along. Because it is important that group members feel the group values their contributions, group members should take especially important care to avoid appearing neutral.

Equality Versus Superiority

Equality and superiority deal with how group members minimize or maximize their individual differences. A group member engaging in **equality** treats all group members the same and believes the contributions of all group members are equally needed, desired, or required. A group member engaging in **superiority** treats all group members differently because he does not consider them equals. Such factors as power, wealth, intelligence, and physical appearance exemplify what makes a group member feel superior (Gibb, 1961). By engaging in superiority, a group member implicitly states he does not find the group members' contributions credible, does not value their input, and is not interested in receiving feedback. In the case study, Julie uses equality when she lists each member's contributions to the group process. Shanika, on the other hand, demonstrates superiority in several instances. Can you identify these instances?

Provisionalism Versus Certainty

Provisionalism and certainty center on group members' degree of inflexibility or rigidity when communicating with each other. A group member engaging in

Photo 12.3   In certainty, one aspect of a defensive communication climate, a group member believes there is only one way to approach a task.

Source: ©iStockphoto.com/endopack.

provisionalism makes tentative judgments about the task and the group members whereas a group member engaging in **certainty** sees only one way to approach a task. According to authors Charles and Elizabeth Beck (1986), a provisional group member will adapt, experiment with alternatives, and try new behaviors. A group member using certainty has highly dogmatic thoughts and remains convinced his way is the "right" way. In the case study, Shanika displays certainty when she tells the group it would have performed more efficiently had it followed her suggestions.

Now that we understand the distinctions between the dimensions of a supportive communication climate and the dimensions of a defensive communication climate, let's examine how a defensive communication climate can turn into a supportive communication climate.

Turning a Defensive Climate Into a Supportive Climate

What happens when your group consistently works in a defensive communication climate? According to researchers William Gardner and Nancy Masztal (1985), a

group has two choices: either remain in a defensive mode or turn the defensiveness into supportiveness. To make the group experience as productive and as
enjoyable as possible, we recommend you and your group members actively work
toward developing a supportive communication climate in one of four ways.

First (and perhaps easiest), monitor your relational communication by
reviewing the negative messages associated with each dimension of a defensive
communication climate and actively working toward replacing the negative message with a positive message. Consider the following messages: (1) "You're stupid
to think that," (2) "I'm the one in charge here, and you're going to do things my
way or else," (3) "I'm going to maneuver you into doing exactly what I want you
to do," (4) "I don't care about you," (5) "I'm better than you are," and (6) "I'm
right, you're wrong" (Gordon, 1988, p. 55). Take a few minutes and review the six
dimensions of a defensive communication climate. Now, match each of these six
aforementioned statements with the appropriate dimension. If you matched these
statements correctly, you answered (in order) evaluation, control, strategy, neutrality, superiority, and certainty. Now, replace each negative message with a positive message. If you can do this at this point, you should be able to do so when
working with a group.

Second, use confirming messages and avoid the use of disconfirming messages. A **confirming message** recognizes the value and importance of a relational
partner. In a small group, the use of confirming messages relates positively to
group member agreeableness (Sager &
Gastil, 2002), meaning that when
group members agree with each other,
they acknowledge each other's contributions. A **disconfirming message**
makes a relational partner feel devalued. Disconfirming messages cause

> **?** In your work group, how common
> is the use of these disconfirming
> messages? How could the use
> of these messages be prevented
> or avoided?

individuals to feel as if other people aren't listening to them, their contributions
aren't important, or their participation is neither welcomed nor needed (Cissna &
Sieburg, 1981), which can occur easily in any small group. Communication scholars Frank Dance and Carl Larson (1972) identified a variety of disconfirming
messages, contained in Table 12.2.

Third, reduce the use of discounting messages. A **discounting message**
disparages or fails to affirm a new idea (Weaver, 1993) that emerges in either a
verbal (e.g., "The trouble with that is . . ." or "That's stupid") or a nonverbal
(e.g., rolling the eyes or smirking) form (Smith, 1983). Unlike a disconfirming
message, which devalues a group member, a discounting message devalues a
group member's ideas. Unfortunately, many members do not recognize this distinction and, as a result, retaliate against the discounting message by using
another discounting message, termed the discount/revenge cycle (Weaver, 1993).
To avoid triggering the discount/revenge cycle, consider whether you use such

Table 12.2   Disconfirming Messages

Type	Definition
Impersonal	A message that is nonimmediate and cliché-ridden
Impervious	A message that is not acknowledged by the receiver
Incoherent	A message that is difficult to follow
Incongruous	A message that contains contradictory verbal and nonverbal components
Interrupting	A message that is cut short by the receiver
Irrelevant	A message that is unrelated to a prior message
Tangential	A message that is taken in a new direction

Source: Based on Dance, F. E. X., & Larson, C. E. (1972). *Speech communication: Concepts and behavior.* New York: Holt, Rinehart & Winston.

common triggers as "I have a problem with that," "I know what I'm talking about," or "Based on my experience, I think . . . " (Weaver, 1993).

Fourth, engage in feedback. If you recall from Chapter 8, feedback describes the response a listener gives to a speaker about the speaker's behavior (Ogilvie & Haslett, 1985) and provides members with a chance to correct their performance, develop their abilities, and/or change wasteful practices (Harris, 1988). With the perception of group members as a useful and valuable feedback source, the number of feedback attempts among group members increases (Gordon, 1985). If your group members frequently provide feedback, your group likely has established a supportive communication climate. Additionally, as group members engage in feedback, their self-confidence increases and their anxiety decreases (Hansford & Diehl, 1988), which means that group member self-confidence and anxiety may reflect the cohesion and climate present in the group.

A Final Note About Cohesion and Climate

Given the importance of cohesion and communication climate in a group, it may seem odd that they are covered in the last chapter of a textbook devoted to developing an understanding of the small group communication process. We placed this chapter here for three reasons. First, as psychology professor Marvin Shaw and his colleagues (1979) discovered, the social-emotional aspect of group members' communication becomes more important as the group matures and works together. In the initial phases of group work, the effective functioning of group members' interpersonal relationships is not integral to task accomplishment, particularly with short-term group membership. As such, it is essential to create a climate in which group members feel comfortable: Be flexible and empathic, respectful, and specific and direct in your comments; listen (Haslett & Ogilvie, 2003; Samares, 1980; St. John, 1996); and avoid the use of discouraging messages (Reynolds, 2006). Second, cohesion occurs over the life span of a group (Drescher, Burlingame, & Fuhriman, 1985), which means that at any given time, cohesion will affect how group members communicate with each other. Third, as you may recall from Chapter 2, the exit stage of the group socialization process becomes part of a group member's antecedent stage for the next group he joins. As you enter the exit stage of socialization with your classroom group, reflect on how your group developed cohesion, used the dimensions of a supportive communication climate, and used the dimensions of a defensive communication climate.

Conclusion

This chapter introduced you to the concepts of cohesion and climate. To do so, we reexamined cohesion and explained its importance to small group members. We then defined communication climate, focusing specifically on the six dimensions that comprise a supportive communication climate and the six dimensions that comprise a defensive climate. Finally, we examined four ways a group can turn a defensive communication climate into a supportive communication climate. Hopefully, you will consider this information the next time you work in a small group.

Discussion Questions

1. Refer to Chapter 3. To what degree does your ability to engage in a supportive communication climate depend on your own communication traits?

2. Reflect on the verbal and nonverbal communicative behaviors you use in one of the groups to which you belong. How did your behaviors contribute to the development of a supportive communication climate? How did your behaviors contribute to the development of a defensive communication climate?

3. Which dimension(s) of a defensive communication climate are you most likely to use in a small group? Why? What could you do to turn the defensive dimension(s) into a supportive dimension(s)?

4. How has the discount/revenge cycle emerged in your work group? How has this cycle had a negative impact on the communication climate of your group?

5. In your work group, would you rate the communicate climate as being generally supportive or generally defensive? How does the climate affect cohesion?

References

Anderson, J. D. (1985). Working with groups: Little-known facts that challenge well-known myths. *Small Group Behavior, 16,* 267–283.

Beck, C. E., & Beck, E. A. (1986, January/February). The manager's open door and the communication climate. *Business Horizons, 29*(1), 15–19.

Carron, A. V., & Brawley, L. R. (2000). Cohesion: Conceptual and measurement issues. *Small Group Research, 31,* 89–106.

Cissna, K. N. L., & Sieburg, E. (1981). Patterns of interactional confirmation and disconfirmation. In C. Wilder-Mott & J. H. Weakland (Eds.), *Rigor and imagination: Essays from the legacy of Gregory Bateson* (pp. 253–282). New York: Praeger.

Craig, T. Y., & Kelly, J. R. (1999). Group cohesiveness and creative performance. *Group Dynamics: Theory, Research, and Practice, 3,* 243–256.

Dance, F. E. X., & Larson, C. E. (1972). *Speech communication: Concepts and behavior.* New York: Holt, Rinehart & Winston.

Drescher, S., Burlingame, G., & Fuhriman, A. (1985). Cohesion: An odyssey in empirical understanding. *Small Group Behavior, 16,* 3–30.

Evans, N. J., & Jarvis, P. A. (1986). The group attitude scale: A measure of attraction to group. *Small Group Behavior, 17,* 203–216.

Fujishin, R. (2007). *Creating effective groups: The art of small group communication* (2nd ed.). Lanham, MD: Rowman and Littlefield.

Gardner, W. P., & Masztal, N. B. (1985). Communication climate: How to create a positive atmosphere. *Management World, 14*(1), 30–31.

Gibb, J. R. (1961). Defensive communication. *Journal of Communication, 11,* 141–148.

Gordon, R. D. (1985). The self-disclosure of interpersonal feedback: The "dyadic effect" in a group context. *Small Group Behavior, 16,* 411–413.

Gordon, R. D. (1988). The difference between feeling defensive and feeling understood. *Journal of Business Communication, 25,* 53–64.

Hansford, B. C., & Diehl, B. J. (1988). Verbal comments, ideas, feedback, and self assessment during small-group discussions. *Small Group Behavior, 19,* 485–494.

Harris, T. E. (1988). Mastering the art of taking back. *Management World, 17*(3), 9–11.

Haslett, B. B., & Ogilvie, J. R. (2003). Feedback processes in task groups. In R.Y. Hirokawa, R. S. Cathcart, L. A. Samovar, & L. D. Henman (Eds.), *Small group communication theory and practice: An anthology* (8th ed., pp. 97–108). Los Angeles: Roxbury.

Kavanaugh, R. R., Jr., & Bollet, R. M. (1983). Levels of verbal intimacy technique (Lovit): An initial validation study of the measurement of verbal intimacy in groups. *Small Group Behavior, 14,* 35–49.

King, C. P. (1986, July). Crummy communication climate (and how to create it). *Management Solutions, 31*(7), 30–31.

Kjormo, O., & Halvari, H. (2002). Two ways related to performance in elite sport: The path of self-confidence and competitive anxiety and the path of group cohesion and group goal-clarity. *Perceptual and Motor Skills, 94,* 950–966.

Larsen, S., & Folgero, I. S. (1993). Supportive and defensive communication. *International Journal of Contemporary Hospitality Management, 5*(3), 22–25.

Ogilvie, J. R., & Haslett, B. (1985). Communicating peer feedback in a task group. *Human Communication Research, 12,* 79–98.

Reynolds, R. A. (2006). Discouraging messages. *Communication Reports, 19,* 16–30.

Rosenfeld, L. R. (1983). Communication climate and coping mechanisms in the college classroom. *Communication Education, 32,* 167–174.

Sager, K. L., & Gastil, J. (2002). Exploring the psychological foundations of democratic group deliberation: Personality factors, confirming interaction, and democratic decision making. *Communication Research Reports, 19,* 56–65.

Samares, J. T. (1980). Two-way communication practices for managers. *Personnel Journal, 56*(8), 645–648.

Shaw, M. E., Ackerman, B., McCown, N. E., Worsham, A. P., Haugh, L. D., Gebhardt, B. M., et al. (1979). Interaction patterns and facilitation of peer learning. *Small Group Behavior, 10,* 214–223.

Smith, B. L. (1983). Interpersonal behaviors that damage the productivity of creative problem solving groups. *Journal of Creative Behavior, 27,* 171–187.

St. John, D. (1996). Forget the global communication climate for a minute: How's the weather inside your own organization? *Communication World, 13*(3), 24–25.

Veiga, J. F. (1991). The frequency of self-limiting behavior in groups: A measure and an explanation. *Human Relations, 44,* 877–895.

Weaver, W. T. (1993). When discounting gets in the way. *Training & Development, 47*(7), 55–59.

Appendix A

Connecting Small Group Communication Concepts

After reading this appendix, you should be able to:

1. differentiate among the four connections of group work,
2. identify the core small group communication concepts associated with each connection,
3. explain how small group communication concepts can make small group interactions productive,
4. explain how small group communication concepts can make small groups enjoyable, and
5. apply small group communication concepts to future group interactions.

Case Study

Jamal, Selena, Joe, Sophia, and Mary are students enrolled in COMM 400: Advanced Small Group Communication. For their final assignment, they must write a paper on applying small group communication concepts to a learning group. Their professor, Dr. Wright, plans to incorporate the best paper into the next edition of the course textbook. The group meets at Starbucks to discuss its options for writing the paper.

Jamal:	I've been thinking about this paper assignment for a few days, and I'm at a loss for a topic. Does anyone have any ideas?
Mary:	I think we should write about coffee shop employees getting laid off and then starting their own restaurant together.
Sophia:	That's a bad idea, Mary. Based on what we've learned in class, wouldn't the employees of a coffee shop be considered a work group rather than a learning group?
Jamal:	Sophia, we shouldn't judge each other's ideas until we have heard all of them. Besides, why do you always have to be so negative?
Sophia:	I'm not trying to be negative, just trying to keep it real. I think Mary's idea is terrible.
Selena:	I agree with Jamal. We should save our critiques until we have finished generating ideas.
Sophia:	Maybe we could write about a group of adolescents dealing with peer pressure and the temptations of drugs, alcohol, and sex.
Jamal:	I don't like that idea at all.
Sophia:	(sarcastically) I thought we agreed not to judge each other's ideas until we have heard all ideas, Jamal.
Jamal:	Well, Sophia, I'm just trying to keep it real, too.
Joe:	Knock it off, you two. We can only evaluate ideas that meet the requirement of the assignment. Once we actually develop some ideas that meet the requirements, then we can evaluate them.
Mary:	I've got it! Why don't we write about our own group's experience completing the course assignments, including this paper?
Jamal:	Wow! That's a great idea, Mary, but do you think Dr. Wright will be down with that?
Sophia:	Yeah. Doesn't it seem a little odd to write a paper about our own group? I think we should choose another topic.
Joe:	It sounds like a good idea to me. Since we fit the definition of a learning group, we can use real-life examples of how our group works and how our group communicates.

Selena: I like this idea. I will e-mail Dr. Wright tonight and ask if this topic is acceptable.

Mary: I don't think Dr. Wright will have a problem with this topic because it will be the most creative paper in the entire class!

Jamal: Now I'm getting excited about this assignment! Hopefully Dr. Wright will use our paper in the next edition of the course textbook!

Somehow, someway, you find yourself in a small group, perhaps by choice or by chance. Whether you realize it, at this point you have acquired the knowledge base from reading this textbook to set the foundation for a positive small group experience—not to suggest that simply reading this textbook will make all future small group interactions enjoyable. The odds, however, of having more positive than negative small group experiences have just increased. You need only to start applying what you have learned to your small group interactions.

This appendix aims to demonstrate how the combination of small group concepts can make future small group experiences more productive and enjoyable. We will connect the small group concepts covered in the chapters of this textbook to small group interactions so you can determine how these topic areas cooperate when accomplishing various small group activities in the future. Following each point is the corresponding chapter so you can reference information on that topic in greater detail.

Connecting Textbook Content to Small Group Interactions

This section will explore four small group interactions that you may encounter in the future. Within each connection, we discuss pertinent knowledge that you have gained from the textbook. Hopefully, these connections will provide you with some of the possibilities for applying your knowledge about small groups to future group interactions.

Connection One: How to Make Social Groups Work

Throughout your life, you likely will be a member of numerous social groups, ranging from the most informal (e.g., playing basketball on Thursday afternoons with three friends from high school) to formally established social organizations (e.g., fraternities and sororities). You may not play basketball with the same group of friends years from now, but you won't necessarily play only by yourself in the future. If you can determine how to make your social groups work well now, you should be able to apply these skills in future social groups.

> ? Based on what you have learned in this course, what is the single most important tip you would give to group members on how to make a social group work?

To think about how to make social groups work, we selected six chapters. These chapters focus on socialization processes (Chapter 2), member communication and personality traits (Chapter 3), small group roles (Chapter 8), relational communication (Chapter 10), conflict (Chapter 11), and cohesion and climate (Chapter 12).

1. Social groups are not created instantaneously. Just like any other group, certain processes need to occur when new members first join the group or when the group is just getting started. Sometimes these processes are stated formally, but the majority of social groups do not have formal processes for socializing new members.

2. Although members may share many communication or personality traits, they may display these traits to others in various ways. Furthermore, one member's dominant trait could influence group interaction. As a result, it is important to be aware and sensitive of people's tendencies in social groups.

3. Although you may not consciously think of this, members may take on different roles in social groups. For example, often someone takes on the role of planner for the group. In the case study, Mary adopts the leader role when she offers a suggestion for the paper. Another member regularly may supply comic relief when the group gets together. As a result, group roles prove just as important in social groups as they do in task groups.

4. Membership in social groups, usually voluntary, often provides an outlet for members to think about something other than school, work, or family. As a result, group members tend to get to know one another on a more personal level. After all, we most readily acknowledge these individuals as our friends. Our communication patterns, as well as our expectations for them, may differ based on these relationships.

5. Social groups not uncommonly experience conflict, but these conflicts primarily contain a relational component. Disappointing a friend is not quite the same as disappointing a coworker; we well may tolerate coping with a friend's

misbehavior (e.g., always running late, never having any money). As a result, we deal with some issues in a timely fashion, if at all. However, this does not mean we're unfazed by these issues.

6. Changes to social groups can traumatize some members because social groups are often very cohesive. Changing some of the traditions in social groups, often steeped in traditions, proves extremely difficult. An equal challenge occurs when members of social groups change. Not doing this by choice, such as when a member graduates and moves to a new city, presents an even greater challenge. These changes have the potential to change the dynamic of social groups.

Connection Two: How to Make Work Groups Work

As you have discovered, college courses—particularly small group communication courses!—often incorporate the use of work groups. Think of work groups, typically created to complete a particular task, as task groups. In addition, note the underlying sense of "business" associated with most work groups. Thinking that members who do not know how to "play nice" with each other could complete many tasks successfully, however, is premature.

> **?** In your work group, how do members "play nice" with each other? Based on what you have learned in this course, what additional recommendations would you make to encourage group members to "play nice"?

To think about how to make work groups work, we selected eight chapters. These chapters focus on member and personality traits (Chapter 3), diversity among small group members (Chapter 4), small group tasks (Chapter 6), small group decision-making procedures (Chapter 7), small group roles (Chapter 8), small group leadership (Chapter 9), small group conflict (Chapter 11), and cohesion and climate (Chapter 12).

1. Always important is understanding group members' tendencies. How will members likely interact with others? Furthermore, how do different environmental factors influence members' communication and personality traits? For example, who handles stress well when something unexpected happens, and who doesn't? Consider, from the beginning, how group members' communication and personality traits will impact the ability of the group to successfully complete its assignment. Unfortunately, this information is not easy to acquire the first time you work with someone, so being able to identify various messages or behaviors when interacting with others is important.

2. Not all work groups consist of heterogeneous members. In fact, work groups usually comprise individuals with varying backgrounds, talents, abilities,

and attitudes toward group work. Recognizing the group's composition will allow for furthering the strength diversity plays in group decision making and problem solving by capitalizing on the unique characteristics and perspectives that diverse members bring to the group.

3. As stated earlier, work groups typically are created to complete a task. Therefore, understanding characteristics of small group tasks will help you succeed. In the case study, Jamal demonstrates this understanding when he establishes a procedural norm in order to maximize the group's ability to choose a paper topic. Subtle features may be associated with the task you must complete, and this knowledge can help you troubleshoot issues accordingly.

4. Work groups likely will encounter many decision-making situations. Time constraints and the tendencies of the group leader play a part in determining the type of decision-making procedures selected.

5. The roles of work group members could vary based on whether the group is completing a task, which will dissolve the group upon completion, or if the group exists to complete a task on a regular basis. The first type of task might entail different roles for members than the second type of task.

6. Work groups commonly have a designated leader; however, the leadership characteristics necessary to help a work group succeed may vary based on the task, as well as the characteristics of the group members. What type of leadership does completing this task require? Are the group members motivated, or do they need direction? Consider these important questions when assessing how to lead a work group.

7. Work conflicts, problematically, may impact the career inspirations of members. As a result, it is important to know the type of conflict being experienced by work groups. Strategies for managing personality conflicts in work groups will not exactly match the strategies selected for managing conflicts associated with procedural choices. Most (but admittedly not all) work group members realize that the group's performance on a task reflects the entire work group. As a result, work group members tend to have a vested interest in helping the group successfully complete its task, even if the conflict is not resolved.

8. Cohesion and climate also may impact the performance of work groups. How important is it that the group completes its assignment well? Will members fail the course, or will they be fired? In addition, how much support does the group get from its instructor or superiors in the organization? Assessing the degree of unity both within and outside the group in regard to the assigned task can set the tone for how the group proceeds through stages to completion of the task.

Connection Three: How to Become a Better Group Member

Whether you are an athlete or a fan, you undoubtedly have heard the phrase "There is no *I* in team." In many respects, this represents the ultimate compliment to give a member on a sports team. In some instances, group members evaluate each other's performance. While this feedback can be rewarding to receive if your group members think you did a good job for the group, it can be a bit embarrassing if your fellow group members believe that you did not give your all to the group and essentially coasted through on other members' efforts. So what should you pay attention to if you want to become a better group member?

To think about how to become a better group member, we selected seven chapters. These chapters focus on socialization processes (Chapter 2), member communication and personality traits (Chapter 3), diversity among small group members (Chapter 4), small group roles (Chapter 8), small group leadership (Chapter 9), relational communication (Chapter 10), and small group conflict (Chapter 11).

1.   Helping socialize new members into the group will help you become a better group member. Joining an established group can prove a bit intimidating—just think about your first semester as a first-year college student, and you'll be in the ballpark! Helping other members acclimate to the group shows that you care about new members and the group's success. A group composed of all new members presents a somewhat different challenge. In this case, remember that it may take a little time for everyone to get to know each other. Thus, group members should feel free to spend time informally getting acquainted.

> ? Based on what you have learned in this course, what could you do to become a better group member?

2.   Becoming aware of your own and your group members' communication and personality traits also will allow you to become a better group member. In the case study, Sophia reminds the group that her criticism of Mary's idea should be attributed to her personality rather than considered a personal attack. If you know how you or your group members tend to respond in various circumstances, you may try to modify the environment to allow or inhibit the likelihood of interacting in certain ways.

3.   Developing an awareness of how group members differ in their cultural, demographic, and cognitive diversity presents yet another way you can become a productive group member. Take this awareness a step further by recognizing and

responding competently to the diverse attributes of group members when working on a task or getting to know each other socially.

4. Becoming a strong group member proves easier if you know (in advance) what is expected of you. Are you supposed to double-check the details, or will someone else complete this task? Not knowing your role and the corresponding expectations reduces the likelihood of successfully completing your portion of the task.

5. If you find yourself in the leadership position of your group, your challenge will include demonstrating the appropriate leadership style for the task at hand. At times, as the leader, you may be forced to keep your group members on task (even if members want to fool around); at other times, as the leader, you may need to know when to step out of the way to let members do their jobs. Successfully modifying your leadership style, more difficult than it sounds, takes practice, as well as demonstrating sensitivity toward the needs and requirements of the task and your fellow group members.

6. Improve your group member skills by being open to the verbal and non-verbal messages group members send your way. Taking time to accurately process these messages offers great benefits. Other members will see that you are caring, considerate, and responsive to the needs of others in your group, and these relational characteristics could increase your value to the group in others' eyes. After all, who wants to work with a selfish jerk?

7. One of the best strategies for becoming a better group member during a conflict is to listen to your group members. Many conflicts occur between group members as a result of misunderstandings. If you cannot admit that you may be wrong or that other reasonable viewpoints to an issue exist, you may find your interactions with group members become strained.

Connection Four: Understanding How and Why Groups Function

You may not realize now that you could find yourself in a position where you must decide if a group (or "committee" as groups so often are referred to in the workplace) is needed to complete a task. Therefore, the more you know about how groups function and the more knowledge you recall about small groups from this course and textbook, the better.

To think about how and why groups function the way they do, we selected six chapters. These chapters focus on socialization processes (Chapter 2), models of small group development (Chapter 5), small group tasks (Chapter 6), small group decision-making procedures (Chapter 7), small group roles (Chapter 8), and cohesion and climate (Chapter 12).

1. It is important to understand how groups initiate new members. You don't become an "official" member immediately; usually, a socialization process introduces people to groups and helps them become active, contributing members. Interestingly, groups unable to recruit and retain new members at some point in time will dissolve. Therefore, understanding the role of socialization is important.

2. Groups develop in a variety of ways. Oftentimes the task the group must complete determines the path taken. Probably the most important thing to remember is that group formation is a *process*. Groups do not emerge from a vacuum. Members need to put forth the necessary time and energy for strong groups to develop, and as your textbook indicates, groups can take a variety of different paths to attain the same outcomes.

3. Groups receive a variety of assignments. Fortunate groups receive a clearly identified task. In the case study, Dr. Wright provides the students with the task, although the group itself must determine its options for task completion. However, the original assignment of the group may change. Even worse, some groups never really understand their assignment. As you might guess, these groups are truly at a disadvantage when it comes to completing a task.

4. Groups have a surprisingly large number of options available to them when it comes to making decisions. Most groups, however, tend to use a default decision-making procedure, even if it is not always effective. Understanding that groups may want to expand the procedures used when making decisions could assist group members in making better decisions overall.

5. If your interests lean toward learning more about how groups function, observe the role(s) that members perform. Members receiving assigned roles does not guarantee that they will complete their assignments. Some instances involve no formal role assignments. If this happens, it is interesting to see what group members will do to help the group succeed.

6. Although a group need not comprise cohesive membership in order to complete its task, cohesion never hurts! In fact, if group members had their choice, they undoubtedly would choose to have cohesion and bonding with their fellow group members. Some might go so far as to say that cohesion makes group successes sweeter, but it also helps groups survive difficult circumstances. To assess a group's cohesion, examine the messages exchanged between members. What is said (as well as what is not said) may reveal a lot about the group's cohesion.

A Final Note About Connecting Small Group Communication Concepts

Hopefully, this appendix (a) reminded you of the knowledge you have acquired about small group communication and (b) opened your mind to the endless possibilities for applying this knowledge base to future small group interactions. Like it or not, small groups play a pivotal part in our professional and personal lives. Not all small group interactions are perfect, however; in fact, most small group interactions don't occur by chance. Many factors influence any small group experience. Therefore, your challenge is to determine how to navigate through the issues that shape how small groups function. But know this: This challenge can be met successfully. Besides, because you belong to a small group, you happily do not need to meet it alone.

Conclusion

This appendix demonstrated how a combination of small group concepts potentially can make future small group experiences more productive and enjoyable. We made connections between small group concepts covered in the chapters from this textbook and small group interactions so you can determine how these topic areas cooperate when accomplishing various small group activities in the future. Following each point, we listed the chapter so you can reference information on that topic in greater detail. When you engage in future small group communication encounters, consider yourself prepared.

Discussion Questions

1. Of the four connections, which connection is the most relevant to understanding the importance of small group communication? Why?

2. Develop a connection for "How to Make Learning Groups Work." Identify six chapters you would include with this connection.

3. Based on the course content, identify and explain the three most important concepts you have learned about the small group communication process.

Appendix B

Designing and Delivering
Small Group Presentations

After reading this appendix, you should be able to:

1. identify and explain the five components of designing a small group presentation,
2. explain how to organize a presentation,
3. differentiate between a panel discussion and a symposium,
4. identify the three performance strategies that enhance presentational speaking, and
5. list the three rules for selecting a visual aid.

Case Study

The members of WV Unexplored!, an extension of the West Virginia Department of Tourism, which plans trip packages for tourist groups visiting West Virginia, meet to decide on a destination for their upcoming promotional campaign. The members consist of Tammy Whitzard, the group's director, and employees Kristy Tittleton-Maarten, Kate Hoagland, and Maritta Raj.

Tammy: It is important that we decide on a destination quickly so we can spend the rest of our time designing our presentation to the secretary of tourism slated for next week. I'd like to remind everyone about the criteria for choosing this year's focal destination: The trip can't take more than five days, the trip cost must be under $200 per person, the

trip must take place during the summer months, and no more than 15 people can go on the trip. Let's go around the room and share our ideas. If possible, I'd like for you to hold your questions until after everyone has spoken. Kristy, how about if we begin with you?

Kristy: That's fine, Tammy. I thought we could begin the trip at Bluestone State Park and go camping for a few days. We then could stop at the New River Gorge National River and go whitewater rafting or stop at Tamarack and look at the handicrafts. It can take an afternoon to walk around Tamarack and look at the paintings, photographs, pottery, food items, jewelry, clothing, and books made by the artisans living in West Virginia.

Tammy: Kate?

Kate: Anyone who loves country music would love Jamboree in the Hills outside Wheeling. This year, Reba McEntire, Sugarland, Brad Paisley, Miranda Lambert, and Montgomery Gentry are slated to perform.

Tammy: I keep forgetting you're from Wheeling. Maritta?

Maritta: What about sponsoring a trip to Seneca Caverns in Riverton?

Tammy: These sound like viable ideas, but we need to determine whether each idea meets our criteria. I see the biggest issue being money. How much would each trip cost? Remember, the maximum amount a person can spend is $200, and we can't go a penny over.

Kristy: It won't cost much to camp at Bluestone State Park, but there is a two-day minimum for renting a campsite. The big cost would be the whitewater rafting, which runs around $60. It doesn't cost anything to go to Tamarack.

Maritta: Jamboree in the Hills might be too expensive, then. A four-day pass cost $160 last year.

Kate: Not if we bought a one- or a two-day pass. While in Wheeling, we also could go to the Good Zoo and the Benedum Planetarium at Oglebay Park.

Maritta: The trip to Seneca Caverns wouldn't cost much either.

Tammy: Even though money is an issue, so is time. Most of these trips could be taken in a day, which defeats the purpose of exploring West Virginia.

Kristy: What about if we combined several ideas? We could go camping at Bluestone State Park for two days, go to Beckley and spend an afternoon

	exploring Tamarack, drive to Fayetteville and go whitewater rafting for a day, and stop at Seneca Caverns for another afternoon. Surely this trip could be taken for less than $200 per person.

Kate: Or we could go to Wheeling, spend a day at Jamboree, spend another day at the zoo and the planetarium, and then splash down the water slide at Wheeling Park.

Maritta: If we timed it right, we also could go to the Upper Ohio Valley Italian Festival on the waterfront and take in a show at the Victoria Vaudeville Theater. I know there is a toy and train museum nearby, and there is an artisan center similar to Tamarack located downtown. Maybe Wheeling would be the best option.

Kate: Plus, since I know the area, I could give the presentation, which would save us some time.

Tammy: Well, before we start planning our presentation, we need to choose a destination. But as usual, regardless of which one we choose, I think we have come up with a great way for visitors to explore West Virginia!

As this case study demonstrates, when groups face a task, they must make a decision or solve a problem. For many small groups, however, making a decision or solving a problem is just the first part of the task. The second part of the task centers on presenting the decision or solution in an oral, a written, or an oral and written format conducive to the group, the audience, and the topic.

This appendix aims to provide you with some basic information on how to design and deliver a small group presentation. To reach this end, first we will identify and explain the five components of designing any small group presentation. We then will discuss the difference between a panel discussion and a symposium, two types of oral group presentations. Finally, we will offer three performance strategies to enhance presentational success and identify the components of a written report.

Designing the Small Group Presentation

A successful small group presentation begins with a thorough design plan. The five components of designing a presentation include (1) analyzing the audience, (2) selecting a topic, (3) identifying the primary points, (4) organizing the presentation, and (5) choosing supporting materials.

Analyzing the Audience

Before deciding on the content or delivery of any small group presentation, it is essential that you and your group members engage in an audience analysis, which emerges as the first important component of presentation design because without an audience, the presentation is not necessary (Weinholdt, 2006). Audience analysis consists of an analysis of demographic, psychographic, and situational variables. **Demographic variables** refer to the observable characteristics of an audience that provide you with some basic information about the audience. Examples of demographic variables include sex, age, race, ethnicity, religion, educational level, and socioeconomic background. **Psychographic variables** refer to the attitudes, values, and goals commonly shared by an audience. If you recall from Chapter 6, an **attitude** reflects how favorable a person judges a person, a thing, or an event; a **value** reflects a belief or feeling about a person, a thing, or an event; and a **goal** reflects the end state of group activity (Gouran, 1997). **Situational variables** refer to the variables contained with the physical location of the presentation. Examples of situational variables include the lighting, temperature, physical layout, and availability of technology in the space where the group will deliver its presentation.

In addition to the demographic, psychographic, and situational variables, consider such other variables as the time of day or day of the week of the presentation, whether the audience members attend the presentation voluntarily, and whether the presentation occurs during a peak work time or project time. Still other variables include audience size, whether your group is the only speaker or one of several groups of speakers, and the benefits (or costs) the audience might associate with attending the presentation (Krannich, 2002; Morrisey, Sechrest, & Warman, 1997).

? If your work group had to design a presentation for the members of your organization, what additional demographic, psychographic, and situational variables would your group need to analyze?

Although audience analysis might seem like a heady task, taking the time and effort to analyze the audience offers multiple benefits. Not only will your group be able to target a message specifically to your audience; your group also will progress more effortlessly into the next stage of presentation design, selecting a topic.

Selecting a Topic

When faced with selecting a topic, it is essential that you and your group choose an appropriate topic for the audience and the occasion. In some cases, a person external to the group will assign your group a topic; in other situations, your group will be assigned the task of selecting a topic, in which case your group might consider choosing a topic its members are knowledgeable, experienced, or enthusiastic about (Kelly, Phillips, & Keaten, 1995). In the case study, Kate exemplifies this notion when she chooses Wheeling as a destination based on the fact that she grew up there.

Regardless of how it selects a topic, your group must follow three steps to narrow the topic into an appropriate and manageable form. First, determine the general purpose of the presentation, which often is to inform, to persuade, or to entertain. When the general purpose is **to inform**, the group presents the information in a concise, clear, and unbiased manner. When the general purpose is **to persuade**, the group presents the information in a manner that advocates a particular point of view or position. When the general purpose is **to entertain**, the group presents the information in an amusing, lively, or humorous manner.

After identifying its general purpose, the group needs to construct a specific purpose statement. The **specific purpose statement** identifies exactly what the group wants to accomplish with its presentation. To ensure effectiveness, the specific purpose statement should contain one idea, not be vague or general, and not use figurative language. "The specific purpose is to inform the audience about three inexpensive trips to explore West Virginia" exemplifies an effective specific purpose statement the WV Unexplored! group could use as a guide for its presentation; "The specific purpose is to inform the audience that there are lots of things to do in West Virginia" exemplifies an ineffective specific purpose statement.

The specific purpose statement then serves as the foundation for the thesis statement. Similar to the thesis statement you use in your written communication, the **thesis statement** serves as the primary assertion for the content that you want your audience to retain. Typically a one-sentence statement, the thesis statement provides a focus for the organization of the presentation.

By identifying your general purpose, constructing a specific purpose statement, and writing a thesis statement, your group then can determine the content of the presentation. More specifically, your group will be able to identify the primary points to address in the presentation.

Identifying the Primary Points

Public speakers must wrestle with such issues as identification of the primary points of the presentation. This issue proves important because if a presentation does not cover enough content, the audience members may regard the presentation as neither helpful nor useful. Conversely, if a presentation covers too much content, the audience members may feel overloaded and tempted to dismiss the content instead of retaining it.

To combat this issue, experts recommend that any presentation contain between two and five primary points (McCarthy, 1989), with three primary points as the preferred number. We consider three points ideal because with only two points the presentation may not be as developed as possible, and with more than five points audience members will find retaining the content difficult. Limiting your presentation to three primary points encourages the audience to feel empowered instead of overpowered (Johnson, 2006).

Organizing the Presentation

Once you and your group members determine the primary points you want to cover, it is time to organize the presentation. Any presentation will have three primary components: the introduction, the body, and the conclusion. Because the majority of the time spent delivering a presentation focuses on the body, your group should organize this section first to ensure that enough content exists and you allot enough time to cover the content.

To keep your presentation organized, use an organizational pattern that parallels the specific purpose and thesis statements. Although you can organize a presentation in many ways (Detz, 2000), the organizational patterns most commonly used in presentational speaking include the chronological pattern, the topical pattern, the spatial pattern, the cause-effect pattern, and the problem-solution pattern. The **chronological organizational pattern**, used to show how something developed over time or to indicate the steps to a process, follows a particular sequence key to understanding the concept or process. The **topical organizational pattern** is used to link several independent aspects of a topic or when a topic can be divided into types, categories, components, or parts. The **spatial organizational pattern** is used to demonstrate how space, direction, or physical arrangement link several aspects of a topic. The **cause-effect organizational pattern** is used to illustrate the relationship between an existing issue and the ramifications of the issue. The **problem-solution organizational pattern** is used to identify a problem and propose a solution.

Once you organize the body of your presentation, your group needs to construct an introduction and a conclusion. Both the introduction and the conclusion should be relatively brief; each component serves to introduce and conclude the presentation, respectively, without presenting any extraneous information. Due to the brevity of each competent, the combined speaking time spent on the introduction and conclusion should consume no more than 20% of the total presentation time.

The introduction prepares the audience for the presentation by gaining its attention, orienting the members to the purpose of the presentation, and providing the members with a preview of the primary points. Use a host of devices to gain attention, including posing a rhetorical question; making a reference to the occasion for the presentation or to a preceding speaker; asking a provocative question; describing a shared experience; using an example, an unusual fact, a quotation, a brief story, or an anecdote; making a reference to a recent or historical event; or making a startling or humorous statement (Krannich, 2002; Smith & Tague-Busler, 2003; Wilder, 1999).

Regardless of the chosen device, its appropriateness is imperative given the topic, the audience, and the occasion. Once you hold the audience's attention, you must orient the members to the purpose of the presentation and provide a preview of points statement. Orient the members to the purpose of the presentation by using your already written thesis statement, followed by a preview of points statement that contains a list of the primary points (in order) that you will cover in the presentation.

The conclusion signifies the end of the presentation for the audience. In the conclusion, it is necessary to remind the audience about the purpose of the presentation, review the primary points that you covered in the presentation, and close the presentation succinctly. To do so, restate the thesis statement used in the introduction and follow it with a review of points statement that contains a list of the primary points (in order) covered in the presentation and a closure statement. This closure statement can take the form of a memorable statement, a link back to the attention-getting device, a reminder about the significance of the content, or, in the case of a persuasive presentation, a call for a specific action or the issue of a challenge (Krannich, 2002). Because the closure statement allows your group to make its final impression on the audience, never introduce new or tangential content or make a disparaging comment about the topic, the audience, or the occasion. Plus, as you already know, statements such as "That's all," "I'm done," or "That's all the time we have" never conclude a presentation effectively.

Choosing Supporting Materials

Supporting materials refer to the evidence offered by a group used to reinforce the primary points covered in a presentation. Most presentations require supporting materials because they not only clarify or "prove" the primary points covered in a presentation; they also add interest, make a presentation memorable, and build the group's credibility (Krannich, 2002).

Although supporting materials can take many forms, the three most commonly used forms in presentational speaking include the statistic, the example, and testimony. The statistic refers to the use of a number to express a fact or an idea, the example refers to a factual or hypothetical instance that makes a general point, and testimony refers to the use of a quotation or paraphrase from an expert (Myers, 1997). Other forms of supporting materials include facts, definitions, descriptions, personal observations, analogies, and personal anecdotes (Detz, 2000; McCarthy, 1989). As Tammy, Kristy, Kate, and Maritta work on designing their presentation, what forms of supporting materials might they consider using?

When selecting supporting materials, it is important to select those proximate to the audience. Based on the audience analysis, your group should have a firm grasp on the types of evidence to which your audience will acknowledge, respond favorably, or respect. The audience will be more receptive to supporting materials with which it can identify. Also important, consider whether your supporting materials are recent (e.g., how old is the material?), relevant (e.g., does the material relate specifically to the topic of and the purpose behind the presentation?), and reliable (e.g., is the material biased?), particularly because we can obtain so many of these materials through search engines and databases on the Internet.

> **?** What supporting materials has your work group used in a prior presentation? How proximate were these materials? How recent, relevant, and reliable were these materials?

When your group faces the task of designing a presentation, consider the five components of analyzing the audience, selecting a topic, identifying the primary points, organizing the presentation, and choosing supporting materials. Once your group has designed its presentation, it can move to the next task, deciding how to deliver the presentation.

Delivering the Small Group Presentation

As the deadline for project completion draws near, many groups face the task of presenting their work, whether in oral form, written form, or both. In this section, we will discuss the two types of oral group presentations, offer three performance strategies to enhance presentational success, and identify the components of a written report. Because group members make their impression on the audience through the oral or written presentation, they must plan, organize, rehearse, and present their work in a professional manner.

Oral Presentations

Group presentations comprise more than just members presenting individual speeches. If you recall from Chapter 1, group members use two types of oral presentations: the panel discussion and the symposium. A **panel discussion** consists of a group whose members respond to a series of questions posed by a moderator, who may or may not belong to the group. The moderator generally delivers the introduction and the conclusion, poses questions to the group members, and leads the question and answer session that follows the discussion. Group members receive the questions prior to the panel discussion so that they can develop their responses fully in order to contribute to the discussion.

A **symposium**, on the other hand, occurs when each member presents a speech on one aspect of a topic. Unlike the panel discussion, a symposium does not require the presence of a moderator. Instead, one member delivers the introduction, one member delivers the conclusion, and one member coordinates the question and answer session.

Whether your group presents its content in the form of a panel discussion or a symposium, consider three important performance strategies to enhance your group members' success as presentational speakers. The first strategy involves using multiple speakers. Doing so keeps the audience interested, paints a brighter picture of group involvement, and demonstrates group solidarity. Your group can create a common theme for the presentation, which each speaker repeats or which acts as a transition from point to point and from speaker to speaker. For instance, if the members of WV Unexplored! chose Kristy's idea as their featured destination, Kristy could discuss camping at Bluefield State Park, Tammy could highlight Tamarack, Kate could focus on whitewater rafting in Fayetteville, and Maritta could concentrate on Seneca Caverns, with the common theme being exploring West Virginia. Because some groups even use dress to create a nonverbal message of unity, the members could wear matching shirts. As a rule of thumb, each speaker should contribute five minutes or more to the total speaking time.

The second strategy involves incorporating visual aids (e.g., overhead projectors, video and LCD projectors, handouts, flipcharts and whiteboards, workbooks and manuals, and models) into the presentation. Visual aids increase audience retention, sustain audience interest, clarify content, and help convey complex information (Booher, 2003). When selecting a visual aid, your group should follow three rules: (1) A visual aid should support but not substitute for or sabotage your presentation (Booher, 2003; Morrisey et al., 1997); (2) a visual aid should complement, not duplicate, the presentational content (Johnson, 2006); and (3) the content on a visual aid should be kept simple. Too much content simply overwhelms, which can frustrate or annoy audience members. Because PowerPoint often negates this rule, remember to limit the amount of text and color, use bulleted lists or pictures rather than paragraphs, insert animation and music where appropriate, and provide references for content other than your own (Booher, 2003; Dolasinski, 2004; Morrisey et al., 1997).

The third strategy involves being prepared for questions from the audience to which your group will have to provide answers, otherwise referred to as the **Q&A session**. During the Q&A session, which occurs after the presentation concludes, the audience directs questions to either an individual member or the group as a whole. This provides one critical reason each group member should familiarize him- or herself with all members' parts. Additionally, during the design component of your presentation, your group should anticipate some questions that the audience might ask. Most speakers manage a question from the audience by repeating the question and then respond by drawing from the material already presented. If neither you nor your group members know the answer, tell the

> **?** What are some additional performance strategies your work group could use?

audience member you will get back to him once you have obtained the answer. By all means, create a low-risk environment for the Q&A session by treating all questions with respect and patience (Dibble & Langford, 1994). After the last question, one group member should thank the audience, restate the thesis and review of points statements, and conclude the presentation.

In some instances, your group may be asked to submit a written report, in addition to or in lieu of an oral presentation.

Written Reports

Consider written materials tools that also convey the message the group wants to send. If the materials accompany an oral presentation, group members should follow and use the oral presentation as a guide to construct the written report. The report should include a title page, a table of contents, a listing of the speaking order with names and titles, an abstract of each presentation, a disc of PowerPoint slides, all research materials, and any other critical information specific to the project. If your group used a presentational theme, it must incorporate this theme into the report. Then, along with any additional materials, your group should place the report, free of spelling and grammatical errors, in an appropriate folder or binder.

If the report is in lieu of an oral presentation, more specific format guidelines exist—see Table B.1—that most group scholars would consider important. Remember, however, to always format your report with the audience (reader) in mind.

Table B.1   Suggested Guidelines for Written Reports in Lieu of an Oral Presentation

Section	Content
Cover Page	Includes date, title, name of the group, and name of recipient
Table of Contents	Lists each important section with corresponding page number
Executive Summary	Contains recommendations, followed by an abstract of each section
Introduction	Provides background, introduces goals for project, and prepares reader for information to follow
Body	Describes the group process, research used, decision-making process, and data findings
Discussion	Interprets and explains the relevance of the findings tied to the group's goals
Conclusion	Lists specific conclusions tied to the group's goals and answers any questions raised

Knowing how to design and deliver a presentation contributes to group members' repertoire of group skills and experience. Through this process, members build competence and gain confidence in their ability to perform as a group.

A Final Note About Designing and Delivering the Small Group Presentation

As your group works on designing and delivering a presentation, know that groups not uncommonly experience preperformance concerns, or concerns faced by public speakers that can affect their speaking performance adversely and emerge in the form of performance (e.g., the use of visual aids or notes), environment (e.g., the room size), audience (e.g., the size, a particular member), preparation (e.g., audience analysis, the use of supporting materials), and self (e.g., communication apprehension) concerns (Daly, Vangelisti, Neel, & Cavanaugh, 1989). To combat these preperformance concerns, experts recommend that groups thoroughly prepare (i.e., design) and practice (i.e., deliver) their presentation, preferably in front of an audience, because preparation and practice leads to a better performance (Menzel & Carrell, 1994) and practice leads to more favorable audience evaluation (Smith & Frymier, 2006). Moreover, view the chance to design and deliver a presentation "as an educational experience and not as a final judgment" (Maxey & O'Connor, 2007, p. 79); there is always an opportunity for growth as a presentational speaker.

Conclusion

This appendix provided you with some basic information on how to design and deliver a small group presentation. To reach this end, first we identified and explained the five components of designing any small group presentation. We then discussed the difference between a panel discussion and a symposium, two types of oral group presentations. Finally, we offered three performance strategies to enhance presentational success and identified the components of a written report. Hopefully, the next time your group faces the task of designing and delivering a presentation, you can design and deliver with relative ease.

Discussion Questions

1. Choose one of the textbook chapters to design a presentation for your classmates. Working as a group, identify the general purpose, construct a

specific purpose statement, and write a thesis statement for this presentation. Then, identify three primary points, select an organizational pattern, and write an introduction and a conclusion.

2. Refer to the decision-making procedures discussed in Chapter 7. How appropriate is the use of these procedures to select a topic or identify primary points? Why?

3. Refer to the PRCA-24 scale you completed in Chapter 3. According to your scores, are you apprehensive in the public speaking context? If so, what can you do to alleviate your apprehension? If not, what can you do to help your group members alleviate their apprehension?

References

Booher, D. (2003). *Speak with confidence! Powerful presentations that inform, inspire, and persuade.* New York: McGraw-Hill.

Daly, J. A., Vangelisti, A. L., Neel, H. L., & Cavanaugh, P. D. (1989). Pre-performance concerns associated with public speaking anxiety. *Communication Quarterly, 37,* 39–53.

Detz, J. (2000). *It's not what you say, it's how you say it.* New York: St. Martin's Griffin.

Dibble, L. A., & Langford, B. Y. (1994). *Communication skills and strategies: Guidelines for managers at work.* Cincinnati, OH: South-Western.

Dolasinski, M. J. (2004). *Training the trainer: Performance-based training for today's workplace.* Upper Saddle River, NJ: Prentice Hall.

Gouran, D. S. (1997). Effective versus ineffective group decision making. In L. R. Frey & J. K. Barge (Eds.), *Managing group life: Communicating in decision-making groups* (pp. 133–155). Boston: Houghton Mifflin.

Johnson, D. (2006, October). Top ten secrets for a successful workshop. *Library Media Connection, 25*(2), 30–35.

Kelly, L., Phillips, G. M., & Keaten, J. A. (1995). *Teaching people to speak well: Training and remediation of communication reticence.* Cresskill, NJ: Hampton Press.

Krannich, C. R. (2002). *101 secrets of highly effective speakers: Controlling fear, commanding attention* (2nd ed.). Manassas Park, VA: Impact.

Maxey, C., & O'Connor, K. E. (2007, March). Dealing with blunders. *T+D, 61*(3), 78–79.

McCarthy, E. H. (1989). *Speechwriting: A professional step-by-step guide for executives.* Dayton, OH: The Executive Speaker Company.

Menzel, K. E., & Carrell, L. J. (1994). The relationship between preparation and performance in public speaking. *Communication Education, 43,* 17–26.

Morrissey, G. L., Sechrest, T. L., & Warman, W. B. (1997). *Loud and clear: How to prepare and deliver effective business and technical presentations.* Reading, MA: Addison-Wesley.

Myers, S. A. (1997). Evidence. In S. A. Myers (Ed.), *Speak easy: Principles and practices of public speaking* (pp. 46–50). Needham Heights, MA: Simon and Schuster.

Smith, T. E., & Frymier, A. B. (2006). Get "real": Does practicing speeches before an audience improve performance? *Communication Quarterly, 54,* 111–125.

Smith, T. L., & Tague-Busler, M. (2003). *Icebreaker: A manual for public speaking* (5th ed.). Long Grove, IL: Waveland Press.

Weinholdt, R. (2006, November/December). Taking the trauma out of the talk. *Information Management Journal, 40*(6), 62–67.

Wilder, L. (1999). *7 steps to fearless speaking.* New York: John Wiley and Sons.

Glossary

Ability   a group's collective knowledge, skills, and experience

Abstract   a word or phrase without an identifiable referent and a less-than-clear meaning

Acceptance level   the degree to which group members find the task outcome acceptable

Accommodator   a group member who learns through a combination of feeling and doing

Action-oriented listener   listener who prefers concise, efficient, and error-free messages

Additive task   a task in which members work individually on a task or one aspect of a task

Adjourning   phase where the group reaches the end of its involvement; last of five stages of Tuckman's five-phase model of group development

Affection   member is motivated to communicate to feel liked and to like others; one of six interpersonal communication motives

Affective conflict   conflict centered on individual group members' communication and personality traits

Affective dimension   the negative emotions group members associate with conflict

Agenda   an outline of the specific objectives a group hopes to accomplish during a meeting

Ambiguous feedback   feedback that is neither positive nor negative and offers little information to the member

Androgynous individuals   individuals who possess high levels of both masculine and feminine behaviors

Antecedent phase   the first phase of the socialization model that includes the beliefs, attitudes, traits, and demographic characteristics that individuals bring to the socialization process in groups

Anticipatory phase   the second phase of the socialization model in which individuals decide what they expect from group membership as well as each group member

Appointed leader   a member who assumes the role responsibility of controlling and directing the group

Appreciative listening   the desire to listen for reasons of enjoyment

Area of freedom   the amount of authority or responsibility the group possesses when it comes to implementing the task

Argumentativeness   an individual's ability to defend his position on a controversial issue while simultaneously attempting to refute another person's position on the same issue

Assimilation phase   the fourth phase of the socialization model where new members accept the established group culture and begin to identify with the group and its members

Assimilator   a group member who learns through a combination of thinking and watching

Attitude   how favorable a person judges a person, a thing, or an event

Attraction theory   feelings of liking for a particular group or group member(s)

Audience-based apprehension   a form of apprehension linked to communicating with a specific audience

Authority rule   someone in a position of power makes a decision on behalf of the group

Autocratic style of leadership   belief that group members need controlling

Avoiding conflict-handling style   style in which a group member has a low concern for both the self and the group members; one of five conflict-handling styles

Behavioral dimension   the behaviors group members use during conflict

Black hat   member approaches the decision in a cautious manner by centering on the negative aspects of the decision; one of six thinking hats

Blue hat   member approaches the decision in a procedural manner by monitoring the decision-making procedures used by the group; one of six thinking hats

Brainstorming   a decision-making procedure used to creativity in the idea generation process that allows groups to generate more ideas or solutions to problems than individuals might generate working alone

Breakpoint   a switch from one track activity to another

Buzz group   a decision-making procedure in which a larger group breaks into 3- to 5-member subgroups, each of which then generates ideas to take to the larger group for discussion and decision making

Cause-effect organizational pattern   a pattern used in presentational speaking to illustrate the relationship between an existing issue and the ramifications of the issue

Central negative   group member who challenges the group's decisions; one of five informal group roles

Certainty   a member sees only one way to approach a task

Charge   the direction given to a group about how to proceed with the task

Charismatic approach to leadership   a leader possesses the ability to accomplish extraordinary things while simultaneously exerting a powerful influence on members

Charter   a list of the goals the group hopes to achieve

Chronemics   the use and structure of time

Chronological organization pattern   a pattern used in presentational speaking to show how something developed over time or to indicate the steps to a process

Closed-mindedness   a group relies solely on its members to gather and evaluate information

Cluster   the use of several communicator style attributes at the same time, which represents an individual's communicator style

Code of conduct   a list of behaviors by which members agree to abide

Cognitive dimension   differences in opinion among group members in conflict

Cohesion   a member reaches an acceptable level of desire to stay in the group

Collectivistic culture   a culture that values the group over the individual

Communication apprehension   an individual's level of fear or anxiety associated with either real or anticipated communication with another person or persons

Communication climate   the relative acceptance or rejection a group member feels based on the social and psychological tone of the relationships established among group members

Communication satisfaction   a member experiences positive feelings of fulfillment from the group experience

Communication trait   an individual's consistencies and differences in message-sending and -receiving behaviors

Communicator style   the way an individual uses verbal and nonverbal communicative behaviors to indicate how literally others should take a message

Completion   final group meeting when the group absolutely must finish the task

Comprehensive listening   the need to listen to comprehend information in order to learn

Compromise   some members may not agree with the decision, but the group as a whole stands by the decision

Compromising conflict-handling style   style in which a group member agrees to be agreeable and strives to find a middle ground between satisfying his own needs and satisfying his group members' needs; one of five conflict-handling styles

Concrete   a word or phrase with an identifiable referent and a clear meaning

Confirming message   a message that recognizes the value and importance of a relational partner

Conflict   the process that occurs when group members, due to their interdependence, their real and perceived differences, and their emotions, engage in an expressed struggle that impedes task accomplishment

Conformity   a member agrees with the group's decision because the majority of the group members agrees

Conjunctive task   a task that requires members to coordinate their efforts

Connotative meaning   the personal response to a word

Consciousness-raising talk   talk centered on group identification and pride

Consensus   all group members agree with and commit to the decision

Content-oriented listener   listener who evaluates information before forming an opinion

Context-based apprehension   a form of apprehension tied to a specific context (i.e., small group, meetings, interpersonal, public speaking)

Control   member is motivated to communicate to have the power to manipulate the environment; one of six interpersonal communication motives (Chapter 2) **OR** a member attempts to impose his point of view on other members (Chapter 12)

Converger   a group member who learns through a combination of thinking and doing

Conversational sensitivity a person's ability to pay attention to and make inferences about the meaning generated in a conversation

Counteractive influence approach to leadership when the group encounters an obstacle, the leader draws upon a repertoire of communication skills that (a) counters what other group members have said or done and (b) influences members to resolve or remove whatever caused the obstacle

Creativity the process by which group members engage in idea generation

Critical advisor member who challenges group members' ideas in a constructive manner; one of three formal group roles

Cultural diversity the sum total of beliefs, values, attitudes, meanings, perceptions, customs, practices, language, and other artifacts of social life that are learned, shared, and passed on by a group of people

Decision characteristics the parameters surrounding task assignment as experienced directly by the group

Decision making the group chooses one option from a set of already selected options in which no externally correct option exists

Decision-making context the organizational parameters surrounding task assignment that are independent of the group

Decision-making procedures structured methods of decision making that coordinate members' communication, keep members focused on the issues at hand, and guide members through the process of problem diagnosis, solution selection, or solution implementation

Defensive communication climate group members feel their contributions are neither welcomed nor valued

Delay breakpoint a group decides to reexamine a position or repeat some part of a task

Democratic style of leadership belief that members should be involved in the decision-making or problem-solving process

Demographic variables the observable characteristics of an audience that provide some basic information about the audience

Denotative meaning the dictionary or literal meaning of a word

Depersonalizing conflict occurs when group members recognize that conflict forms part of the small group process and thus do not attribute conflict to a specific member

Description   a member describes her feelings and presents her viewpoints as her own

Deviance   a member disagrees with the group's decision, even though the majority of the group members agrees

Deviant behaviors   behaviors enacted by members that violate group norms

Deviant roles   individual member behaviors that are negative and destructive to the group's productivity and success

Disconfirming message   a message that makes a relational partner feel devalued

Discounting message   a message that disparages or fails to affirm a new idea

Discriminative listening   the ability to differentiate among various stimuli

Disruption breakpoint   conflict forces the group to stop working or failure forces the group to reevaluate its position

Distance   the amount of physical space that exists between two or more group members as they communicate

Diverger   a group member who learns through a combination of watching and feeling

Diversity   the joining of individuals who differ in cultural, demographic, and cognitive backgrounds

Dominating conflict-handling style   style in which a group member places a priority on satisfying her own concerns instead of satisfying the concerns of group members; one of five conflict-handling styles

Elaborated code   use of complex, extensive, and precise language

Elected leader   a member elected from the group membership to lead the group

Emergent approach to leadership   a group member emerges as a leader based on communicative behaviors and persuasive influence

Empathic listening   the willingness to listen to understand how someone feels

Empathy   a group member identifies with other members and attempts to understand their feelings, needs, and interests

Encounter phase   the third phase of the socialization model where individuals come together for the first time, either face-to-face or through other media, and begin the process of establishing group goals and roles

Encounter talk   talk that is interpersonal in nature

Equality a group member treats all group members the same and believes the contributions of all group members are equally needed, desired, or required

Escape member is motivated to communicate to avoid other activities or stressful situations; one of six interpersonal communication motives

Ethical responsibility requires group members to act in a way that not only promotes caring for both themselves and each other but also requires members to share equally in assuming responsibility for the consequences of their actions

Ethics the process of making judgments (e.g., good-bad/right-wrong/worthy-unworthy) about a person's behaviors or actions

Ethnocentrism the tendency for individuals to use the values, attitudes, and behaviors of their ingroup as the basis for judging and evaluating another group's values, attitudes, and behaviors

Evaluation a group member passes judgment, assigns blame, and interrogates other members

Evaluative listening the need to listen to evaluate information in light of some criteria

Example a factual or hypothetical instance that makes a general point

Excursion a three-stage process that requires group members to (1) put the problem or task out of mind, (2) focus on an irrelevant yet unrelated topic, and (3) force-fit the characteristics of the irrelevant topic to the original problem or task

Exit phase the fifth phase of the socialization model that includes how members leave the group, how groups disband, and how members retain relationships

Facial expression how a group member conveys meaning through the face

Facilitator an individual whose purpose is to ensure that group members follow the decision-making procedure in the time allotted for the procedure

Feedback the response a listener gives to a speaker about the speaker's behavior

Feminine individuals individuals who possess high levels of feminine behavior and low levels of masculine behavior

Formal role specific role position assigned to one group member through appointment or election as part of the group's structure

Forming phase where group members meet the group process with their own reasons for joining the group; first of five stages of Tuckman's five-phase model of group development

Functional approach to small groups   a focus on the communicative behaviors used by group members during group meetings

Functional perspective of small group communication   a group's performance directly relates to the communicative functions performed by a group

Gender   the social beliefs and values associated with being male or female

Gersick's punctuated equilibrium model   a model of group development in which groups progress through a period of inertia punctuated by a period of concentrated change

Goal   the end state of group activity

Green hat   member approaches the decision in a creative manner by exploring alternatives of the decision; one of six thinking hats

Group building and maintenance roles   roles that strengthen the group's collective bond

Group efficacy   members' belief in their collective (i.e., group) ability to perform a task

Grouphate   feelings of dread that arise when faced with the possibility of having to work in a group

Group structure   the behaviors and characteristics unique to the group

Group task roles   roles that facilitate group movement toward task accomplishment

Groupthink   a mode of thinking members engage in when they are deeply involved in a cohesive group, which overrides their motivation to realistically appraise alternative courses of action

Grouptyping   arises when a nonmember makes assumptions (either positive or negative) about a person based on the person's group memberships

Haptics   a group member's use of touch

Heterogeneous group   a group comprising members who differ in cultural, demographic, and cognitive backgrounds

Historical context   the group's history of working together

Homogeneous group   a group comprising members similar in cultural, demographic, and cognitive backgrounds

Ideawriting   a decision-making procedure that focuses on a single topic that produces a written product

Identity   the psychological and/or physical boundaries that distinguish a group member from a non–group member

Impersonal message a disconfirming message that is nonimmediate and cliché-ridden

Impervious message a disconfirming message not acknowledged by the receiver

Inclusion member is motivated to communicate to have a sense of belonging; one of six interpersonal communication motives

Incoherent message a disconfirming message that is difficult to follow

Incongruous message a disconfirming message that contains contradictory verbal and nonverbal components

Individualism-collectivism whether attention is focused on the group or the individual

Individualistic culture a culture that values the individual over the group

Inequity conflict conflict centered on a group member's perceived imbalance between his contribution to the group and the contributions made by the group members

Informal role role that emerges through group member interaction; used by the member with the appropriate communicative and group skills needed to fulfill the role function

Information provider member who exercises the ability to synthesize information; one of five informal group roles

Informational diversity differences among group members based on their education, work experience, group experience, and expertise

Institutional context the group's position within a larger group membership

Integrating conflict-handling style style in which a group member works toward developing a solution that satisfies the needs of all members; one of five conflict-handling styles

Interdependence the process by which a change in one part affects the other parts; occurs when members coordinate their efforts to accomplish their task

Interpersonal communication motive one of six reasons—inclusion, affection, control, escape, pleasure, and relaxation—a person has for communicating with people

Interrupting message a disconfirming message cut short by the receiver

Intrinsic interest what each member finds interesting or fascinating about the task

Irrelevant message a disconfirming message unrelated to a prior message

Kinesics   a group member's use of body movement, including posture and gestures

Laissez faire style of leadership   belief that members should function independently, with little direction or personal involvement by the leader

Leader   member who must move the group toward its goals and convince external audiences the group is achieving or has achieved its goals; one of three formal group roles

Learning group   a group whose members hope to enhance their skills, abilities, or cognitive processes

Learning styles   individuals' preferences for acquiring information in a learning environment; influences how individuals listen to and present information

Life span approach   groups have a beginning, a growing stage, and an ending

Listening   the process of receiving, constructing meaning from, and responding to spoken and/or nonverbal messages

Loneliness   a member feels powerless from not being able or allowed to participate in the group process

Machiavellianism   an individual's ability to manipulate a situation in order to influence and control it for his own purposes

Majority rule   group members take a vote, and the alternative that receives the majority of the votes becomes the group's decision

Masculine individuals   individuals who possess high levels of masculine behavior and low levels of feminine behavior

Maturity   the ability and willingness a group possesses as it moves through the developmental process

Mentoring   an interpersonal relationship between an experienced member and an inexperienced member whereby the experienced member facilitates the professional and social development of the new member

Mindguarding   a group member's attempt to keep adverse information from the other group members

Model of small group socialization a   five-phase (i.e., antecedent, anticipatory, encounter, assimilation, exit) model that illustrates how communication influences the socialization process

Negative feedback   feedback that helps members identify weaknesses and make improvements

Neutrality a group member indicates her indifference toward other members and their feelings, needs, and interests

Nominal group technique a decision-making procedure that allows group members to independently and silently generate ideas; members work alone, combine ideas afterward, and later view the process as one in which they worked as a group

Nonverbal communication all communication other than words through which meaning is created

Norm a guideline or rule designed to regulate the behaviors of group members

Normal breakpoint a group shifts focus or examines another aspect of a task

Norming phase where the group and its members work together on the task and attempt to get along; third of five phases of Tuckman's five-phase model of group development

Obliging conflict-handling style style in which a group member concerns herself highly with the needs of her group members; one of five conflict-handling styles

Oculesics a group member's eye behavior

Olfactics scent and smell

Orientation behaviors a group's tendency to examine the procedures it uses while engaging in the decision-making or problem-solving process and to include the use of verbal behaviors that direct members to handle conflict, make helpful suggestions, lessen tension, and facilitate agreement

Panel discussion a public group whose members engage in a discussion about a topic

People-oriented listener listener who listens primarily out of concern for other people's feelings and emotions

Performing phase where the task is readied for output and evaluation by an external audience; fourth of five phases of Tuckman's five-phase model of group development

Personal appearance encompasses many dimensions of how a group member looks, including height, weight, body shape, and clothing

Personality trait an individual's psychological makeup comprising attitudes, values, beliefs, experiences, and behaviors

Phase one time period in which members make sense of the task in light of their own experiences, viewpoints, and biases

Phase two   time period in which members recognize they have work to complete but lack the urgency to finish their task

Pleasure   member is motivated to communicate to have fun; one of six interpersonal communication motives

Population familiarity   the degree of group members' familiarity with the task

Positive feedback   feedback that helps members distinguish between typical and optimal behavior concerning task performance and relationship building

Power distance   the inequality that exists between a less powerful person and a more powerful person

Primary group   a group whose members are engaged in an intimate relationship

Primary tensions   tensions that reflect the anxiety members feel about being in the group and the uncertainty surrounding the roles they will play

Problem orientation   a group member collaborates with other members by seeking a mutually defined and acceptable solution

Problem-solution organizational pattern   a pattern used in presentational speaking to identify a problem and propose a solution

Problem solving   the group engages in several activities: defining the problem, identifying the solutions, and choosing one solution from the set of identified solutions

Problem-solving talk   talk centered on accomplishing the group task

Procedural conflict   conflict centered on the procedures group members use to critically evaluate ideas or confront member behavior

Procedural norm   a norm that indicates the procedures the group will follow

Promotional leadership   the behaviors a group leader uses early in the decision-making process to promote one idea rather than encourage the generation of multiple ideas

Provisionalism   a group member makes tentative judgments about the task and the group members

Proxemics   a group member's use of space (i.e., distance, territory)

Psychographic variables   the attitudes, values, and goals commonly shared by an audience

Public group   a group whose members interact for the benefit of an audience

Q&A session   a time after a presentation during which the audience directs questions to either an individual member or the group as a whole

Question of conjecture charge given to a group to determine the possibility of whether something might occur

Question of fact charge given to a group to determine whether something holds true

Question of policy charge given to a group to determine whether a plan of action should be adopted

Question of value charge given to a group to determine whether something is viewed favorably or unfavorably

Recorder member who takes the minutes of meetings and records any other actions of the group that need to be stored as permanent records; one of three formal group roles

Red hat member approaches the decision in an emotional manner by legitimizing members' emotions and feelings about the decision; one of six thinking hats

Relational communication the use of verbal communication, nonverbal communication, and listening to develop and maintain relationships between and among group members

Relational obstacles differences in attitudes, values, and goals that arise among members that impede a group's ability to effectively accomplish its task

Relaxation member is motivated to communicate to unwind and lower anxiety; one of six interpersonal communication motives

Restricted code use of short, simple, and conventional language

Role a repeatable pattern of communicative behaviors that members come to expect from each other

Role conflict two or more members vie for the same role

Role flexibility possessing the skills and abilities needed to engage in a variety of group member roles

Role rigidity members do not play a variety of roles

Role strain the group requires members to assume a new role, and they feel reluctant, at least initially, to do so

Role talk talk centered on the specific role each group member plays in the group

Sanction a punishment in response to a norm violation

Second-guessing a listener questions the literal meaning of a message to determine the truthfulness of the message; if the listener doubts the truthfulness of the message, the second guesser attempts to attach an alternative meaning to the message

Secondary tensions   tensions that emerge as members seek to influence others, develop norms and roles, and explore the issues surrounding the task

Self-censorship   members monitor their reactions and contributions to the group discussion, making sure never to reveal their doubts and questions

Self-esteem   a person's overall self-worth

Self-help group   a group whose members share a common problem or life situation

Self-monitoring   the extent to which a person pays attention to the social requirements of a situation and, striving for appropriateness and effectiveness, adapts her verbal and nonverbal behaviors

Service group   a group whose members, largely volunteers, help others in need of a particular service or who lack something that would help them lead a functional life

Sex   the biological difference between men and women as evidenced by an individual's external genitalia and internal sexual organs

Shared leadership behaviors   the behaviors any group member can enact to demonstrate leadership

Situational apprehension   a form of apprehension a person experiences when communicating with a given person in a particular situation

Situational approach to leadership   the idea that leadership behavior depends on situational variations (i.e., power, the task, leader-member relations)

Situational variables   the variables contained with the physical location of a presentation

Six thinking hats   a decision-making procedure designed to simplify thinking by having a group focus solely on one aspect of a decision at a time

Small group communication   three or more people working interdependently for the purpose of accomplishing a task

Social cohesion   the level of positive affect among group members

Social complexity   the degree of ego involvement present among members in accomplishing the task

Social-emotional leader   group member who is concerned with the building and maintenance of group member relationships; one of five informal group roles

Social group a group whose members share a common interest or engage in a common activity

Socialization a two-way process of influence and change whereby group members use verbal and nonverbal messages to create a new and unique group culture

Socialization guidelines ideas for the successful socialization of members to help ensure success, from the perspective of both the new member the group

Socialization outcomes how group members and the group as a whole feel about how they cooperated and succeeded in completing goals

Social loafing the process by which individual member efforts decrease as the number of group members increases

Social norm a norm that governs how members engage in interpersonal communication behaviors

Solution multiplicity the number of alternatives that exist for accomplishing the task

Spatial organizational pattern a pattern used in presentational speaking to demonstrate how space, direction, or physical arrangement link several aspects of a topic

Specific purpose statement a statement that identifies exactly what the group wants to accomplish with its presentation

Spontaneity a group member openly expresses her thoughts, feelings, or emotions upfront

Stakeholder a person external to the group who has a vested interest in the task

Statistic the use of a number to express a fact or an idea

Storming phase where group members begin to actively participate by sharing ideas and talents; second of five phases of Tuckman's five-phase model of group development

Strategy a group member shares her thoughts, feelings, or emotions less than honestly

Style approach to leadership the idea that leaders display different styles, which then a differently impact group outcomes

Substantive conflict conflict centered on group members' critical evaluation of ideas

Superiority a group member treats all group members differently because he does not consider them equals

Supporting materials   the evidence offered by a group used to reinforce the primary points covered in a presentation

Supportive communication climate   group members feel their contributions are welcomed and valued

Symposium   a public group in which each member presents a speech on one aspect of a topic

Tangential message   a disconfirming message taken in a new direction

Task   an activity in which no externally correct decision exists and whose completion depends on member acceptance

Task cohesion   the degree to which group members work toward a common goal

Task difficulty   the ease of task accomplishment

Task leader   member who "takes charge" of the group; one of five informal group roles

Task norm   a norm that enables a group to work toward task accomplishment

Task-related obstacles   informational, analytical, and procedural problems that impede a group's ability to effectively accomplish its task

Tension releaser   member who uses light humor strategically to ease tensions in the group; one of five informal group roles

Territory   the ownership of space

Testimony   the use of a quotation or paraphrase from an expert

Thesis statement   the primary assertion for the content in a presentation that the group wants the audience to retain

Time orientation   how quickly a culture assumes important aspects of life (e.g., relationships, careers) should develop

Time-oriented listener   listener who prefers brief interactions and lets the speaker know time is an issue

To entertain   the group presents the information in an amusing, lively, or humorous manner

To inform   the group presents the information in a concise, clear, and unbiased manner

To persuade   the audience presents the information in a manner that advocates a particular point of view or position

Topical organizational pattern a pattern used in presentational speaking to link several independent aspects of a topic; often used when a topic can be divided into types, categories, components, or parts

Trait a relatively enduring behavior that people tend to use consistently across their life span

Trait apprehension a relatively enduring level of apprehension across a variety of situations

Trait approach to leadership the idea that members inherently possess characteristics that distinguish them as either a leader or a follower

Transition midpoint of a group's allotted task time

Trust group members' willingness to "take a chance" on each other

Tuckman's five-phase model a model of group development that covers group structure and task behavior across five phases: forming, storming, norming, performing, and adjourning

Uncertainty avoidance the amount of stress that a culture associates with an unknown future

Undifferentiated individuals individuals who possess low levels of both masculine and feminine behaviors

Value a belief or feeling about a person, a thing, or an event

Value diversity differences among group members in terms of what they consider as their group's goals, mission, and purpose

Verbal aggressiveness the tendency for an individual to attack the self-concept of another individual for the purpose of inflicting psychological harm

Verbal communication the words and phrases used by members through which meaning is created

Verbal information probes statements made by group members intended to probe the accuracy of the information under examination by the group

Virtual community a group that meets regularly in cyberspace for members to share their experiences, opinions, and knowledge on a particular topic or interest

Virtual group a group whose members work interdependently on a task but from different physical locations via communication technology

Vocalics the qualities of a group member's voice

White hat   member approaches the decision in a neutral and objective manner by providing facts and figures; one of six thinking hats

Willingness   a group's collective motivation and confidence

Work group   a group that occurs within an organizational context whose members complete and take collective responsibility for a common task on behalf of the organization

Yellow hat   member approaches the decision in an optimistic manner by focusing on the positive aspects of the decision; one of six thinking hats

Zero history group   a group whose members never worked together before

Index